W9-BTD-650

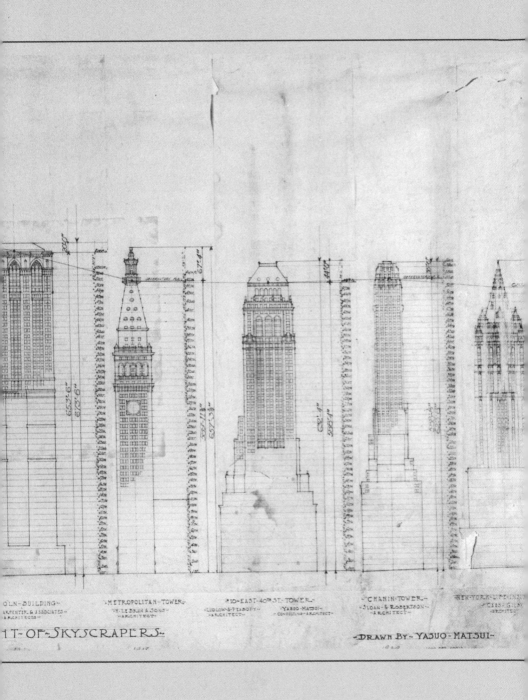

HIGHER

Doubleday

New York   London   Toronto
Sydney   Auckland

51984970

HIGHER

A Historic Race to the Sky
and the Making of a City

Neal Bascomb

PUBLISHED BY DOUBLEDAY
A division of Random House, Inc.
1745 Broadway, New York, New York 10019

DOUBLEDAY and the portrayal of an anchor with a dolphin are trademarks of
Doubleday, a division of Random House, Inc.

Title page photograph: *View from River House: Cloud Study, Noon,*
December 15, 1931, by Samuel Gottscho. The Gottscho-Schleisner Collection.
Museum of the City of New York (39.20.1)

Library of Congress Cataloging-in-Publication Data

Bascomb, Neal.
Higher : a historic race to the sky and the making of a city / Neal Bascomb.—1st ed.
        p. cm.
Includes bibliographical references.
1. Skyscrapers—New York (State)—New York—History—20th century.
2. Manhattan (New York, N.Y.)—Buildings, structures, etc. I. Title.

NA6232.B37 2003
720'.483'097471—dc21
2003048888

Book design by Donna Sinisgalli

ISBN 0-385-50660-0

Copyright © 2003 by Neal Bascomb

All Rights Reserved

PRINTED IN THE UNITED STATES OF AMERICA

October 2003

First Edition

1 3 5 7 9 10 8 6 4 2

For My Parents

Contents

HIGHER

The Soaring Twenties

"What floor, please?" said the elevator man.

"Any floor," said Mr. In.

"Top floor," said Mr. Out.

"This is the top floor," said the elevator man.

"Have another floor put on," said Mr. Out.

"Higher," said Mr. In.

"Heaven," said Mr. Out.

—*F. Scott Fitzgerald, "May Day"*

Like other races—to build the transcontinental railroad, discover the North Pole, scale Everest, or land on the moon—the race to build the tallest skyscraper in the world demanded sheer determination, deep pockets, terrific speed, unbridled ambition, grand publicity campaigns, and a dose of hubris. It began in 1924 with architects William Van Alen and Craig Severance, who had just passed into their partnership's tenth year. In the course of a few short months, a bitter rivalry would begin to take shape—one that would ultimately bring their celebrated union to an end and cause a much greater battle ahead.

In the winter of 1923–24, Severance & Van Alen, Architects, was riding a wave of critical and financial success. They had recently completed the Bainbridge Building on West Fifty-seventh Street, and a review was imminent in one of the leading journals, *Architectural Record*. This was the latest in a string of commissions the partnership had won for high-profile projects in New York, including the Prudence Building at 331 Madison Avenue and the Bar Building on West Forty-fourth Street, where the firm now had its offices. Their client list consisted of the most reputable names in the city, including the Standard Oil Company of New York, the Title Guarantee & Trust Company, and E. E. Smathers, Esq. Scores of draftsmen worked in their "factory," as large architectural practices were called at the time.

The two men went into business together when they were in their early thirties and were anxious to make their way in New York. Both had struggled for years in the same kind of draftsmen factories that they now ran, where long hours and meager wages went hand-in-hand with T-square and tracing paper. In Van Alen, Severance found a talented designer who dazzled clients with his eye for style and form, not to mention his training at one of the most exclusive schools of the time, Paris's Ecole des Beaux-Arts. In Severance, Van Alen gained a charismatic partner who managed the business. What one lacked the other supplied. Leonardo da Vinci wrote that "an arch is two weaknesses which together make a strength." So it was with their partnership.

This kind of balance between partners had given rise to many of the most famous firms, including McKim, Mead & White, Carrère & Hastings, Sullivan & Adler, and Burnham & Root. Affectionately called "the steersman of the ship" as William Mead was, or "the plumber" as John Carrère once said of his role in the firm, partners like Severance managed the firm's staff, smoothed the ruffled feathers of the clients, oversaw the finances, and dealt with the less glamorous engineering elements, including heating, plumbing, and electrical details. Severance's role, quite simply, was to keep the ship sailing and the big commissions coming.

Like Stanford White and Thomas Hastings, Van Alen was helpless when it came to business affairs, but he could draw brilliantly, and he distinguished his firm from the host of others through his inventive designs. With each passing year, Van Alen's plans grew bolder. Breaking with tradition, he chopped off useless cornices from the tops of buildings and set windows flush with the wall. Architects in New York stopped by to see his designs. When Richard Haviland Smythe came by the J. M. Gidding store on Fifth Avenue, a writer asked the architect, "Well, how do you like it?" Smythe replied, "How I don't like it is what you mean . . . Van Alen's stuff is so darned clever that I don't know whether to *admire* it or *hate* it." Similar things were said of White and Hastings in their time.

As it turned out, however, this partnership between Van Alen and Severance was not immune to the perils that threaten many successful firms: petty jealousies, questions of direction, money, and who was *really* responsible for the firm's success. For the two architects, both of whom enjoyed more than their share of ego, a rift eventually developed. The fact was they were very different men. Van Alen spent evenings at the Architectural League of New York, debating with his fellow architects, many of whom he had studied with in Paris. Severance went to the Metropolitan Club after a long day, passing his time with industrialists and financiers, men who could give him jobs. When Severance needed a drink, he often joked about his command of a language his partner spoke fluently: "All my French is coming back to me . . . *Entrez le boite!*" The differences that made the two effective as partners also diminished their chances of resolving the conflicts that arose between them.

By their tenth year, the architects had long since left behind the personal warmth that had characterized their early partnership, when they had spent weekends together in the country, and Van Alen had asked Severance to be the best man at his wedding. In 1923 they became embroiled in a lawsuit over their commission on the Hotel Empire on Sixty-third Street. The owners had cancelled their contract, complaining that the plans, for which Van Alen was responsible, had been consistently late. They lost out on more than half their fee.

Then the February 1924 issue of *Architectural Record* finally arrived with the review of the Bainbridge Building. The critic Leon Solon liked the building, praising the design as "most satisfying" and an "imaginative reaction." He thought that it made a bold new step in design, particularly because of the façade's light treatment, which revealed the building's steel structure rather than hiding it behind some heavy masonry details. Solon concluded: "In William Van Alen's work we welcome the identification of design with structure after its long architectural dissociation." The problem with the review was that Van Alen was the only one praised. It mentioned Severance only as a name on the partnership's letterhead. One can appreciate the bitterness this engendered in Severance. After all, Bainbridge Colby, the former secretary of state under Wilson, was a personal friend, and short of this relationship the commission never would have happened.

Not only had Van Alen earned all the recognition for the building, but the review also established Severance & Van Alen, Architects, as a practice showing "the greatest energy in shaking off the shackles of purposeless convention." As Raymond Hood, one of the decade's leading architects, learned in the first days of his practice, clients often disdained innovation. The story went that Hood had submitted preliminary sketches for a bank commission he hoped to win in Providence, Rhode Island. Hood was known as somewhat of a rebellious and bold designer, and the bank president came back to him and said, "We're going to ask McKim, Mead & White to do it."

"But you can't," said Hood. "Those men are dead. . . . If it's an old firm name you want, I'll give you one. How about Praxiteles, Michelangelo & Hood?"

Many big-spending clients whom Severance sought and wooed were like Hood's banker. They closed the door on firms that strayed too far from classical tenets. Severance decided he didn't need a partner who upset convention. He could just as easily hire talented designers who would follow his lead, and keep all the profits to himself. A few short months after the review, the partnership officially ended, and so did their friendship. Van Alen moved out of their office, never to return.

Within months, Van Alen sued Severance. They skirmished over money and how the client list would be divided. The suit dragged out over a full year; eventually Severance won. Van Alen appealed the decision, but failed to have it overturned. Neither man took on another partner in his career, nor did either forget what had happened between them.

Several years later, in 1929, Severance and Van Alen were locked into yet another struggle—one that would change New York's skyline and challenge each man to build higher than anyone had gone before. It also would lay down the gauntlet for a third skyscraper to stretch even higher. It began as a contest between their egos and became a race involving many players, each with their own agendas. They included two rival automobile giants, a young Wall Street titan in it for the game, a political hero on the mend, and two brothers out to crown their building careers. As the long shadow of the Great Depression began to darken the edge of the Roaring Twenties, the race to build the world's tallest building captured the nation's imagination.

———

To understand this chase into the sky, one must look further back in history—far beyond the building of the first skyscrapers in America. In man's earliest days, he constructed basic shelters of wood, leaves, and earth. As the burden of survival lightened, he began to develop beauty and grandness in his designs. Man wanted to make his mark on the world, and the structures he built became a statement of self.

So humankind built, at times with great ambition. On the Nile's west bank, the Great Pyramid of Giza, reaching 450 feet high with over two million stone blocks, served as the tomb for King Khufu. On a hilltop in Athens the Greeks built the Parthenon, a temple that towered over the city below. Triumphal arches and the Colosseum marked Rome, while on the hills of San Gimignano, rival Italian families built hundreds of towers—one taller than the next—to declare their power. In Southeast Asia, the Khmer empire erected massive tiered stone spires, the earthly representation of Mount Meru where their Hindu gods lived. Great Chinese pagodas, French cathedrals, ziggurats, lighthouses, bell towers, and even the simple steeple that stands above a countryside village—what they may not have in common purpose or scale, they shared in command of height. This height expressed preeminence, whether of their gods, their engineering skill, their power, their wealth, or their position above others.

The demand for height was equally strong in America. In the days before the Revolutionary War, rebels raised tall liberty poles in city squares, risking the bayonets of British soldiers, to declare their freedom. By 1850 sightseers offered up a shilling to climb the wooden stairs inside Trinity Church's steeple for a bird's-eye view of New York at 284 feet. In the nation's capital, the 555-foot Washington Monument completed in 1884 honored America's first president. Soon thereafter, the demand took form in mountains of steel and stone that many called "skyscrapers," a term used by the end of the nineteenth century, when rival insurance companies and newspapers competed for the title of New York's tallest building—or at the least the tallest building in their particular industry.

Home Life battled with New York Life and Equitable. The headquarters of the *Tribune* beat out the *Sun*, then lost to the *World* at 309 feet in 1890. After its construction, architect Harvey Wiley Corbett recalled, "Architects said nothing would be higher; engineers said nothing could be higher; city planners said nothing should be higher, and owners said nothing higher would pay." Nonetheless, by 1899 the Park Row Building in New York City held the height crown at 386 feet, outstretching its tallest Chicago rival, the Masonic Temple, by 84 feet. Of course, one had to disregard the Times Building, which proclaimed that it reached the "extreme height" of 476 feet, if one included the basement floors in the measurement. Its owner was neither the first, nor the last, to manipulate what "tallest" meant, but the man on the street knew.

By the turn of the century, architects had mastered these man-made mountains, if not in style then in engineering. Only their owners' ambition limited their height, and if there was one thing hard to limit in a country coming into its own—having built a railroad from coast to coast, won the Spanish-American War, and transformed itself with the Industrial Revolution—it was ambition. In 1903 the Fuller Building was completed at Twenty-third Street and Broadway, and though not the tallest at 285 feet, the city marveled at its distinctive flatiron shape. Photographer Alfred Stieglitz expressed what many saw: "With the trees of Madison Square covered with fresh snow, the Flat Iron impressed me as never before. It appeared to be moving toward me like the bow of a monster ocean steamer—a picture of the new America still in the making . . . The Flat Iron is to the United States what the Parthenon was to Greece."

The attention sparked by the Fuller Building inspired ever taller skyscrapers. It was part advertising, part proof of their company's success, and part economics in deriving the most office space from the narrow plot of land.

In 1906 came the Singer Building, a monument to Isaac Merrit Singer, the manufacturing genius of the sewing machine. Originally the company settled on a thirty-five-story tower, but wanting it to be the tallest, they doubled its height, moving ahead with plans for a skyscraper designed by Ernest Flagg that rose 612 feet tall when completed in 1908. A year later, the slender Singer tower with its three-story curved mansard roof (and flying from its flagpole a thirty-foot-long banner with S-I-N-G-E-R spelled out in giant letters) lost its crown to greater aspirations, those of John Hegeman, the president of the Metropolitan Life Insurance Company. From sidewalk to crown, the fifty-story tower, modeled after Venice's Campanile of San Marco, measured 700 feet tall. Then came Frank Woolworth, the five-and-dime store king, who had a score to settle with Metropolitan Life for denying him a much-needed loan years before. The loan denial cost Hegeman his crown and in 1913 set the Woolworth Building, at 792 feet tall, as the skyscraper to beat in the years ahead.

The tale of the Woolworth Building and its owner foreshadowed the skyscraper race in the Roaring Twenties. Born in upstate New York, Frank Woolworth escaped the family farm to be a dry-goods store clerk. He had an instinct for attracting customers, acting on the novel idea of placing items for sale in the shop windows. His efforts boosted sales but didn't fill his own pocket. Soon enough he went out on his own. In February 1879 he opened a shop in Utica, New York, full of small items—baby toys, buttons, note tablets, soap, harmonicas—and hung a sign that read "The Great Five Cent Store." Thirty years and millions of nickels and dimes later, F. W. Woolworth Company owned 596 stores across the country, plus Canada and England. He had mastered the art of "location, location, location" and of giving the public a good show; it paid for his extravagant lifestyle and thirty-room mansion off Fifth Avenue. Woolworth ate well, drank well, and fancied the latest cut in suits. When his bankers refused to give him a loan for a skyscraper in New York, he financed the $13.5 million structure out of his own pocket.

For his site, he chose Park Place and Broadway, a perfect spot near City Hall, the financial district, and the Brooklyn Bridge. For his architect, he hired Cass Gilbert, a young star who had apprenticed at McKim, Mead, & White, the training ground for many of America's greatest architects. Woolworth wanted a Gothic tower, suggesting the

Victoria Tower of the Houses of Parliament in London as a model, but the question remained how high to build. He fretted about the cost: one had to sell quite a few marbles, Christmas ornaments, and dolls to build a skyscraper, particularly the tallest. Twenty-five stories seemed more manageable. If he wanted to continue higher later, then Gilbert could design for that possibility. Gilbert cast aside the old drawings to begin again.

But while on tour in Europe, Woolworth kept hearing about the Singer Building, how grand and tall it was. He and Gilbert then settled on a third proposal for a 620-foot skyscraper. In November 1910 the *New York Times* published a stark, black-and-white rendering of the tower. At night the tower would have so many lights that a couple sitting on their back porch fifty miles away could see the skyscraper's apex. Still Woolworth remained unsatisfied: second highest was second highest. He sent Gilbert off to measure the exact height of the Metropolitan Life Building. The architect returned to Woolworth's office with the answer.

"How high do you want the tower now?" asked Mr. Gilbert

"How high can you make it?" Mr. Woolworth asked in reply.

"It is for you to make the limit," said Mr. Gilbert.

"Then make it fifty feet higher than the Metropolitan Tower."

In January 1911 Woolworth acquired another parcel of land at the corner of Barclay Street for his site, a sure sign he meant to go higher. Gilbert returned to his drawing board. His builder, Louis Horowitz, tried to rein in this modern Croesus. One had to think about costs and economic return. After all, Cass Gilbert said a tall building's purpose was "to make the land pay." Woolworth feigned indifference whenever someone presented this reasoning to him. Later he confessed to Horowitz, "There would be an enormous profit outweighing any loss. . . . The Woolworth Building was going to be like a giant signboard to advertise around the world [my] spreading chain of five-and-ten cent-stores."

Two years later, after hundreds of changes to Gilbert's designs, Woolworth planned an opening worthy of an emperor's coronation. Dubbed the "Cathedral of Commerce" by the popular reverend Parkes Cadman, the Woolworth Building dwarfed the spire of Trinity Church by over five hundred feet. Its final height was 792 feet and one inch above the sidewalk. On April 24, 1913, crowds gathered out front in City Hall Park. Invited guests were brought into New York from Washington and Boston on special trains and put up at the finest hotel, the Waldorf-Astoria, to dress. At 7:30 in the evening, President Woodrow Wilson pressed a button in Washington and "80,000 lights instantly flashed throughout the Woolworth Building. The event marked the completion, the dedication and the formal opening of that regal edifice, the tallest and most beautiful building in all the world. . . . Assembled there was a great host of statesmen, captains of industry, merchants, journalists, scholars, poets—all representative Americans, proud to break bread with and honor the man who had realized his dream." So read the building's purple-prose brochure.

For all of the master showman's announcements of "highest in the world," the Eiffel Tower actually reigned as tallest at 984 feet. Europe still led the world culturally and symbolically. From entrance to tower, the Woolworth Building was an adaptation of European style and design. In his office, the Empire Room, Woolworth kept Napoleon's portrait hung at eye level and a bronze bust of the conqueror as well. Soon, though, a Great War would catapult Europe into unimaginable horror and cause a dramatic shift in the balance of world power. Only then would Americans look within their own shores for heroes. Only then would its architects dare to go higher and do so in a style of their own. A young architect named William Van Alen, fresh from school and with an office in the same building where Gilbert designed the Woolworth Building, planned to explore the new frontier.

First, however, came the darkness.

———

At dusk on August 3, 1914, Sir Edward Grey, England's Foreign Secretary, stood at a window in Whitehall. The night before, a telegram had come in warning that Germany was set to invade Belgium. France would be drawn into the struggle, then England herself. The killing of Austria's Archduke Franz-Ferdinand on June 28, 1914, was the spark; centuries of history fueled the flames.

"Could this country stand by and witness the direst crime that ever stained the pages of history and thus become participators in the sin?" So spoke Grey earlier that day as he tried to rally England into the war. Now he was tired. Down below men lit the street lamps. Grey turned to his friend in the room and uttered what may have been the most prophetic words of the war: "The lamps are going out all over Europe; we shall not see them lit again in our lifetime."

Millions of Grey's countrymen and allies threw themselves into the cauldron of the war. In the trenches men fought to defend a few hundred feet of charred earth. The soldier-turned-artist Paul Nash described the horror: "The rain drives on, the stinking mud becomes more evilly yellow, the shell-holes fill up with green-white water, the roads and tracks are covered in inches of slime, the black dying trees ooze and sweat and the shells never cease . . . they plunge into the grave which is this land . . . It is unspeakable, godless, hopeless." Men with machine guns mowed down thousands. Soldiers didn't even have to aim, they just fired into the mass of bodies. Gas poisoned the fields. Flamethrowers spilled death into dugouts and pillboxes. Lice, flies, mites, mosquitoes, mutilated parts, and rats the size of cats served as a soldier's companions in the trench. Worse than all of it, though, was the waiting: the waiting as the shells shot down from the sky, the waiting for the hunger to pass or sleep to come, the waiting for death. As the months and years passed, this wasteland swallowed up a whole generation of Europe.

President Wilson hesitated to move America into the Great War. The country wanted little to do with it. When Wilson could delay no further, he ruthlessly prosecuted the war. He issued the draconian Espionage Act and launched a vicious propaganda campaign against the Germans. He instituted the draft and by war's end the United States had a standing army of four million, half of whom saw action. He called on legions of businessmen to direct America's industrial might for the fight. He spared no effort.

America brought the war to a close. Her efforts decided the outcome at a cost of 112,432 men, many of whom suffered in the trenches, but in sheer brutal numbers, there was no comparison: Germany lost 1,773,000; Russia, 1,700,000; France, 1,363,000; Austro-Hungary, 1,200,000; Britain 908,000. In total, Europe lost 8,500,000 people and suffered 21,000,000 wounded.

By March 1919, with America's troops marching down Fifth Avenue to raucous cheers and brass bands, much had changed. The United States ranked as the mightiest economic and financial power. The country discovered it need not look back to Europe to help find its way forward. The horror the war had wrought left few to admire the past. Staid Victorian values and old governances held little power, yet what was to take their place? People had few answers. If life was so cheap as to merit the loss of millions, then what was its meaning? Congress rejected Wilson's idealistic League of Nations. Most people refused to think of what might come to pass if reparations cut too deeply, or of consequences at all. Instead they danced and drank; they slashed away at convention and wanted experience for experience's sake. F. Scott Fitzgerald, the poster boy for the decade to come, gave words to what everyone felt: "A fresh picture of life in America began to form before my eyes—America was going on the greatest, gaudiest spree in history and there was going to be plenty to tell about it. The golden boom was in the air."

While Europe was forced to tend its wounds, America accelerated at a dizzying pace into the 1920s. The decade saw the first pilot to cross the Atlantic in a solo flight and declare in France, "I am Charles Lindbergh." It saw the spread of mass production, mass marketing, and mass consumption. It brought us flappers, short skirts, the Harlem Renaissance, a woman's right to vote, the martini, celebrity scandals, the cult of youth, talkies, mobsters, the great Babe Ruth, speakeasies, 104 words for "intoxicated," Dorothy Parker's Round Table, the fast-step, and lots of cigarettes and sex. Passion was liberated, and there seemed no end to it: there were million-dollar-bout fights, ticker-tape parades, pole-sitting contests, the tabloid boom, mah-jong, hip-flasks, the handsome and hapless President Harding followed by Coolidge's prosperity, stock market mania, marathon dancers, and movement, always movement. The decade was best described by a boy in Muncie, Indiana, who when asked by his Sunday-school teacher to "think of any temptation we have today that Jesus didn't have," answered: "Speed."

A deep ocean now separated the old from the new, and New York became the lighthouse for all to seek. The modern spirit arrived upon its shore, with a generation of artists seeking the truth in their work, a truth that reflected their life and spoke American. This spirit revealed itself in theaters and musicals across the city. Jazz musicians played it in clubs and sold it on vinyl in the millions. Fashion designers, advertisers, publishers, writers, aviators, painters, architects, and businessmen gave the spirit expressions never before seen or heard or read. As Sherwood Anderson said about New York, "It is a European city no longer. It is America. It is itself. Imperial New York. Plenty of time yet. Men and machines. We are all so young yet. Wait and see. Wait and see what New York will do."

The stage was set and fittingly located in a place whose flags were emblazoned with the motto "Excelsior," meaning "ever higher."

Part One

CHAPTER ONE

A Hunch, Then a Demand

NEW YORK
The heart of all the world am I!
A city, great, and grim and grand!
Man's monument to mighty man!
Superb! Incomparable! Alone!
Greater than ancient Babylon,
The giant walled! Greater than Tyre,
Sea-Queen! Greater than Nineveh,
Pearl of the East! Greater than Rome,
Stupendous reared, Magnificent!
Greater than Paris, city fey!
Greater than London, fog-enmeshed!
Greater than Venice! Vienna!
Or Petrograd! Greater than these!
That I am! Mark my high towers!

—*Arthur Crew Inman*

T he lobster shift returned home from a long night of pouring drinks, driving taxis, scrubbing floors, or walking the beat on the mad city streets. A few bands still shouted and hollered in Harlem speakeasies, their lawbreaking patrons eased back in their chairs, glad not to have gone to bed on the same day they got up—the Mayor Jimmy Walker way of living high in the era of Prohibition. Liner ships cut through the fog toward the island of Manhattan, arriving from Liverpool, Rotterdam, Genoa, and a dozen other cities. On the waterfront, dockworkers threw back their coffees and stamped out their Lucky Strikes, ready for the cargo hauls from North Africa, Sumatra, Capri, and Costa Rica.

Downtown, milkmen left crates of bottles for the army of office clerks to drink that day. In the gray of dawn, the clanking of ash cans echoed through the streets. A horse-drawn cart turned the corner. At the fish market, mongers spun and heaved three-hundred-pound barrels of flounder onto handtrucks and took them away. The morning chill bit their wet hands. Ferries and tugs shuttled across the harbor. Valets and maids prepared for their blueblood bosses to awake. The newsboys wiped the sleep from their eyes and shouted their first headlines: "Rothstein Shot . . . Hoover in a Landslide . . . Get your paper . . . Two cents . . . Just two cents." It was November 5, the day before the 1928 presidential election between Al Smith and Herbert Hoover, for most New Yorkers simply another day in a decade gone mad.

In Fifth Avenue suites and tenement apartments across the city, alarm clocks rang a thousand rings. *Time to chase another buck.* Trains, buses, and cars approached the city; their passengers—perhaps today an actor from Poughkeepsie, a playwright from Chicago, a bank teller looking to hit it rich on Wall Street—bounced up and down on their seats as the sun struck gold on the Metropolitan Life Tower. A second later they shot underneath the Hudson River, the towers of New York lost to the darkness. As the sun lifted into the sky, a crowd, one thick swell of dissonant voices, headed for work. They slipped nickels into turnstile slots and waited for the IRT or BMT to come down the elevated rails or screech through the tunnel. Some rushed from ferries once they docked and the gates were pulled aside. One man passed an old friend, tipped his hat, and said "Good Morning" before hurrying on his way. *No time to stop for a chat and catch-up. Got to move. Got to go.* Hawkers hawked their wares. Dynamite blasted. The ground shook. The first rivet thundered. Reporter and raconteur Damon Runyon knew what he was talking about when he said, "The bravest thing in New York is a blade of grass. This is not prize grass, but it has moxie. You need plenty of moxie in this man's town, or you'll soon find yourself dispersed hither and yon."

The morning sun slanted through the Prospect Park West apartment of William Van Alen in Brooklyn. Out his window the white oaks surrounding the Long Meadow were shedding their last leaves. Cars rumbled around Grand Army Plaza, some speeding despite the big round sign that read "Slow Up . . . What's Your Hurry?" Bankers and lawyers rushed toward the subway, passing mothers heading into the park with their children. In the crisp late fall day a slight breeze blew in from the northwest. Van Alen put on a fine wool suit and cinched the knot on his tie. Leaving his wife, Elizabeth, he headed out the door. It was not just another day for Van Alen; it was a big day, perhaps the most important of his life.

An architect differed from other artists: a musician could jab out a few notes with his horn, hear the pitch and tempo; a painter could draw a brush stroke across the canvas and see what she had done; a writer could finish a page, pull it from the typewriter, and read his words. An architect needed more to realize his vision. Van Alen could sketch his designs, order his draftsmen to work out the elevation details in quarter-inch scale, and have blueprints of the same made on fine linen paper that would last for years. But without an owner to finance his plans, a builder to order the steel and brick, and workers to connect the columns and beams hundreds of feet in the air, Van Alen had little more than lines on a page. Without a patron, he was like a composer with a great score and no orchestra.

Over the past two years, Van Alen had drawn countless sketches for the site at Forty-second Street and Lexington Avenue, sketches for a grand skyscraper to tower over Grand Central Station and all of midtown. Three weeks before, William H. Reynolds, the real-estate speculator behind the project and the man to whom Van Alen was under contract, had sold the site to the automobile man Walter Chrysler. With the lease's assignment, Reynolds informed Van Alen that his services were no longer required, neither to draft any more proposals nor to oversee the construction of a new building on the site. The architect insisted that he remained "ready, able, and willing" to continue the job, but this was now a decision for Chrysler, who owned the plans—to do with them (or not do with them) as he pleased. Regardless, Reynolds assured Van Alen that the new owner would honor the balance remaining on the hundred thousand dollars in fees due the architect.

Van Alen pressed for a meeting with Chrysler, motivated by something far greater than securing the remainder of the balance due him. The architect wanted his plans to be built in steel and stone, and Chrysler agreed to meet with him. Today was that day.

Chrysler was the kind of client architects fought over. He was rich, willing to break with tradition, and obviously had a point to prove. He would want a different design, something that distinguished his skyscraper from all the others sprouting up across the city. Although it was still unclear what kind of building would rise at 405 Lexington Avenue, the site teemed with activity. The tenants had moved out; the United Cigar store on the corner had shuttered its doors; and the wreckers had erected a fence around the building. Already demolition crews were tearing down the walls of the five-story office building there.

Anyone exiting Grand Central would hear the din of pneumatic hammers and foremen shouting, "All right, boys!" It wasn't just 405 Lexington; all of Forty-second Street appeared to be under construction. Derricks lifted another tier of columns on the fifty-three-story Chanin Building going up across the street. Down the block, J. E. R. Carpenter, an architect Van Alen had promoted for membership in the

Architectural League, had designs for his own skyscraper: great lumbering trucks threaded their way through traffic to deliver materials to the future Lincoln Building.

Two blocks from Chrysler's site, Van Alen made his way toward his office on Madison Avenue, the same office he had occupied since the split with Severance four years before. When he arrived, the two ex–Vassar College shot-putters, as a visitor once described Van Alen's secretaries, knew to keep away most callers. Sitting in his office before his meeting with Chrysler, the architect must have worried about what questions his potential client would ask. Was Van Alen willing to make significant changes to his original designs? Were he and his firm up to the task? Why shouldn't a more established firm get this plum commission or at least serve in an advisory capacity? How long would the whole operation take? Or maybe he just wanted to meet Van Alen and get a feel for him. But what if Chrysler asked him if he drove one of his cars? Van Alen would have to tell him it was not a Chrysler. He drove a car built by E. L. Cord, even though he had trouble with the clutch and often ground the gears. Chrysler had to understand that Cord offered the latest in styling. Or maybe he wouldn't understand. There was a reason Severance pitched all the clients when they were partners. Van Alen was too introspective and made a weak first impression.

———

Reynolds first hired Van Alen in 1921 when he was still working with Severance. The developer wanted a penthouse designed for the five-story building at 405 Lexington Avenue. Reynolds promised many improvements to the site, but carried few of them to completion. Despite a lack of results, Reynolds hired Van Alen yet again in March 1927, and again asked him to design something for 405 Lexington: this time, a forty-story hotel. Van Alen hired Chesley Bonestell, an illustrator who freelanced with a number of firms around town, to collaborate with him on the preliminary studies for the hotel. He fired up his factory of draftsmen to prepare for the detailed, scaled drawings they would make from his sketches. Several months later, however, Reynolds scrapped the hotel plans. He wanted an office building instead—a skyscraper.

He called Van Alen, and the two revised their contract for the new structure. The skyscraper was not to exceed sixty stories and would contain "stores and other improvements as may be required, such as banking offices, cafeteria, grill room, subway connection and all the appurtenances that may be necessary." Van Alen was to prepare the plans and specifications and confer with architect Robert Lyons on the initial sketches. The dry legal jargon fails to convey the opportunity this skyscraper presented to Van Alen, who wrote:

> In designing a skyscraper there is no precedent to follow for the reason that we are using a new structural material, steel, which has been developed in America and is different in every way from the masonry construction of the past.
>
> Structurally, and in their purpose, our tall buildings are wholly unlike any buildings of an earlier day. To apply to our tall office buildings, apartment houses and hotels the familiar architectural features characteristic of the comparatively low palaces, temples and churches that were built before the advent of steel as a building material, is not economical or practical, and it is artistically wrong since it is not truthful.

This skyscraper, described by Reynolds as "a fire-proof office building similar to such buildings as are competitive in the City of New York" was to be for Van Alen a statement of the truth. More importantly, he needed the commission, one that could catapult him to the top of his profession, as the Woolworth Building had Cass Gilbert.

Since severing his partnership with Craig Severance, Van Alen had

floundered. Without his partner to score the big commissions, his designs of critical note were limited to a chain of Childs restaurants and
a pair of show windows for stores. Meanwhile New York underwent a
building boom the likes of which had never before been seen. Many of
the architects Van Alen had known as draftsmen and studied with in
Paris now enjoyed flourishing practices. Although the *New Yorker*
would first say it several years hence, most in the architectural community knew already that "leading the New York modernists [are]
Ralph Walker, Ely Jacques Kahn, and Raymond Hood. They are three
little men who build tall buildings, and who probably rake into their
offices more business than any other architects in the city . . . They eat
and drink and lunch and confer constantly . . . They plan great projects. They lead the Architectural League . . . They are constantly publicized, interviewed, quoted. They dash to Boston. They race to
Chicago. They have a glorious time." It was these three that newspaper
journalists visited when they needed a quote on the essentials of good
architecture—not Van Alen.

Of course, Reynolds cared as much for Van Alen's statement of
truth and place in the architectural community as he did about the
color of the architect's tie. Reynolds was a jack-of-all-trades and a
master of only one: the art of self-promotion. Employment as a real-
estate developer was a good match. Born and raised in Brooklyn, his
first job entailed clearing the plaster and debris from the houses his
father worked on as a carpenter. Reynolds studied law, but left before
finishing to make his initial investments in real estate. In his first
year, he earned over forty thousand dollars, a king's sum at the time. By
his twenty-fourth birthday, Reynolds found himself elected to the state
senate, the youngest member in Brooklyn history. Despite serving only
a few years, he maintained the "senator" imprimatur throughout his
life. He also worked as an oil promoter, copper mine owner, racetrack
developer, amusement park operator, theatrical promoter, and proprietor of a trolley line and water company. Known for crooked deal-

ings, true or purported, he was twice indicted by the courts, but never served any time in jail. The last charge, grand larceny, was overturned on appeal in March 1927.

Nearly bald, with eyebrows arched so perfectly they could have been painted, Reynolds was a tireless showman. His most notable achievement in real estate remained the 1903 development of Coney Island's Dreamland Park, featuring a tower with a hundred thousand lights, the largest dancehall in the country, and spectacles with titles such as "Fire and Flames" and "Trip to the Moon." In 1911 a few of the lightbulbs exploded on the Hell Gate attraction and eighteen hours later Dreamland Park smoldered in ashes. That same year Reynolds maneuvered his way into acquiring the lease on Lexington Avenue and Forty-second Street, which was owned by Cooper Union and had the benefit of being tax-exempt. Originally Reynolds signed a twenty-one-year lease with an annual payment of fifty-four thousand dollars a year in rent. Cooper Union approved of Reynold's alterations to the building on the site, except to say that "the flourishes in the two gables" should be toned down and made simpler. After the construction in 1913 of Grand Central Terminal, Reynolds shrewdly returned to Cooper Union's trustees to ask for an extension. Over the next fifteen years, Reynolds finagled revaluations, extensions, and options on the lease by pledging multimillion-dollar developments on the site, yet the showman's promises for the site remained as empty as the air above the five-story building.

Regardless, Van Alen sketched, studied, and modeled a skyscraper. Reynolds helped pay his bills, and the opportunity was too big to pass on simply because of impatience. Early in 1928, Van Alen started a game of one-upmanship with the developer of the Lincoln Building and its architect, J. E. R. Carpenter. Carpenter announced he would build a fifty-five-story skyscraper at the old Lincoln warehouse site across from Grand Central. Fellow designer and critic Kenneth Murchison chronicled Van Alen's next move in a leading architectural journal: "In a rich baritone voice, [he] sang something to the effect that only a block away he proposed putting up a fifty-six-story building! This, of course, made the Lincoln people perfectly furious so they proclaimed that they would probably make theirs sixty-three stories high, to which Mr. Van Alen said, 'Hold, men, we will make ours SIXTY-FIVE stories high!' " Carpenter backed down and Van Alen finished plans for a skyscraper one story less than he boasted.

On April 7, 1928, Reynolds finalized a new sixty-seven-year leasehold—the longer the duration, the more valuable the lease. He was so pleased with the result that he offered to pay the legal fees that Cooper Union incurred from the long negotiations. They accepted his check for ten thousand dollars. Now Reynolds heated things up. On June 3 he called a meeting of the National Association of Building Owners and Managers to review Van Alen's plans and specifications for his sixty-four-story skyscraper to rise eight hundred feet in the midtown skyline: the tallest office building in the world by eight feet. The association reviewed proposed buildings for their viability as income-producing investments. They would provide the seal of approval Reynolds needed to promote his skyscraper and cause a stir in the real-estate community. Over afternoons playing golf at his Lido Beach Golf Club and grand dinners back in the city, Reynolds wooed and coaxed the collection of engineers, building managers, and rental agents. He proclaimed the leasehold for the site had a value of $17 million. He carted out Van Alen to discuss his plans, as well as the contractors and structural engineer. He hosted a theatrical performance for the attendees. After three days of schmoozing, the inspectors heralded the building to the press, saying it would be a "successful addition to the skyscraper group of mid-Manhattan . . . [and] serve to revolutionize store values and the class of tenants in 42nd Street and Lexington Avenue."

In August Reynolds released Van Alen's final rendered drawings for the skyscraper, which now stretched sixty-seven stories high. The

American Architect credited Van Alen for his modern design and how he "has departed from certain of the old-time principles on which the skyscraper was developed . . . the design of the Reynolds Building is developed to be of interest throughout its entire height." The first twelve floors would have corners wrapped in glass, and a giant glass dome to be lit from within would sit atop the skyscraper's tower. Most important, the skyscraper had $7.5 million in financing from S. W. Strauss & Company. With nine hundred thousand square feet of rentable space, the building would generate over a million dollars in rent every year.

Van Alen had fulfilled his end of the deal, providing plans, specifications, models, large-scale and full-size detailed drawings as well as all blueprints for the building in its many forms. Reynolds accepted all of them, but by September 1928 he still delayed the beginning of construction. The architect shouldn't have been surprised. As it turned out, Reynolds, who had financed his first real-estate investment from monies earned on the two percent commissions his father's creditors paid him to collect on his delinquent debts, had no way to finance the completion bond, which meant no skyscraper. All of Van Alen's designs and hopes were in jeopardy.

But with his well-crafted publicity campaign, Reynolds had baited the hook and thrown out his line. He owned a valuable lease on an extraordinary site. Now he only had to wait for a big fish to strike. This was the speculative builder's modus operandi, landing millions in the sale of a lease "without turning a spadeful of earth," as builder William Starrett said. Wasting Van Alen's designs was just an unfortunate part of the business.

In October 1928, as the Governor of New York ran for the presidency and the Yankees swept the favored St. Louis Cardinals in the World Series, one of the biggest fish of all, Walter P. Chrysler, came biting. Reynolds landed over two million dollars in profit on the deal. All Van Alen got was a notice that his services were no longer needed.

———

Walter Chrysler was a bear of a man. Hard-driving at business, he had built one of the country's leading automobile companies in the short span of four years. When he wanted something, he seized it. If a struggle ensued, all the better—Chrysler liked a good fight. If he saw a way to improve an engine, he donned his overalls and set about the task, no matter how dirty his hands became. He spoke plainly, didn't suffer fools well, and had created an empire with his tireless energy and commitment to look twice before accepting the old way as the right way. Chrysler loved machines and thought that with science and invention the world could reach some sort of apotheosis. He was a modern individual in the most modern of times.

The builder of the Woolworth skyscraper, Louis Horowitz, once offered Chrysler a ride uptown after a board meeting they had attended in New York. Outside, Horowitz directed Chrysler toward his old Rolls-Royce. Seeing the car, Chrysler stopped cold.

"Where did you get this be-something-er-other ark?" he asked.

Horowitz urged Chrysler to get in the car so he could take him to his office. Chrysler acquiesced, but throughout the ride uptown he berated the old car, saying he expected to be carted out the door with a broken back.

"Tell you what," Chrysler said as he opened the car door when they arrived at his office. "If you will take this thing and run it off a ferry-boat into a deep place in the bay, I'll give you a decent car."

On November 5, 1928, Van Alen had his chance to go face-to-face with Chrysler himself. Little did the architect know when he was ushered into Chrysler's office at 347 Madison Avenue that the automobile magnate was determined to change the city's skyline in the same way he had the car industry in the last decade—forcefully. The previous year had been his most commanding yet. He had acquired the Dodge Brothers, a move that one observer compared to the minnow swallowing the whale. Next he had premiered the Plymouth: "A New Car . . . a New Car Style, a New Zenith of Low Priced Car-Luxury and Performance." Ad slogans aside, Chrysler produced the Plymouth for one reason: to strike at Henry Ford's new Model A. The day the first car rolled off the assembly line in June 1928, he drove it to Ford's River Rouge plant. Ford inspected the car and said with his usual aplomb: "Walter, you'll go broke trying to get in the low-price market. [We] have that market sewed up, and as sure as you try to step in, we'll stop you." In October Chrysler broke ground on the largest automobile plant ever built—covering 22.7 acres of ground under a single roof—to produce the Plymouth, whose sales were surpassing every expectation.

Chrysler dreamed of a building that would leap into the sky like a beacon, a reflection of the Chrysler Corporation's leap to become one of the top three automobile companies. The *New York World* reported that the skyscraper would serve as the next "step in the campaign which Mr. Chrysler has planned against the General Motors Corporation for supremacy in the automobile world." His competitor had recently opened a twenty-six-story skyscraper at Fifty-seventh Street and Broadway on New York's Automobile Row. Nonetheless, Chrysler insisted that his purpose was a selfless one. When asked why he was financing the skyscraper out of his own pocket, the former railroad journeyman replied that his two sons needed a place to work. "I was well aware that a rich man's sons are likely to be cheated of something. How could my boys ever know the wild incentive that burned in me from the time I first watched my father put his hand to the throttle of his engine? I could not give them that, but it was through this thinking that I conceived the idea of putting up a building." Despite what its owner told the press, the Chrysler Building would be more than a place for his two sons to work.

Chrysler had wanted to build a great skyscraper in New York for years, and he'd had realty men looking for the perfect site for him. When Reynolds offered his lease on the land at Forty-second Street and Lexington Avenue, he attacked in negotiations led by his Harvard-trained lawyer Nicolas Kelley. Chrysler always hired the best. The deal took two and a half weeks in a series of nonstop meetings.

Kept from his wife, Kelley wrote to her about the furious pace of negotiations: October 5—"After a long harrowing day, we passed one stage"; October 9—"I went into a difficult meeting with lawyers who have been treating us as if we were rogues"; October 10—"The whirl still continues"; October 13—"Here it is five o'clock on the warmest, muggiest and most drizzling of Saturday afternoons. We are making progress with our land deal"; October 16—"We closed the Chrysler land business yesterday!"

There were two main issues. First, Gano Dunn, the lawyer who represented Cooper Union, had barely heard of Chrysler and only thawed after Kelley presented his own credentials as a member of the Century Club and the Downtown Association. Second, Dunn needed to be sure that Chrysler had the security to see the building to completion. Chrysler had many millions in his company stock and municipal bonds, but it was a question of what to put forward. Kelley pleaded with his boss to secure a larger amount up front rather than a lesser amount whose value he had to guarantee. Kelley warned him that if the market collapsed, as it had many times before, he would suffer a financial disaster. Chrysler finally agreed, and Cooper Union accepted the deal. Not at issue during these early stages was whether he intended to construct the tallest building in the world. Even Kelley's young daughter knew, writing to her father on October 22 after he was given the position of vice president of the Chrysler Building Corporation. "I think it's great—and the biggest building—gosh!"

On that fateful November 5 morning, Chrysler and Van Alen looked across at one another in the automobile man's office. The architect was the taller of the two at over six feet, but he was awkward in his frame, as if not quite sure how to move about with so much leg. He had a great crown of a nose and a spare smile, one of a man uneasy around others. He seldom spoke unreservedly and when he did, it was quietly. When out in social situations, he let his wife carry the conversation for the both of them. His boldness came out in his designs, or when he spoke of them.

Seven years the architect's senior, Chrysler offered a study in contrast. With a head shaped like a bullet and sharp blue eyes, the automobile man struck those he met as a man to follow. He shook a man's hand hard and liked to settle back after a long day with a cigar, stiff drink, and ribald jokes among friends. He hunted, golfed, yachted, played the tuba, entertained well, and owned a Gatsbyesque estate in Long Island with a twenty-three-room mansion, eight-car garage, and 150-foot pier and boathouse. Although devoted to his wife and children, he enjoyed a taste for showgirls. When he arrived in New York one evening, word leaked that he had a girl with him for the overnight trip. Reporters peppered him with questions. Chrysler scoffed off the suggestion, but after stepping away from the scene with a colleague, he remarked, "Actually, I had two."

Over the past month Chrysler had wavered on whether to use the plans as Van Alen had drawn them. As the meeting continued, Chrysler must have sensed in Van Alen the kindred spirit of a maverick. Obviously he knew his craft and liked to push the envelope. Chrysler had hired and fired legions of people, many times on projects that cost millions and whose success depended on such decisions. Once asked how he picked his people, he responded, "I don't know. You just do it." In that way, Chrysler decided Van Alen was the architect for him. Yet although he hired Van Alen, Chrysler didn't intend to use the skyscraper designs presented to him. Van Alen was to abandon the plans he'd drawn for Reynolds.

Chrysler spoke plainly, "I want a taller building of a finer type of construction and it's your job to give the best that's in you." He told Van Alen to travel, study buildings in Western cities, and examine their designs and use of materials. "Improve upon them to the best of your ability," Chrysler said. "Spare no effort or time." Van Alen could hire whomever he needed, spend whatever he needed, and unlike the deal with Reynolds, no consulting architects would have a say or veto power over his plans. As far as a fee, neither even pegged a figure, nor did they sign a contract.

Chrysler demanded that Van Alen give him his best. For Van Alen, whose best was often limited by a client's budget, oversight, and absence of daring, this was the commission of a lifetime.

From the beginning it was clear that the two were ideally suited for one another. Their intention was the same: make a statement in steel and stone. Van Alen burned to innovate as much as Chrysler did. The architect had endured two years of false hopes and frustration thanks to Reynolds—and in nearly two decades as an architect he had never lived up to his early promise. Now was his chance.

CHAPTER TWO

The Architect-Artist

You shall no longer take things at second or third hand, nor look through the eyes of the dead, nor feed on the spectres in books.

—*Walt Whitman*

Fifty years before a skyscraper rose at Forty-second Street and Lexington Avenue, there was Mrs. White. She lived in a small white farmhouse on that rocky knoll, surrounded by a pasture for her goats and some squatters' shanties. The land was valued at two cents a square foot. Across the street sat a dilapidated building shaped like a radish bulb, the Hospital for the Ruptured and Crippled. Nearby, Doctor Tyng preached to his flock in what some called the Church of the Oily Cloth. Other neighbors included the druggist Schoonmaker, butcher Tyson, baker Gibson, grocer Brandeis, and the man who owned the oyster shack. A few years later, Schoonmaker installed the first all-night telephone service in the city; neighboring hotels sent guests there if they needed to make a late call. Up the block, Commodore Vanderbilt kept his horse, Maud S, and his grandson planned a chateau on Fifth Avenue and Fifty-second Street so he could have "air and breathing space around it." At night, gas lamps lit the way on Forty-second Street for those who climbed the hill east of Second Avenue to watch the Boston and Harlem boats scoot up the river.

Most banks, insurance and trust companies, industrial corporations, and law firms were located downtown near Broadway and Wall Street. Furriers and garment producers ran their sweatshops just north of Canal Street. For shopping, Macy's and Hearn's on Fourteenth Street fit the bill. Despite a few tall buildings and premature cries of a "high-building epoch," the city was primarily a rectangular stretch of low, flat roofs, crossed by a gridiron of streets. For most, Forty-second Street was "that place north."

This was the shape of the city when William Van Alen was born across the river in Williamsburg on August 10, 1882. The architect came from a family steeped in the history of America. With his wife and three children, the first Van Alen set foot in the New World off a ship from Utrecht, Holland, in 1658. Settling in Beaveryck (now Albany), he traded beaver skins. Before the Revolutionary War, John Evert Van Alen worked as a surveyor and civil engineer. A close friend of George Washington, he later served in Congress between 1793 and 1799. Letters written to John Evert from Washington survived through the years and were prized by the family. Another civil engineer, William's great-grandfather, surveyed land for the Erie Canal and drew one of the first maps of Albany. His son Benjamin charged General Mosby's command in the Civil War as part of the Army of the Potomac. He distinguished himself in battles at Harper's Ferry, Cold Harbor, and the bloody fight at Wilderness. The architect's father, Jacob Van Alen, married Eleda Squire in 1881 and had William eleven months later. Although the family traced its roots to the days when the Dutch West India Company stole Manhattan for a mere sixty guilders, they were by no means landed gentry. Jacob Van Alen ran a small company called New York Stove Works, producing potbellied cast-iron stoves. He worked hard to bring in the sales, like other budding industrialists around him.

At the end of the nineteenth century, Williamsburg was crowded with distilleries, sugar refiners, breweries, glass factories, iron foundries, and shipyards. For three cents, passengers took a ferry across the East River to the markets on Twenty-third Street. On the docks, cats followed around the fishmongers. Vendors peddled hot corn on the streets and a poor fellow named Bismarck was often seen turning the corner, ordering the troops of his "army" to rally against an unseen foe. Most of the houses were two stories and wooden framed. As the first steel-framed buildings went up in Manhattan, the best Williamsburg offered for a skyline was the dome of the local savings bank and a string of six-story grain elevators along the waterfront. But it was as fine a place as any in the city to raise a family.

While returning home from Jamaica Bay on July 22, 1897, Jacob Van Alen was struck by a LIRR train and killed. William was fourteen, his sister eleven. Two years later William left public school in Brooklyn to work as an office boy for architect and developer Clatence True. True paid him a meager wage and "Will" or sometimes "Bill" took to his role as errand boy for the senior draftsmen and the "boss," as the head of an architect's office was always called. Clarence True was the owner, contractor, and architect of most of his buildings: he seldom compromised. Known for developing rowhouses up and down Manhattan's Riverside Drive, True turned heads when he first advertised his firm. The journal *Pencil Paints* said: "His name, tripping the light fantastic on the signboards of New York, was then as familiar as are those of 'Camel,' 'Chesterfield,' and 'Spearmint' . . . for the rather exclusive circles of men who considered themselves as the standard-bearers of the learned profession and fine art of Architecture, it was the unfittest of things unfit to do." The advertising worked though, and True's office rushed to complete his many jobs. While many of his peers studied at the handful of schools that taught architecture, like MIT and Columbia, Van Alen earned his start as once all architects had, with his hands. The futurist True played the mentor, showing the teenage tyro that architecture was in part about advertising and that the disdain of others could be the best indicator that one was on the right path. In his career ahead, Van Alen would exhibit a flair for showmanship in his designs and certainly earn a harsh word—several in fact—from the standard-bearers.

Half a century before Van Alen apprenticed with True, most people considered architects simply carpenters putting on airs. In Chicago in 1853, several builders sat down to discuss who should forgo contracting to spend his time solely drawing up plans in order that they all could meet the demand for new buildings. When one of the builders volunteered, the group guaranteed that if he didn't earn at least two dollars a day, they promised to make up the difference. Such was the state of the profession at the time. The few practicing architects distrusted one another and secreted their designs. There were no schools, no national publications of import, no society, and the few architecture books these men owned were prized and kept under lock and key.

Finally in 1857, Richard Upjohn, architect of New York's Trinity Church, and several others came together to share what they knew, adopt some guidelines, and form an official group: the American Institute of Architects (AIA). Architect George B. Post said of these days: "It was torn by dissensions and jealousies, and its few members were engaged in a war of styles. The Medievalists could see no merit in Classic art; the devotees of the Renaissance considered modern Gothic worthy of no consideration; and the Pre-Raphaelites believed in neither. The American painters and sculptors were frankly outspoken in their opinion that there was no art in Architecture." Architects fought for the occasional church or public building where they could show their skill, but few of their designs were of consistent character. Only after the Civil War, with the rising influence of the American Institute of Architects, and the development of architecture schools at MIT, the University of Illinois, and Columbia, among a handful of others, did a formalization of style begin to emerge.

When Van Alen first began to trace drawings and scour dusty tomes filled with Ionic orders, Roman vaults, and Gothic buttresses, architecture in America was under the spell of the 1893 World's Fair in Chicago. Daniel Burnham with his aide-de-camp, the firm of McKim, Mead & White (Charles McKim, William Mead, and Standford White), managed to set the style for the kind of architecture they decided America needed, rather than the more democratic approach of giving the individual what he wanted. According to Stanford White, it was fine for H. H. Richardson to design a few buildings with an inventive use of mass, as long as others didn't follow in his path; what the crude tastes of the American public needed was some classical European refinement. Charles McKim set about to establish the American Academy of Rome, for students to study classic Italian architecture and steer clear of "Yahoo or Hottentot creations." Soon New York and cities across the country turned to Classical, or Renaissance design for their libraries, train stations, court houses, office buildings, and houses. In an imperial rebirth of ages past, architects put up little Romes everywhere. In his last couple years, Richard Morris Hunt, considered the dean of American architecture, must have been bleary-eyed with the number of Italian palazzos the wealthy asked him to design. The Beaux-Arts movement that soon followed, though drawing on a range of styles and benefiting from a stress on a building's plan, was mostly a language of French neoclassical design with a heavy emphasis on ornament. Sullivan commented: "the damage wrought to this country by the Chicago World's Fair will last half a century. It has penetrated deep into the constitution of the American mind, effecting there lesions of dementia." It would be years before clients wanted anything other than amended copies of classical architecture.

Although aware of this cultural nod to all things European, Van Alen had other concerns, like mastering his trade. Many architects' offices at the time were housed in barren lofts. Tables crowded the room where the draftsmen labored in shirtsleeves. Ventilation was a luxury and a spot by a window the prize of seniority. The men attached string to the lamps hanging from cords overhead to illuminate a section of their drawing board. Cigarette butts and torn pieces of tracing paper littered the cement floor. Drawings were pasted over most of the walls. Between shelving materials and taking measurements, a neophyte like Van Alen spent his days learning the basics. He copied classical orders and traced floor plans; he went on-site and watched the progress of the masons and carpenters. If asked, he cleaned the office floor of pencil shavings. Practices of the day were open six days a week and most the draftsmen were paid less than the bricklayers and carpenters on the jobs (some started at as little as eight to ten dollars a week). They had to be fast and accurate with their work.

After three years and three months, Van Alen made draftsman's grade. Draftsmen were responsible for taking rough designs (sketched out by True and the senior men) and developing them into working drawings and specifications for the builders to use on site. If a change in the plan was needed—additional windows, alterations in story heights or exterior details—draftsmen such as Van Alen were called to make a new drawing. Head draftsmen rarely hesitated to criticize an uneven or too bold line. Occasionally Van Alen was asked to make a preliminary sketch in soft pencil in addition to the final drawings. The total number of drawings required for a single building stacked up into the hundreds.

Although exhausted by the end of the day, Van Alen attended night school at the Pratt Institute in Brooklyn, a school of art and design founded with the motto: "Be True To Your Work And Your Work Will Be True To You." It was a young school, started only a decade before the burgeoning architect enrolled. What free time Van Alen had left, he spent like most draftsmen with aspirations to be great designers—looking for inspiration and an opportunity to learn. As one contemporary described, young apprentices "herd by themselves. They do not often go to parties, they do not go much to the theatre; they are always walking about the Metropolitan Museum . . . or taking trips out to see old colonial houses or working on problems in the ateliers . . . There is certainly something in the profession that gets the men as does no other profession that I know of."

In his last days of apprenticeship with True, Van Alen left Pratt to study at an atelier run by Emmanuel Masqueray, a Frenchman and one of the founders of the Society of Beaux Arts Architects. The organization was formed in 1893 by several alumni (mostly American) of Paris's Ecole des Beaux-Arts, who wanted to bring the famed school's method of study, the atelier system, to the United States. Its members sponsored ateliers, or studios, where students gathered to study the craft and participate in a succession of competitions with various design problems to solve. In a sense, the organization ran a loose-knit collection of mini-academies, some affiliated with universities like Columbia, MIT, and the University of Pennsylvania, others run independently by teachers or architectural clubs. Atelier teachers strove to instill in budding architects the principles of design—balance, flow, utility, truth, scale, proportion, and beauty—rather than rote adherence to historical style.

Van Alen chose one of the more eccentric characters running an atelier in the city. The red-bearded Masqueray had a flair for the dramatic. Once asked by a patron to add more color to his drawing, Masqueray pulled on his handlebar mustache and said, "Oh! You make it twenty-five dollar more, an' I put on *all ze colours in ze box!*" Underneath the good humor, there was a bit of a revolutionary in Masqueray. He insisted his students break from the past. Van Alen learned from him that while the Parthenon may be fine architecture, "it might not make the best design for an office building if a dozen Parthenons were piled one upon another and hung to a steel skeleton."

Masqueray pleaded with his students to make things simple. The Frenchman may have had praise for Vignola's rules for Renaissance order and decoration, but he also knew that "Vignola has been dead a long while and besides, he didn't know everything when he was alive." After work and late into the night, young men like Van Alen discussed theories of design, made colored perspectives, and critiqued each other's drawings in the loft on east Twenty-third Street. They copied plates of Greek temples and simmered in Masqueray's thoughts on architecture.

In 1901 Van Alen left True's office to cut his teeth at the large firm Copeland & Dole. He stayed there a few short months and then jumped to the conservative firm Clinton & Russell for a higher salary. While working on the grand Hotel Astor for his new firm, he switched ateliers, joining the one run by Donn Barber, the ninth American to graduate from the Ecole des Beaux-Arts. Van Alen wanted to follow in his steps, but had little money to go gallivanting off to Europe. There was only one way he could attend: win the Paris Prize. First awarded in 1904, the prize offered a scholarship to the famed school and a stipend for travel to the winner of a nationwide design competition sponsored by the Society of the Beaux-Arts Architects and funded by the likes of Andrew Carnegie and J. Pierpont Morgan. It was *the* honor for an atelier student.

Van Alen first tried in 1906, but was eliminated. In 1908 he entered again. The competition was closed to anyone twenty-seven or older, since one had to be younger than thirty years old to be at the Ecole des Beaux-Arts and it took roughly three years to graduate. At twenty-six, this would be Van Alen's last chance. The competition ran in three rounds of elimination. In the first program, students had twelve hours to draw a decorative motif. Judges from the Society chose who continued to the second program, which called for a plan for a single building or group of buildings. For the third round, the five finalists gathered in New York and in thirty-six hours made preliminary sketches for the auditorium floor and principal façade of a theater. The program read: "This theater for a large city is designed for lyric and dramatic representations, the former comprising opera, ballet, and the latter tragedy, comedy. Like all theaters, it comprises two grand divisions: 1. the part for the public; 2. the part for the artists." After the sketches, each finalist was given ten weeks for study, then returned to finish rendered drawings *en loge*—or, "in the box"—without the benefit of any books or consultation with another architect. Van Alen delivered his final drawings by the deadline, two showing plans for the ground and auditorium floors, as well as an elevation for the façade for his "Grand Opera House" and a longitudinal section drawing at one-sixteenth scale. The drawings revealed an architect with a fine sense of scale and a clever eye, but more important, one with more promise than the thousands of others who aspired to the Paris Prize. The judges issued their decision: Van Alen was to sail for Paris in September.

Before he left, Clinton & Russell entered their firm into a competition for a New Orleans bank. Van Alen was chosen to represent them. Contrary to classical rules of design, he chose to split the façade with a pilaster and won the commission for the firm. Clinton & Russell took the job, but removed the pilaster. They had no intention of mocking good fashion. As Van Alen departed for his education at the Ecole des Beaux-Arts, he left behind an architectural community desperate to know the name of the designer who had dared to upset convention.

————

Marco Vitruvius Pollio, the architect for Emperor Augustus of Rome, set down his principles for the training of an architect in his legendary treatise, *De Architectura*: "He must have both a natural gift and also a readiness to learn. For neither talent without instruction nor instruction without talent can produce the perfect craftsman. He should be a man of letters, a skillful draftsman, a mathematician, familiar with historical studies, a diligent student of philosophy, acquainted with music; not ignorant of medicine, learned in the responses of jurisconsults, familiar with astronomy and astronomical calculations." Nearly two thousand years later, those principles were at the core of the Ecole des Beaux-Arts when Van Alen presented his papers for entrance.

Beyond architectural theory and design, students at the Ecole des Beaux-Arts were taught mathematics, geometry, history, sculpture, mechanics, painting, and even the principles of construction. Although the school only enrolled forty-five French and fifteen foreign applicants each term, thousands descended upon rue Bonaparte to take the five-part entrance examinations. The caliber of students, particularly among Americans, was high. They included architects who later made their names designing skyscrapers, among them William Lamb, Raymond Hood, George Howe, and Ely Jacques Kahn. But Van Alen was the only one in 1908 to walk through the doors with a scholarship courtesy of the Paris Prize and a pass on the entrance examinations.

Students spent little time at the school itself. Lecture attendance was optional. Typically, each student joined an atelier connected with the school, where they worked on their architectural studies. Van Alen spent most of his waking moments at the atelier of Victor Laloux, the architect of the Gare de Quai d'Orsay and one of the most revered instructors. Many of his students claimed top awards at the school, and he was known for his emphasis on the plan of a building, rather than on decoration like Redon taught at his atelier. *Nouveaus* of the atelier were subjected to ritual hazing. The *anciens* tore their clothing, painted them blue and red, drew mustaches on their faces, reddened their cheeks with rouge, stuck plaster on their noses, and forced them to parade through the streets. Some were ordered to buy pastries or sing at the top of their lungs. Although everyone had a good laugh at their expense, a greater purpose was gained by these pranks: in a student's first year, humility was necessity.

The new initiates then spent the next six months in service to the *anciens,* meaning Van Alen performed menial tasks like buying materials for the atelier and mounting paper for the older members. The arrangement served both parties: the atelier won free labor, the *nouveaus* learned techniques of craft and a sense of duty to what would be their family in the coming years. Every two months the professors called the students into the school to make a sketch solution for a particular architectural problem, like a decorative treatment for a wrought-iron door or the plan of a museum. After the preliminary sketch, they returned to the atelier to study their original sketch and to render a final solution (based on the original, or it was disqualified) in the next two months. There they worked night and day with the others: the *anciens* guided the younger students; the *nouveaus* helped the older members with detail work, retrieved books from which to study or ran for baguettes and cheese. Their patriarch Laloux oversaw the work, guiding with broad strokes; the students adored him like a father.

The day before the Saturday two o'clock deadline for the final solution, the atelier went wild. Members scrambled over one another for paste brushes and mounting boards. If the candles shed inadequate light, some waited until dawn to put the last finishes on their watercolors and ink-wash renderings. Then the last hour came. Clarence Stein, a student at the atelier with Van Alen, described the scene:

> Everyone was shouting and running around. The whole atelier seemed to have gone mad. Finally we had loaded all the drawings mounted into small *charettes*—carts. I, as last nouveau, was commanded to act as horse for the last *charette*. It was five minutes of two . . . The cart-load was heavy—it seemed to be pulling me back, but I jogged along. A tram came along and al-

most ran us down, and we in turn came near to knocking down innumerable old men and children . . . One final spurt and we were at the school. My, I was tired when it was all done. I felt like sitting down there on the stairs and dying.

Van Alen and Stein, who later became well known for his efforts in city planning, often ran together. They traveled to Fountainbleu, where they got lost in the woods outside the town. They shared drinks at the brass-edged tables of Café des Deux Magots; they attended grand balls and costume parades, sometimes ending the night at a bonfire before the Pantheon and the hustle of police; and they worked together. Once they spent the last weeks of December, including Christmas and New Year's Eve, toiling on a competition design for a terra-cotta building. Friends stopped by the atelier or their apartments to help, or at least share in a tea, but Van Alen kept calling Stein back to the drafting table, even while he was writing letters home to his parents. There was work to be done. Ely Jacques Kahn said of his time in Paris with Van Alen and Stein, "Unless you were really serious about trying to do a job, nobody gave a damn about who you were or anything about you whatsoever." To graduate, students earned points from competitions held throughout the year; rivalry among students, especially from different ateliers, was intense. To dare step into another atelier earned one a pail of water poured from overhead.

Despite the constant competition, Van Alen remembered the time spent in the old Louis XV–style private house near the school as one of the finest of his life. He lived up to the promise of a Paris Prize winner, earning special remark from Laloux and medals for his design of a bathhouse, a City Hall, and a naval monument on an island in the sea. He was praised for his cleverness and understanding of scale. One critic commented: "The training was providing him with the mental freedom necessary to think independently, instead of merely the school-cargo of elements of architecture and a technique of composition by rules." The school taught him the necessity of a logical plan rather than a blind adherence to one style or another; the broad range of study gave him knowledge of all the arts and an insight into the physics of construction. He mastered the technique of rendering so that he might provide future clients a vision in ink and color of how their buildings would look. He modeled in clay, competed with painters, and was won over by the school's bent toward monumental, large-scale projects.

His instructors also stressed beauty in design, a lesson that motivated Cass Gilbert to say: "Aim for beauty; originality will take care of itself." In Paris beauty was a student's constant companion, from the Palais du Luxembourg, to the arcades of the Rue de Rivoli, to the great cathedral of Notre Dame. Van Alen only needed to cross the Pont des Arts, passing the fisherman on the quays, to arrive at the Louvre. Always appearing unexpectedly at the turn of the corner was the Eiffel Tower, looming like a giant over the city at 984 feet. Built twenty years before Van Alen arrived, millions had gone before him up the lifts to the top platform to see the city from the tallest structure in the world. It was a sight that also influenced the artists then carousing at Montparnesse's Lapin Agile and leading the movement of modern art. No matter how hectic the atelier schedule, the pleasures and inspiration of Parisian life were always present to the eager architect.

But most important, the architect, almost thirty years old at his graduation in 1911, learned the art of competition in his three years at the Ecole des Beaux-Arts. At the end, he received his diploma and spent the summer touring through Europe. He met Stein and Kahn in Italy, and for several weeks sketched and made watercolors of the ruins of Rome. That summer Italian cities and villages across the country built pavilions to celebrate Roman arts through the ages. It was as if the past, the architecture of Palladio and Brunelleschi, dared him to challenge their style. Eventually Van Alen returned to Paris and set off back to America, now ready to make his name. His colleague Kenneth

Murchison later characterized the young architect's sentiment: "Van Alen was the only American student who returned from Paris without a box full of architectural books. He foresaw the future. He tingled with the touch of approaching modernism. He threw his pencil compass overboard on the way home."

"No old stuff for me!" Van Alen said. "No bestial copyings of arches and colyums and cornishes! Me, I'm new! *Avanti!*"

CHAPTER THREE

A Proud and Soaring Thing

All great ages have left a record of themselves in
their styles of building. Why should we not try to
find a style for ourselves.

—*Karl Schinkel*

In the first week of November 1928, when Van Alen started the
sketches for Chrysler's skyscraper, the land at Forty-second and
Lexington was worth more than two hundred dollars a square foot.
Only a block away, the Grand Central Terminal was fast becoming the
crossroads of the world. Tall buildings shot up like weeds after a fresh
rain. It was the perfect spot to build a monument to Walter Chrysler,
the master of motion and industry, and Van Alen was eager to see his
designs of a towering skyscraper set in steel and stone. After years of
indentured servitude as an office boy and draftsman, study at the
world's best architecture school, and a partnership settled in lawsuits,
he was ready.

There were few set rules to follow in skyscraper design, particularly in 1928. Past skyscrapers included twenty-story palazzos or
buildings with Greek temples set at their crown. Van Alen scorned
these attempts to use classical architecture on modern structures. It
was high time, as he said, "to recognize that in steel-frame construc-

tion lies the basis for an entirely new, effective and beautiful style of architecture," one absent of the cornices, pediments, and columns that defined buildings made from masonry.

The road to the future looked bleak. Pioneers like Le Corbusier and Walter Gropius urged utility, straight lines, and engineering. To Van Alen and many of his cadre in New York, this radical European movement, of buildings stripped of any clothing or decoration, was tantamount to losing architecture's soul to the devil. As one architect said at the time, skyscrapers must not be reduced to the "stark nakedness of silos and grain elevators."

Instead of mimicking the past or leaping into an uncertain future, Van Alen was looking for "an architectural character that is effective, beautiful, expressive of the purpose of the building, of our method of construction and of the spirit of the times." It was Louis Sullivan, with his Wainwright and Bayard buildings in the late nineteenth century, who first gave expression to the kind of design Van Alen wanted to pursue. To Sullivan, a skyscraper needed to embrace its vertical quality. "It must be tall, every inch of it tall. The force and power of altitude must be in it, the glory and pride of exaltation must be in it. It must be every inch a proud and soaring thing."

In the last decade American architects like Van Alen had begun to embrace Sullivan's words, searching for the skyscraper's true expression. In competitions and sketchbooks, they experimented with obelisks, clock towers, ziggurats, pagodas, and Mesoamerican temples. Some buildings had the shape of a staggered mountain, like a wedding cake; others looked like a "frozen fountain."

Having stripped away the features of classical design, Van Alen and others searched for new methods to dress their buildings. For inspiration, they examined stage and film designs, attracted to the dramatic play of light and color in the sets. Most importantly, they drew upon ideas from the 1925 Exposition Internationale des Arts Décoratifs et Industriels Modernes in Paris, which promoted a movement of interior design and furniture, *style moderne* as it was initially called—later Art Deco—that gave designers the textures, floral patterns, colors, geometric shapes, and materials like rare woods, glass, metal, glazed tiles, and polychromatic terra-cotta to bring their buildings alive.

Not only was Van Alen free to shape his skyscraper in a new way, but he might avail himself of Art Deco designs that could entertain, captivate, evoke emotion, and inspire the imaginations of those on the street. Chrysler wanted such a building. With such freedom and wealth of designs from which to choose, Van Alen took the advice of his Beaux-Arts school and decided to follow his instincts. He started with the sketches he had created for Reynolds. Later the details would change, but the general lines remained the same.

On the initial design of the Reynolds Building in 1928, he had drawn his sketches with a hurried hand, as if getting out his ideas before they vanished. He drew on the tracing paper four step-backs from the street level and then a long tower that terminated in a pyramid. To distinguish certain windows he squiggled dark circles. To allow for light and air he recessed one axis. Then right above the entrance up to the top of the building, he sketched long vertical lines in the center of the tower face. His hand moved up and down over the paper in a flurry, giving the skyscraper its expression of height. Then on each side of that center, he penciled horizontal lines, sometimes so quickly that his hand strayed over the edge of the tracing paper. The lines were uneven and spaced awkwardly, but they managed to emphasize the vertical movement of the building's tower while distinguishing each floor. In the balance of these vertical and horizontal movements, the tower would rise effortlessly to the sky.

The next sketch was absent the nervous doodles to the side of the building that Van Alen had made on the first sketch. Van Alen drew a more cohesive vision of the ground floor and entrance, and in the first setback, he sketched straight lines that crossed one another to identify windows. The long vertical lines in the center of the tower face were now separated into three distinct columns, and the pyramid crown had more distinction. Over the next two years he redesigned the crown with Byzantine domes, curved corner windows, a "top piece which looked for all the world like Governor Smith's famous brown derby," arched entrances, and many brick textures. Still the rough expression of form and height remained.

From these early sketches, he began the plans for the Chrysler Building in November 1928, only days after his meeting with the automobile magnate, wasting no time on traveling to Europe as Chrysler suggested. He had studied enough and now needed to execute. In his Madison Avenue office, he shaped models in clay to get a sense of the proportion and details. His first designs, ones good enough to send to Chrysler, concentrated on the skyscraper's lower floors. Because of city regulations requiring buildings to step back from the street the higher they climbed (so that pedestrians didn't have to walk in dark, crowded canyons), Van Alen accepted that his skyscraper would have a tower that rose out of the massive rectangular base. The key to these "lower masses" was providing tenants proper light and air through light courts and carefully arranged setbacks, organizing the entrances and elevators for efficient access, and designing the façade, primarily through the treatment of the windows, so that these floors gave a sense of stability to the tower above. He planned to achieve this latter element with a gridiron pattern of windows, accentuated by the surrounding brickwork.

As early as November 12, Van Alen began submitting the floor plans for his lower masses, which included the lot dimensions as well as the placement of the windows, elevators, and stairwells. He started with the sixteenth floor and, over the next week, worked his way down to the plan of the basement and cellar. It was a rapid-fire sequence of delivered plans, no doubt many taken in part from his blueprints for the former Reynolds Building.

Starting on November 22, Van Alen and his draftsmen worked out the next eleven stories to the twenty-seventh floor. For the next eight weeks, this was as far as he went in designing the skyscraper, at least in terms of sending blueprints of floor plans or the skyscraper's eleva- tion, which would have provided an idea of the building's overall shape. Short of one attempt in late December, Van Alen had stopped at the point at which the tower would begin to ascend from the lower masses. This was a critical juncture. For Van Alen, the tower—how it rose from the base, how its surface treatment expressed both vertical and horizontal movements "giving life and interest," and how it termi- nated at the apex—was everything. He still needed time to finalize the design from his early sketches.

That was not to say he was idle. There were many meetings with Chrysler and his right-hand man on the project, Frank B. Rogers. After Van Alen delivered the plans for the lower floors at the end of November, Chrysler began requesting revisions, often several times a day. In December, Van Alen made changes to the floor plans for every one of these lower floors, on everything from the position of the ser- vice elevators and stairs to the lot dimensions, floor levels, and place- ment of the exterior columns. Every decision involved a multitude of elements, whether zoning laws, office-unit layouts, construction costs, service facilities, flow of people into and about the building, and struc- tural and mechanical factors—not to mention aesthetic concerns. Both Chrysler and Van Alen were excited by the work, and they got along well.

In January, the deluge of blueprints tapered off; perhaps Van Alen needed some time for reflection. Come the last week of the month though, Van Alen began a six-week burst of creative output on the Chrysler Building that must have taken his client by storm. One could imagine the late nights and early mornings he spent at his drafting board, drawings scattered across the room and his staff peering over his shoulder or waiting outside the door to see what he had done. Van Alen was always relentless and obsessed with his work. If he had time for meetings at his architectural clubs or dinners with his wife Elizabeth, it was limited, and he rarely spoke of what he was doing out-side the office.

During this month and a half, he changed nothing on the lower masses. It was all about the expression of the tower. On January 26, he sent over the floor plans for the fifty-first through the sixty-seventh floors, identifying how the tower made the transition into a multi-tiered dome. This was followed at the first of February by plans for the twenty-eighth through the fiftieth floors, showing the tower rising clear from the final setback at the thirty-first floor. The following week Chrysler was given a look at the brick automobile friezes that wrapped around the floors before this setback as well as how the corners of the building at this level were punctuated by enormous winged gargoyles. The automobile man became obsessed as well, his office strewn with sketches and models of his skyscraper.

By March 4, Van Alen knew how his skyscraper would look from afar. Blueprints were delivered in one-quarter scale for the Lexington Avenue and Forty-third Street elevations, as well as more detailed drawings for the upper part of the tower and the dome. The tower, with its long vertical stretches of windows in the center, looked similar to his earliest skyscraper sketches for Reynolds, though now more de-tailed. The bands of dark brick around the corners also recalled his previous designs. The key difference was the design of the skyscraper's dome. Van Alen had eliminated the awkward glass dome ("a great jew-eled sphere," one critic commented) that interrupted the building's leap into the sky. In its place, he designed a dome above the tower that was shaped in a series of six arches on each side of the building that curved toward one another at the top. The architect never left record of what inspired the design. Some said it spoke to the Singer Building's crown; others thought Van Alen must have drawn the idea from Asian stupas or the Mole Antonelliana in Turin, Italy. Kenneth Murchison, the architect's colleague and unofficial chronicler of the skyscraper race to follow, said that Van Alen returned from a trip to Cuba with the shape of the "neck of a demijohn of Bacardi" in mind.

Whatever the inspiration, Chrysler approved the inventive design for his skyscraper's crown and, by March, was resolved on most of the building's key elements. In the automobile man, Van Alen had indeed found the client of a lifetime. Chrysler pushed him, much as he did his car designers. Chrysler requested hundreds of revisions to the architect's first designs. He knew what he liked when he saw it and would pay whatever it cost, but Van Alen had to come up with the ideas.

When the architect presented Chrysler with the lobby design, showing him a plaster model with walls painted Morocco-marble red, Chrysler said, "It looks a little cramped, to me."

Chrysler pointed to one of four columns in the toy-sized lobby. "A terrific load is carried by those columns in the plans as drawn," said Van Alen.

"But when people come into a big building, they should sense a change, get a mental lift that will put them in a frame of mind to transact their business—how about this?" He reached his fingers into the toy-sized ground floor lobby and hesitated.

"Pull it out," said Van Alen. "That's just a piece of cardboard, pegged in there."

He yanked a cardboard column from the model. "Could it be done?"

Van Alen drew some hurried lines on an envelope with his pencil and then turned it over for him to see. "It could be done this way."

Chrysler smiled. It was all about impressing the millions of people who would walk through the triangular lobby of his building, costs be damned. Van Alen was with him every step of the way.

Once the architect settled on each design element, then came the working drawings and specifications, copies of which were sent to Rogers, the builder Fred Ley, and his subcontractors. These drawings included floor plans, sectional designs, and elevations from every side of the skyscraper. Enough paper passed back and forth to require "several van loads," a member of Chrysler's team quipped.

Throughout this process, materials to be used in the construction also were reviewed and appraised for cost and quality. Van Alen continued to work tirelessly. All his efforts and those of his draftsmen, specification writers, office boys, and secretaries were focused on the Chrysler Building. It must have dominated every conversation. The structural engineer, Ralph Squire, frequently consulted with Van Alen on the size of the columns, beams, and trusses as well as the foundation requirements. The mechanical engineer, Louis Ralston, worked with Van Alen and Squire to draw up plans and estimates for the elevators, plumbing, electricity, and ventilation.

Some of this work, at least the general requirements, had already been mapped out the previous year. This allowed builder Fred Ley and his team to ready the site for the skyscraper to rise according to Van Alen's vision.

———

Nearly from the moment Chrysler took possession of the five-story building at 405 Lexington Avenue, and more importantly, the land underneath, demolition crews hit the site. As the architect, Van Alen oversaw the construction. Beyond providing the plans, Van Alen was responsible for supervising the work, ensuring that Fred Ley was fulfilling his duties on schedule and at the cost that his client had agreed to contractually. His firm answered questions about the architectural plans and specifications and inspected the progress. But for the most part, the builder ran the show.

Born in Springfield, Massachusetts, in 1872, Fred Ley started his career in the construction industry at fifteen years old. He worked for the city engineer, earning a dollar and a half a day, while he learned the basics of surveying. Only six years later, having saved up five hundred dollars, he launched a contracting company, which, except for a brief period when Ley served in the Spanish-American War, grew unimpeded for the next thirty-six years. By the time Chrysler hired him to build his skyscraper, Ley boasted several hundred million dollars of construction projects, some as far away as South America. In New York, he had built the Fisk Building on Fifty-seventh Street and the Liggett Building on Forty-second Street and Madison, only a block away from where he was now engaged. By 1929, business was so good for Fred Ley & Company that he had bought land on Thirty-ninth Street and Fifth Avenue to construct his own skyscraper.

The Chrysler Building dwarfed his other jobs, and he quickly set to the task. By the third week of October 1928, he was in the process of demolishing the five-story office building, which Reynolds had blanketed with advertisements for his beachfront development, Lido Beach. Sometimes these operations could take months. Across the street, the builder of the Chanin Building first had to tear down an old storage warehouse of brick masonry whose walls had been built, in the wake of the city's infamous draft riots, to withstand cannon fire. Ley managed his wrecking job in less than four weeks.

Nonetheless, it was a dirty and noisy operation. Wreckers utilized the "plug and feather" method to take the walls apart. A wedge was stuck between a pair of iron semicylindrical guards, the "feathers," and driven into the masonry to break it loose, a quarrying technique dating back to the Romans. Wreckers also drilled into the top of the wall and pried off sections—the "growler" method. In tougher spots they used quicklime to prompt the expansion of gases and heat to break apart the rock. Chutes carried the old walls down into the trucks. Bricks, glass, stone, pipes, and other junk metal were salvaged for resale; the rest was carried out in barges and dumped into the Atlantic Ocean. The air around the demolition site stank of rotting old lumber and dust stung the eyes. Everything from crowbars to pneumatic drills to acetylene torches were needed to do the job. It took more than a hundred and fifty men from the Albert Volk Company, a demolition subcontractor, working in double shifts to get the site clear enough for the excavators to begin their digging on November 11.

The excavation for the foundations always made for a great street spectacle. People lined the site perimeter and cab drivers slowed to watch the crew dig into the earth. Ley hired the Godwin Construction Company for this task, and over the course of the next four months, they used six steam shovels, twenty drills, forty trucks, and four derricks to chew down sixty-nine feet below the street where the skyscraper's foundations would be set. Laboring night and day, they carried away the debris of the basement walls and floor, plus the fifty-one thousand cubic yards of earth and rock.

Most impressive on the site was the steam shovel, a monstrous machine that belched steam as it clawed and tore its way down below the street. Its shovel carved out a yard and a half of earth at a time. Each rig cost $14,500, and Godwin charged roughly $3.50 per cubic yard of removed earth to a five-foot depth. This escalated to $13.50 once he reached thirty feet from street level. Boilers on the back of the boxcar provided the power. An engineer and helper made up the shovel crew. The former sat in the boxcar behind the shovel and maneuvered the rig, which was unusually agile for its girth. One writer of the time said it could "move in every direction save skyward." Through judicious use of the levers, the engineer moved the shovel forward on its caterpillar treads to where his helper directed, dropped the boom, drew the shovel forward, scooped up his next load, raised the boom, rotated the car (which was saved from tipping over by a five-ton counterweight), and carried it to a dipper lowered from a derrick that then hauled the earth and rock away. The six shovels on the Chrysler Building site repeated this process thousands of times to reach bedrock, and spectators rarely tired of the show.

Unseen by those passing on the street was the tremendous amount of work being done outside of Manhattan Island to prepare for the building to rise. As Van Alen settled on the design as well as specifications for materials, Fred Ley began making the orders, working closely with the manufacturers so that product quality and timely delivery were guaranteed. A skyscraper the size of the Chrysler Building required worldwide efforts. Oak planks would come from West Virginia, spruce from Canada, finer woods from Cuba, Japan, and South America. Brass pipes and copper rods would arrive from Connecticut, aluminum from Tennessee, and asbestos fittingly from Asbestos, Quebec. Quarries from as near as New Hampshire or as far as Italy or Sweden would provide granite and marble. Cement for the foundations usually would arrive from Pennsylvania, while brick came from Michigan. Pennsylvania also would provide much of the steel. Belgians made nice plate glass, and the Portuguese a fine insulating cork. There were thousands of items to purchase, tens of subcontractors to consult for decisions, and millions of dollars in contracts to let.

By the end of February, many of these materials had been ordered and the excavation was nearly completed. Over fifty thousand feet of lumber shored up the walls surrounding the giant chasm that was now 405 Lexington Avenue. Foundation engineers directed the men as they laid the spread footings upon which the columns would stand. These footings distributed the tremendous weight bearing down on each column. Resting on a concrete pier that went down to bedrock, the footing was made of stacks of steel beams placed side by side. Each layer of beams was turned perpendicular to the one below. Once set, the foundation workers constructed wooden frames around the steel and poured concrete inside to weatherproof it. This steel and concrete box weighed over thirty-five tons and could bear a load ten times that weight. It wouldn't be long now before the first columns of the Chrysler Building were raised on top of these footings. Ley was on schedule to live up to the promise of the billboard hung at the edge of the site: "Chrysler Building—Being Erected on this Site—Ready for Occupation Spring of 1930."

And yet with all of this construction and design work over the four and half months since Chrysler had bought the property and declared he wanted the world's tallest building, there was no word of what kind of skyscraper would rise on the land at Forty-second Street and Lexington. Only those involved in the project knew how New York's skyline was about to change forever.

———

Finally on March 7, 1929, Chrysler released the plans and rendering for Van Alen's design to the press. "World's Tallest Edifice to Cost $15,000,000—Topped by Artistic Dome," proclaimed the *New York Times* and "Chrysler Building Will Be City's Highest Tower," promised the *New York Herald Tribune*. Journalists detailed a sixty-eight-story tower of 809 feet, with a total volume of 13.5 million cubic feet and 900,000 square feet of rentable floor space, calling it the "giant of giants" whose neighbors were "such pygmies as the 52-story Chanin Building, the diminutive Graybar Building and the barely perceptible New York Central Building." The skyscraper would house eleven thousand people, run thirty elevators, and have 3,750 windows that needed to be washed on a regular basis. Tunnels would connect the building with Grand Central Terminal, the subway, and the Hotel Commodore. The grand entrance would open into a lobby one hundred feet long, with a dome in the center over three stories tall. The *New York Sun* reported: "At night the tower will be flood lighted with banks of lights on each of the four corners of the terrace at the fifty-sixth floor and another set on the top of the dome to light the pinnacle of the tower. The pinnacle will be in the form of a thirty-pointed star set up on end. It will be of case aluminum and mounted on a figure sixteen feet high." It was a grand announcement, and newspaper editors reproduced the image of the future Chrysler Building on their front pages.

News of "world's tallest" skyscrapers always made for eye-catching headlines, even if most came from developers hoping to spin their hold on a particular spot of land into millions—as Reynolds had done previously for the same site. It had been sixteen years since Woolworth claimed the title, and the possibility of another skyscraper rising higher stirred great interest. The city's height race had been at a slow simmer too long. In 1926 the architect and engineer John Larkin first stirred the pot when he announced a one-hundred-and-ten-story, 1208-foot-tall "super-skyscraper" to dwarf the Woolworth Building. The *New York Times* proclaimed it would make "the Tower of Babel look like a child's toy." Although Larkin failed to meet his promise of world's tallest (ground had yet to be broken by 1929), the possibility was enough to fire imaginations. Others announced plans for towering structures; even the dictator Mussolini promoted a tower for Rome of eleven hundred feet with forty-five hundred rooms, one hundred halls, and a gymnasium for Olympic athletes. But nothing had yet come to pass.

Van Alen, and likely most of the city, knew Chrysler had the will and the money to see his skyscraper soar above any other. The announcements made it clear the Chrysler Building was a personal investment. Now in a decade obsessed with farthest, fastest, and tallest, with the stock market booming and real-estate values climbing, the question was who would challenge the automobile giant and his architect. The answer came soon enough.

CHAPTER FOUR

The Organization Man

I am perhaps a little quick to run and open the
valve. That is about it—a door opener.

—*Daniel Burnham*

In March 1929, Craig Severance waited in his twelfth-floor Fifth
Avenue apartment overlooking the vast stretch of Central Park. He was
dressed in English riding clothes and handmade leather boots. A few
months shy of his fiftieth birthday, Severance had the powerful build
of a younger man. He had a lean jaw and a full shock of dark brown hair;
if one were to qualify him in a word, "vigorous" would fit the bill. His
father squandered the family fortune while Severance was in his teens,
and he had long struggled to build the life he now led as a wealthy man
of business—and yes, architecture as well.

Severance went horseback riding in Central Park every weekday,
short of a morning thunderstorm or blizzard. On weekends he rode in
Point Pleasant, New Jersey, where he had a large Victorian house.
When possible, he brought his only daughter, Faith, along with him.
Usually they trotted along, talking about school, the horses, or the latest adventures of his Pekinese dog, who was so small, he joked, that she
carried a straw instead of a stick. It was just good to spend some time
with Faith now that she was married and away more often. Although he

had separated from her mother years before and remarried, Severance and his daughter were still close. She shared his love for riding and the outdoors. Even from a young age, Faith was a crack shot and every bit her father's daughter.

As light began to fill the streets, the buzzer rang. It was the boy from the stable on Fifty-fifth Street with the horses: Severance's beloved Colonel and a big Irish, Hennessy, for Faith. Once Faith arrived as well, he met her downstairs. They eased onto their mounts and took the reins from the groom. Fifth Avenue was quiet, and the construction crews tearing down the old mansions along Carnegie Hill to make way for yet another fourteen-story apartment building had still not arrived for work. As they waited to cross into the park, Severance calmed his horse and then turned to his daughter. He rarely spoke of his work with her, but this occasion warranted an exception, at least a brief one.

"I'm going to build the tallest skyscraper in the world," he said.

Most daughters would have been shocked to hear this news, and at the least excited—but Faith knew her father too well. Nothing he did surprised her. This was a man who kept a loaded gun by his bedside in the country, and when squirrels or mice rattled around the attic, he fired into the ceiling. He had a huge appetite for life. He settled only for the best. And everyone thought it was inevitable that he would achieve great things. Once, he built a residence for a prominent New York businessman and the completed design came out wrong. Instead of arguing this merit or that, Severance had the walls torn down at his own cost and started again.

"Oh, how wonderful," she finally answered. She was not surprised.

That was the end of the conversation. Severance urged Colonel across the street, and Hennessy followed. After their hour-long circuit through the park, they shared a breakfast of coffee, grapefruit, ham, eggs, and finnan haddie cooked by his Japanese chef, Matsi. The stable boy returned the horses, and the chauffeur delivered Severance on time for the day's first meeting at his office on Forty-fourth Street.

This was the kind of life Faith's father's will and energy had brought him. An architectural journal said that he was "the only architect who owns a Rolls-Royce and rides in it," but the barb rolled off his wide shoulders.

Very few people knew how high Severance's skyscraper was going to be, or of the late arrivals to the deal. The sole public announcement detailed a forty-seven-story office building on a Wall Street site, next to the old United States Sub-Treasury where George Washington had been inaugurated president.

Talking to his daughter, Severance left out the fact that Walter Chrysler, who had attended her large St. Bartholomew Church wedding in January, was also trying to build the tallest skyscraper in the world. But he didn't have to; she read the papers. As for Van Alen, Severance never spoke of his former partner to Faith, and she had yet to forgive the "Beaux-Arts architect" for sitting on a lemon pie she had baked at a weekend in the country. She offered few kind words about Van Alen, who of course hadn't been invited to the wedding. To her, he was a world apart from her father in every way. Van Alen deserved the praise he won as an architect, but regardless he was "an unpleasant, tall funny man and not very distinguished. There was nothing likeable about him." It was obvious to her that their partnership had only prospered because her father had brought in the business.

As for her father, she may have doted on him but there was a frankness in her understanding of his character. She described his thinking as "I want. I get." This business of the tallest skyscraper was simply more of the same.

———

Early in his career, Severance recognized an opportunity to get ahead by shouldering the responsibility many of his colleagues shunned: the business side of architecture. To him, the architect as lonely malcontent, sitting before his drawing board and sketching plans that catered to his needs rather than the clients', was an archaic image. That may have played when architects like Christopher Wren enjoyed the patronage of kings, but this was New York. Here clients sang a different tune: "Make Me Money."

Severance came from a well-established family in Chazy, New York, near Lake Champlain, only miles from the Canadian border. The town was built by pioneers who first trapped and sold furs, then cleared a spot of land with an ax, firebrand, and a pair of oxen. If they needed a fence, they often used the charred stumps remaining from the fire. The calls of wolves pierced the night, and black bears roamed the edges of the woods. Families lived in log cabins and bark huts. They spun their own cloth and made their own shoes. In the winter, the cold set deep into the bones of the town's residents. The grit of a pioneer was in the bones of Craig Severance.

By the time Severance was born on July 1, 1879, the packs of wolves had thinned and the town was coming into its own, thanks in part to the Severance family. His grandfather, George Severance, started as a farmer, but went on to run a general mercantile store that prospered in the Civil War by sending furs and wheat to Union soldiers. He owned great swaths of land and was one of Chazy's leading residents. He financed the Presbyterian Church whose steeple rose over the town, one of his many works. At his death in 1875, his five children inherited his fortune, but not the store, which he had passed on to a clerk who had worked for him for years.

When Craig Severance was a child, his father had yet to lose his inheritance and those of his younger brothers and sisters. They lived somewhat fashionably, with a governess, fine carriage, and a stable of beautiful stallions. Severance rode horses from an early age and scrambled around one of the town's most prominent homes, Slate House. Over the years, though, his father, bitter at not having been given the family store, invested in and ran a number of questionable businesses, including a peanut butter manufacturer, and managed to steadily drain all of the family's money. He was hard on those who worked for him. One time a laborer carrying a wooden plank across their yard asked what they were to do that day. His father answered, "Stand there and hold that plank until I get home." As devout Presbyterians, the family practiced the stricter, rather than the more loving side of the denomination.

After a failed attempt at college, Craig Severance moved to New York. Since his father no longer had the means to support him, Severance took a job with his cousin, Charles Rich, who ran a busy architect's practice. In his first years, Severance had to borrow fifty dollars here and there to get through the lean times, but was always diligent in honoring his debts, writing to his mother about how much he had paid down that month. He lived on West Seventy-ninth Street, and with a twenty-two-dollar-a-week salary, had little money to spare. Like Van Alen, Severance toiled away in a draftsmen factory, learning the trade. Charles Rich and his partner Hugh Lamb never attained the stature of a McKim, Mead & White, but they always had clients coming in the door, everyone from established families like the Colgates and Armours to Broadway theater owners, immigrant bankers, universities, and churches. Among their projects in New York was the fifteen-story Syndicate Building in the financial district, where they had their offices, as well as the Bryant Park Studios and a row of houses on Riverside Drive. They drew praise, but also harsh comments for their designs, particularly from Montgomery Schuyler, the leading critic of the time, who wrote that some of their work called for "the intervention of an architectural police. It is not much of a hazard to say that they are the most thoroughly discreditable buildings ever erected in New York." Regardless of complaints about the quality of their designs, their practice prospered. Rich had the connections, and they managed to juggle a number of commissions at once through good management.

Asked once why he wanted to be an architect, Severance answered:

"It wouldn't have mattered what I decided to do—doctor or lawyer. I would have done them all as well." He drove himself hard, and though he had no great passion for architecture as art, he meant to get ahead. Through his cousin, Severance learned the business of architecture and cultivated relationships with those who later won him commissions. He understood better than most H. H. Richardson's three rules for an architect's practice, "Get the job! Get the job! Get the job!" For Severance, the real classroom for an architect was to be found in the client's boardroom. There an architect pitched his services, closed the deal, budgeted the cost of the building, finalized deadlines, and settled on design and floor plans. Rich set him on the path that the best way to plan a building was through a committee of owner, banker, real-estate agent, architect, engineer, builder, subcontractors, and suppliers. The architect-artist could wait outside. As Richardson also said, "I'll plan anything a man wants, from a cathedral to a chicken coop. That's the way I make my living."

After several years with Lamb & Rich, Severance took a job with the architectural firm Carrère & Hastings—the perfect name to have on his resume before leaving to start his own practice. Thomas Hastings and John Carrère first worked at McKim, Mead & White before setting out on their own. Hastings was the designer of the firm. During the day he sketched out the plans for their latest commissions and ran about the team of draftsmen, offering suggestions, criticizing lines, and then quickly stepping away, sometimes with the praise "I like your architecture. Bully for you! *Chouette!*" Carrère reined in his partner and handled the business end of the practice. As his friend Harold Magonigle said, "There was always Carrère to depend upon or to cancel or mitigate mistakes . . . Hastings was as helpless as a shedder crab when anything practical was in question . . . He was very, very lucky to be able to be relieved of the tedious side of architecture and be enabled to live in the world of his dreams." With this kind of partnership, the firm won the commission for the New York Public Library and distinguished themselves as one of the leaders of the Beaux-Arts movement in architecture.

Severance had scarce patience for the life of an office draftsman, neither the studying of old plates to get the right lines for the Ionic Order's Scamozzi variation, nor suffering the pranks of being sent out by the senior men to bring back a vanishing point since they had loaned theirs out to another office. Severance had other skills, and Carrère & Hastings recognized that he made a fine clerk-of-the-works. The job of superintending the construction site on behalf of the architect was a task he welcomed. He made sure the contractors followed the firm's plans and specifications; he audited the cost figures supplied by the contractors and verified the quality of the materials and workmanship. Severance enjoyed seeing how a building was put together by the sweat and experience of the men on the site. Although liked by the workers, he pushed his weight around when needed. One time while overseeing a man making concrete, Severance told the worker to put more sand in the mixture. It was important to get these things right. Severance walked away and then came back a few minutes later to see the man continuing to do the same as he was before. Severance told him again, but the worker ignored him. Finally, he lifted the worker up by the back of his pants and threw him into a bed of unhardened concrete. From that point forward, the construction men listened to Severance.

During his time with Carrère & Hastings, Severance learned how to manage men and came to understand that more went into a building than some designs and a nice rendering for the papers. It was a business to be mastered. An architect who understood finance and industry, one who recognized the importance of maximizing profit, would go far. Every year since the end of the Civil War, the pump was being primed to enable this kind of architect—one Severance was training to become—to succeed.

The transcontinental railroad brought the economic might of

America into one fold, thereby giving rise to great fortunes and corporate giants. Increasingly industrial juggernauts ruled business, and cities like New York and Chicago held sway over the countryside. In 1907 when Severance went out on his own, he had an intuitive understanding of this modern world and its potential. He was a disciple of Daniel Burnham, even if he was not privy to his words. In his career "Uncle Dan" Burnham advised presidents, designed noted buildings including the Monadnock and Flatiron, ran the American Institute of Architects, city-planned Chicago, San Francisco, and Manila, and earned a fortune in architect's fees on grand projects like Washington D.C.'s Union Station. One day Burnham discovered his partner John Root drawing a minor detail for one of their commissions. Obviously Root didn't yet understand that in this new age one could only harness this "mad and willful humanity" through organization and specialization. Burnham scolded his partner, "John, you ought to delegate that sort of thing. The only way to handle a big business is to delegate, delegate, delegate." Later he told an unimpressed Louis Sullivan, who had witnessed the scene, "My idea is to work up a big business, to handle big things, deal with big businessmen, and to build up a big organization, for you can't handle big things unless you have an organization."

The entrepreneur in Severance had a vision like Burnham's, and it forced him out of Carrère & Hastings. Few architects made their names coming up through the ranks of a practice. It took a decade before architects Richmond Shreve and William Lamb became partners in Carrère & Hastings—and that partnership quickly soured. Most had to strike out on their own, as Severance did. First he needed the commissions. As every architect who ever struggled to pay the electricity bill knew, connections were the key to commissions. Those with access to New York society had a great advantage, and in that respect, Severance had married well. His wife, Faith Griswold Thompson, was from an established Connecticut family and her brother had wedded the granddaughter of *the* Miss Astor. Although Severance's marriage in 1905 may not have brought a dowry of any great note, the door to society and its wealthy inhabitants was open. He also had the pedigree of Carrère & Hastings, plus the contacts he developed in his time with Charles Rich.

Initially Severance worked out of a spare office across from the New York Public Library, taking on minor projects to stay afloat, the kind that didn't warrant mention in architectural journals. Most noteworthy were a string of houses he designed in Locust Valley, New York. In 1911 he partnered with W. Schamm and won praise for the design of a Fifth Avenue shop front that critic Matlack Price said illustrated "the idea of refinement thrice refined in its every member." He was relentless in pitching those with means and influence. He lunched. He dined, entertained, and joined the right clubs, the ones businessmen haunted. "I don't know any architects," Severance said. "They don't get me the jobs." Just as his web of connections began to catch the first of his big clients, he left Schamm to partner with William Van Alen. It was a brilliant move.

Severance and Van Alen first met in the trenches during their draftsmen days. After all, it was a small world. Severance knew the value of having a Beaux-Arts man, and particularly a Paris Prize winner, as a partner. Unlike most of his classmates, when Van Alen returned from France, he chose not to join one of the larger firms. Instead he joined up with a partner and worked on designing cooperative apartment houses—actually introducing the idea of the "garden apartment" with its small patch of a garden in the back—but he was not making any great strides. Thirty-one years old and not yet married, he lived with his mother, her new husband, and his sister in a Brooklyn house on Putnam Avenue. Severance and Van Alen discussed joining forces and a partnership was struck in 1914.

That year they won a commission for a two-story string of shops, the Standard Arcade on Broadway. It won notice for its wide expanse of glass between two Doric columns. As architectural critic Christopher Gray said, it was "unusual for its openness." Next came the Albemarle on Twenty-fourth Street, with which Van Alen proved that an office building didn't need a heavy cornice at its crown. Since ancient Greece, these ornamental slabs had extended out over roofs, and its removal on the Albemarle drew praise for the firm. Soon more commissions for office buildings, banks, hotels, restaurants, stores, and country residences came their way—including the J. M. Gidding Building in midtown, a Fifth Avenue shop front said to have the same breathless inventiveness as Ralph Waldo Emerson's poetry, and a Long Island estate praised for its simplicity. In letters to potential clients, after detailing their list of services and expected charges, Severance & Van Alen would proudly conclude: "Our office is entirely organized, having the Departments to furnish all of the services as outlined; and we have had a wide experience . . . of considerable magnitude with various clients [to] whom . . . we take pleasure in referring you for any outside information regarding our qualification for this work."

The next decade brought Severance the kind of life he had known as a child. When he traveled to Europe, he brought his Rolls-Royce and chauffeur along with him. He owned a yacht and would have belonged to the New York Yacht Club if not for the time when he blocked out Vanderbilt's boat on the Hudson River and was blackballed. Such was society. Anyway, he preferred his hunting trips to Canada. In a private car, he took an overnight train to Montreal, showered and ate breakfast at the Ritz, then went on to Quebec to the Trident Club, a five-hundred-square-mile hunting reserve. Sometimes he took his daughter, sometimes friends. If it was not the Trident Club, it was salmon fishing in Newfoundland. At the Metropolitan Club, he counted among his friends some of the most powerful men in the city. Frank Bailey, the president of the Prudence Company, which financed many of the buildings in New York, was one of his closest and helped him win a number of commissions.

When Van Alen began missing deadlines, earning sole credit for the firm's success, and drawing too much attention to his unconventional designs, Severance put an end to the partnership. Ill feelings or not, this was business. He brought in the clients and deserved to run (and exclusively profit from) his firm.

While fighting through the lawsuit with his former partner, Severance never missed a step. In 1925, he hired two architects, Langfour and Lazinsk, as his head designers. He managed a legion of draftsmen, specification writers, and assistants. He delegated. He invested in real estate, served on corporate boards, and most of all, he brought in ever bigger clients to design ever bigger buildings. If by separating from Van Alen he won the freedom to run his business solo and choose the designs for his buildings, it came at a price, at least in terms of critical praise. The press hammered him. In his first "Sky Line" column in the *New Yorker*, George Chappell (a.k.a. T-Square) reviewed the Delmonico Building on Forty-fourth Street, writing, "Every proportion appears to be unfortunate. The central tower . . . has the grace of an overgrown grain elevator. Of the detail one of the profession said: 'Isn't it curious how a simple element like a band-course or a molding can produce a feeling of nausea? . . . Really, can't the Fifth Avenue Association do something about all this?'" T-Square noted that the older gentlemen architects on their way to lunch at the Century Club found the building so hideous that it caused them to spontaneously "burst into tears. They do not look at the building itself. They can't." Severance sued the magazine on the grounds that it hurt the owner's chances of finding tenants. Architectural snobbery was fine, but not when it hurt his business. Sixteen months too late, he won a meager apology from Chappell, who wrote, "We wish to clear our conscience by saying that we didn't intend to be personal nor to cast any reflection upon the professional attainments of Mr. Severance whom, although we have not had the pleasure of his acquaintance, we know to be one of the leading architects in the city."

It was much more than an isolated case though. Severance was struggling with his firm's designs. His clients may have wanted a familiar, traditional look to their buildings—and that fit nicely with his more conservative bent—but, the demands of height, not to mention the forward-looking critics, urged a more modern look. His 1,250-room Manger Hotel in Times Square, owned by another close friend, came off as cheerless—with the look of a square, cardboard box with holes punched into it for windows. His 50 Broadway skyscraper, which stood on the site of New York's earliest steel-frame structure, the eleven-story Tower Building, served as a lesson on how not to set a tower on a wide lower base. The tower was off-center and set back from the street in such a way that one could hardly see it from Broadway.

What the critics couldn't assail was the great practice he had created. The architect as businessman, someone who knew how to run an orderly, efficient shop, was here to stay. Building in New York City was like running an assembly line, and there was a great deal of money to be made in the process. As for his designs, Severance cared little for skyscrapers and other buildings as practice ground for wild new ideas. His clients paid for him to deliver a "machine that makes the land pay," as Cass Gilbert said of skyscrapers. And the clients continued to knock on his door, with a $2 million building here, and a $4 million headquarters there. At an average fee of six percent of the construction costs of these buildings (a percentage fixed by the American Institute of Architects), Severance reaped a small fortune in commissions every year. With the meteoric rise in construction enjoyed by architects and builders in the twenties, there seemed no end to the possibilities.

If there ever was a time to crown one's career in the twenties, 1929 was the year. Van Alen predicted, "History will record this age as the greatest of all so far as building is concerned." When Severance was approached on the 40 Wall Street development, he must have sensed the chance to live up to Burnham's words: "Make no little plans, they have no magic to stir men's blood and probably themselves will not be realized. Make big plans; aim high in hope and work, remembering that a noble, logical diagram once recorded will never die, but long after we are gone will be a living thing." These were men of money and business, men he understood. The initial plans drawn for the parcels of land at Wall Street and Pine showed a building of forty-seven stories. That kind of building would earn a tidy sum, but the developers and Severance had bigger plans: the taller the building, the more money to be earned. Uptown, Van Alen and Chrysler could raise their fantastic, steel-sheathed tower and drink in the praise of T-Square and others. Downtown, Severance meant to build a skyscraper taller than any in the world and make a good business of it all. That was the legacy he promised to leave.

CHAPTER FIVE

Make the Land Pay

The raison d'être of the skyscraper is therefore not
physical but psychical; it arose in answer to the
desire of the herd to become a super herd . . .
Skyscrapers appear only and always on those sacred
acres which for some mysterious reason have become the blue heaven of the businessman.

—Claude Bragdon

The roots of rivalry ran deep on the land where Severance planned to
design a towering skyscraper. The site at 40 Wall Street marked the
spot where, in 1799, Aaron Burr had deliberately opened a bank across
the street from Alexander Hamilton's Bank of New York, escalating a
feud that resulted in, among other things, Thomas Jefferson's election
as president (Hamilton threw his weight behind Jefferson to block a
Burr presidency) and the famous 1804 Hamilton-Burr duel, in which
Burr killed Hamilton with a shot to the stomach.

New York was steeped in such bloody rivalries. They were the
product of an environment where wealth, power, influence, and ego
flourished. It was only natural then that George Ohrstrom, a master of
negotiating these forces, would find himself interested in the land
where one of its most storied feuds also took root. Burr's bank owned

the final and most critical parcel of property Ohrstrom needed for his skyscraper site. Ohrstrom knew The Bank of The Manhattan Company, which was in the midst of a significant merger, was looking for larger quarters than the fourteen-story building where they now operated. Aaron Burr would have appreciated Ohrstrom's maneuvers to obtain the site, particularly in a real-estate market where a plot large enough to build a skyscraper hundreds of feet into the air was rare at best. An entire plot of land, like the site of the Waldorf-Astoria or Chrysler Building, seldom came on the market. Most often a number of plots needed to be cobbled together, one parcel at a time. Added to the surrounding lots, this last fourteen-thousand-square-foot lot promised great financial returns.

If there was one man who knew about making money, it was Ohrstrom, the "Boy Wonder" of Wall Street. In 1928 when he first took aim at the site, he was thirty-three years old. The son of a Danish immigrant, Ohrstrom grew up in Ford River, Michigan, a town whose population the *Michigan State Journal* said "could be tucked away on one floor" of the skyscraper he intended to construct. His father died when he was fifteen years old, and after he graduated from high school, he toiled away in lumbering and construction yards to earn enough money to go to the University of Michigan.

The call of World War I brought his studies to a premature end, and he enlisted in the air corps to become an aviator with the 104th Aero Squadron, 5th Corps Observation Group. He was shot down once over the French countryside (and rescued by the local resistance group), but then distinguished himself on the day before the Armistice was signed, November 10, 1918, while flying the slow, two-seated Salmson on a reconnaissance mission over the Verdun. A haze of clouds covered the sky. A German patrol of four Fokker planes flying several thousand feet above Ohrstrom sighted his plane and dove down to attack. The lead plane in Ohrstrom's formation, as one account described, "rocked sharply, lifted, then slipped down to the right as a red-tailed

Fokker flashed out of the clouds . . . Ohrstrom kicked the rudder and pulled back on the stick, waiting for the Fokker to pass. As it slid in front of them, he and his observer, Lieutenant Joseph Mallory, fired. The Fokker shuddered, hung for a moment, and then nosed over, trailing smoke and fire in a slow tailspin."

Credited with the last enemy kill of World War I, Second Lieutenant Ohrstrom returned from France to finish his courses at Michigan. After graduating, he moved to New York to take a job with the investment firm P. W. Chapman & Company. In 1926 he jumped headfirst into running his own investment bank and began to underwrite securities, as well as invest in and acquire companies. As luck had it, he made his first great strides in business through owning water companies. Asked by B. C. Forbes how he came to the apogee of success by only thirty-four, Ohrstrom nonchalantly answered:

I haven't reached the top. I was lucky, after being at business only a few years, to see that there was opportunity in a certain field, opportunity that nobody else apparently was going strongly after. I was fortunate in being able to do some financing for water companies at a time when this class of security was very little known. It took a lot of educational work to sell the bonds. I, of course, was sold on them myself. I realized that water is about the most fundamental necessity of man. There is always a demand for it every hour of the day.

So I began to become financially interested in a water company here and a water company there, and we branched out until the Federal Water Service Corporation, for which we are the bankers, controls the largest system of privately owned water supply companies in the United States, with properties valued at close to $150,000,000. Some of the water companies were interested in other utilities, so we became interested in them also, and now the People's Light & Power Corporation, which we have financed, controls electric light and power and gas properties worth more than $40,000,000.

An empire was in the making. Newspaper photographs of Ohrstrom show a young man with a preternatural stare of determination. He was handsome, almost too handsome—with tan, unblemished skin, trim hair parted neatly to the side, and a nose sharpened on a whetstone. Mostly though, it was his eyes that commanded your full attention. In person, he had a politician's skill of making those he met feel they were in the presence of the extraordinary. In a crowded room, he was its center.

And he inspired trust, a quality that proved useful when he asked for money. Sure he understood numbers and the legal nuances of a deal, but more important, he succeeded in his relationships. When the stock market plunged later that year, he went straight to his investors and told them which of his companies would weather the storm and which would not. Those who listened and held on made back their losses and more. As one British investor said, he was the "only person who bothered to come over to England to tell us how he lost our money."

That was Ohrstrom. He took people seriously and expected the same in return. When he hired someone, he rewarded them generously if they achieved and took them out quickly if they did not. He made fortunes for many and ruined others. "There was no bullshit," said one of the men who ran a company for him. Perhaps to remind people with whom they were dealing, Ohrstrom kept the General Order commending him for the "destruction, in combat, of an enemy Fokker" behind a glass frame in his office. That was if they could remove their eyes from his stare.

It was this uncompromising will that earned him a big English manor house on a 135-acre estate in Greenwich, Connecticut, and made securing the thirty-four thousand square feet of land for a sky-

scraper in Wall Street possible. For several years Ohrstrom had dab-
bled in real-estate development, underwriting the financing behind
several buildings in the city before investing himself. With vacancy
rates as low as they were, there was money to be made in development.
Like water, people would always need New York; it was the financial
center of the world, from where all capital flowed. In these endeavors
he chose his partners well. The Starrett brothers, Paul and William, ran
one of the country's leading construction companies and boasted over
one billion dollars in building contracts throughout their careers. They
were respected, envied, and feared by their competitors, and with the
help of Ohrstrom, they were increasingly becoming involved in the
ownership of the buildings they constructed.

In September 1928, Ohrstrom formed a holding company, 36 Wall
Street, to acquire a lease for the first two parcels he needed for his development. On the guarantee of an annual return of at least $175,000 a
year, the Iselin family leased to Ohrstrom the land at 34–36 Wall Street
and 31-33 Pine Street. This served as the first in a chess game of
moves. The key to the attack on the land was not to alert others to the
overall aim. If the six landowners Ohrstrom needed to negotiate with
knew of his intention to assemble a large plot from their individual
parcels, they would bid up the price. After all, this was the heart of Wall
Street. A square foot cost upwards of seven hundred dollars, and
people knew the game: the whole was greater than the sum of the parts
by as much as ten to fifty percent. For his real-estate brokers, he hired
Brown, Wheelock, Harris, Vought & Company in cahoots with Charles
Noyes & Company, so that they could run interference with one another, negotiating separate plots with separate brokers, but holding
the land in trust for Ohrstrom. Secrecy and deception were the tools of
the game. Sometimes even the brokers were kept in the dark about the
developer's ultimate plan.

In a *Fortune* magazine profile of Ohrstrom, the writer likened his
maneuvers to "the reverse of those of Foch on the Marne. The property

is attacked from the principal front, and the lots facing on that street—
say Wall Street—are first secured. Then the secondary lots are taken. By
the time the gentlemen in possession of the rear lots have begun to
suspect that their properties have key value to a great scheme, they find
themselves cut off from the sun and with only one possible profitable
movement—backwards and out."

First Ohrstrom took Lot I, the Iselin property. Because Lot II only
offered much value as an abutment to Lot I, the Iselins gave up that
lease as well. Marshall Field owned 2,105 square feet of land at 38 Wall
Street, Lot III. He turned down an offer to lease the land, but was more
than willing to sell his land outright. The deal was completed. Then
Ohrstrom's brokers acquired Lot IV from J. A. Sisto & Company, given
that Lot V was of only marginal value unless one held the land at Lot II
and Lot IV. The final pawn fell with Hooker Electrochemical's delivery
of Lot V, but there was still the queen to claim and its fourteen thousand square feet of land, Lot VI. To the west, the Assay Office still
threatened checkmate, if another developer bought the land and built
high enough to cause the loss of light and air. Much needed to be done.

Once Ohrstrom had secured the other parcels, he went straight to
the Vice Chairman of the Board of The Bank of The Manhattan
Company, P. A. Rowley. The bank had long ago abandoned its water in-
terests to focus on becoming one of the most prominent commercial
lenders in the city. It had acquired a number of smaller banks and was
set to merge with the International Acceptance Bank founded by Paul
Warburg, creating a company with total resources of $700 million.
Ohrstrom knew the board had formed a committee to explore the erection of a taller building, and he maneuvered his way into the conversation. After telling them he held the leases or owned the properties of
34-36-38 Wall Street and 27-29-31-33 Pine Street, he offered to construct a skyscraper of at least forty stories, providing the bank over one
hundred thousand square feet of space, in exchange for four hundred
thousand dollars annually in rent from the bank and the lease of the

land at one dollar. On January 14, 1929, he called Rowley and then followed up with a letter to explain further that although he hadn't yet secured the financing "there is no intention on our part to build this building, rent it and dispose of it; rather, it is a situation in which we all firmly believe and in which we have chosen to make a large personal permanent investment." Shrewdly, he then told Rowley that he wouldn't trade on the bank's name to win the financing; rather he would call the project the 40 Wall Street Building until he had raised the money, then the skyscraper could carry the name Manhattan Company Building. Still the bank wavered. Ohrstrom needed to move things forward; the clock was running out on the commitments he had made to acquire the other parcels. He risked losing out on the titles of the land, not to mention the options he had paid to have them held. Finally on March 2, he went ahead and announced plans for a forty-seven-story office building.

The bank was coming around, though. Ohrstrom was relentless and the inclusion of the Starretts into the deal as builders and part investors helped smooth the way. The bank would avoid a major investment in the construction of their own building and gain the space they needed at a bargain price—all arguments Ohrstrom made. The bank's directors agreed to meet on March 17 to discuss more definite plans for the site. In the meantime, Ohrstrom needed to iron out some of the financing and have plans drawn up for the skyscraper. He turned to an architect he knew and trusted: Craig Severance.

Severance was called into action to handle the plans. He and Ohrstrom had known each other for years. They inhabited the same world of high business and finance and shared a disdain for the old moneyed New York society. From their work together on a 400 Madison Avenue office building, Ohrstrom had seen the architect in action and understood him as a man who could run the kind of organization needed to design and execute a skyscraper on schedule and at a fair price.

For the financing, Ohrstrom knew his choice of knights and pawns to play on the board. As promised, he put up his own money in the 40 Wall Street Corporation, as did several leading financiers and the Starrett brothers. Then came the pawns to purchase mortgage bonds issued by Halsey, Stuart & Company, thereby funding a good share of the skyscraper.

In the past, money to finance a building was the domain of savings banks, trusts, and insurance companies. Builders sought their loans, and if they so chose, the lenders accommodated after a conservative appraisal to secure the fact that if the developer foreclosed, the exposure of their money, and those who entrusted their savings with them, was limited. In the twenties, mortgage companies took on a much greater role, seeking opportunities to work with builders for the issuance of bonds to the public. They financed upwards of seventy-five to eighty percent of the cost of the building. Their interest, as *Fortune* magazine explained, was more "in earning power than in brick and mortar value." There were risks (sometimes substantial) for those who purchased the bonds, but this only mattered if one thought the demand for office space and/or the spree on Wall Street would come to an end. (Optimism was so great among builders and developers that plans were moving ahead to create a Real Estate Securities Exchange.)

As Ohrstrom prepared the financing and continued to raise the height bar of his skyscraper with every parcel of land added to the site—from thirty to forty-five to fifty to fifty-five stories and beyond—New Yorkers and the nation at large gaped at the frenzy of the stock market and all the money just waiting to be made if they only took the chance—stocks, bonds, buildings, whatever. The only check on Ohrstrom and Severance's drive to go higher was the public's willingness to invest, and in 1929 that willingness was decidedly unchecked. In a real sense, New York leveraged the greatness it sought in scraping the sky.

———

As historian John Brooks noted, New York in the 1920s was the new Golconda. The successor to the legendary city of India, where all who came went away rich, was founded in the canyons of Wall Street. It began with a terrific boom, literally, on Thursday, September 16, 1920. A horse-drawn wagon pulled to a stop in front of the office of the J. P. Morgan Company at 23 Wall Street. The time was 11:55. Herds of stockbrokers, clerks, and secretaries had just begun to come out on the streets to grab a bite for lunch. The Trinity Church bell struck its final note at noon. Suddenly there was an explosion, shattering windows, lifting people off their feet, and sending plumes of smoke and fire a hundred feet high. The bomb blast shot window-sash weights in every direction, cutting into unfortunate passersby and scoring the stone and marble façades of the surrounding buildings. The Manhattan Company bank was only two doors down from the blast. Mayhem enveloped Wall Street. Hundreds were hurt; dozens killed. Radical anarchists were blamed, but never arrested. The next day stretches of canvas covered the shattered windows. The daily flood of workers arrived for the day, some bandaged from shrapnel cuts. The exchange opened on time and rose in a defiant burst of trading and patriotic expression. The day launched a market bound for the clouds.

As jazz musicians played atop buses coming down Fifth Avenue and writers crafted their novels in speakeasies, the real business of America, as President Calvin Coolidge said, was business. "The man who builds a factory builds a temple," he said. "The man who works there worships there." Industrialists Andrew Mellon and Herbert Hoover were put in charge of the Treasury and Commerce departments, respectively. With increased efficiency, much of which was learned during the war, the steel, chemical, petroleum, construction, and automobile industries produced an economic expansion of unparalleled size. Retail chains consolidated into nationwide empires; utility companies brought electricity to the most rural parts of the country, growing power consumption an average of fifteen percent per year throughout the decade. People crowded into stores to purchase what they were convinced they needed: Kriss-Kross razor blades, Lucky Strike cigarettes, combination Electrolux gas refrigerator-stoves, cosmetics, mattresses, caskets, Mother's Day cards, dandruff shampoo, exercise equipment, and gadgets, lots of gadgets. As radio sales rose from $60 million in 1922 to $650 million by 1928, a more than tenfold increase, advertisers from Madison Avenue crowded into the family living room, urging folks to buy, buy, buy. Prizefighters, cowboys, film stars, society mavens helped in the sales pitch: "Reach for a Lucky Instead of a Sweet," "Coca-Cola—The Pause That Refreshes," and "Say It With Flowers." Magazine issues tripled in size thanks to ad pages featuring the latest washing machine or car. The pitches worked. In 1919 approximately 7 million automobiles were running on the nation's roads. Ten years later that number had reached 23 million. America experienced prosperity never known before. Even Jesus Christ was credited. For two years, the best-selling nonfiction title in the country was Bruce Barton's *The Man Nobody Knows*, a book that painted Jesus as the founder of modern business who "picked up twelve men from the bottom ranks of business and forged them into an organization . . . Nowhere is there such a startling example of executive success." Jesus advertised, so why not American business?

The question was how to pay for everything. The age of the machine replaced manpower, and the economic expansion favored the rich, rather than wage earner. The advertisers and salespeople had created the demand and men like John J. Raskob provided the means of payment. As one of the leaders of General Motors, he revolutionized the way automobiles were bought: the installment plan. "No Money Down" and "Nothing to Pay Until——" came the cries from manufacturers, and the people flocked to the doors. Debt rose, the economy expanded; and the stock market mirrored the production gains. "It was a great game," said Will Rogers. "All you had to do was to buy and wait till the next morning and just pick up the paper and see how much you made, in print."

Short of an early stall and a few dips, the stock market rose steadily through 1927. Then it began to climb the sharp peaks of a mountain largely of its own making. Coolidge unburdened the rich of their onerous taxes. Mellon maintained low interest rates, and speculators bought stocks on margin, putting only ten to twenty percent of the price down and borrowing the difference. President of National City Bank, Charles Mitchell, ran a 350-strong sales force to drum up securities investments. To motivate his men, he brought them up to the top of a skyscraper and said, "Look down there . . . There are six million people with homes that aggregate thousands of millions of dollars. They are just waiting for someone to come and tell them what to do with their savings. Take a good look, eat a good lunch, and then go down and tell them." Investors, many of whom experienced the first sweet taste of securities with the purchase of Liberty bonds for the war effort, were eager to buy. Trading volume on the New York Stock Exchange rocketed from 173 million shares in 1921 to 920 million in 1928. When Herbert Hoover crushed Democrat Al Smith in the November presidential election, the bull market surged ahead once again. Trading volume on November 23 went to seven million shares. All-time highs were a daily affair. Hoover, the Great Engineer, promised to live up to the slogan: "Four More Years of Prosperity."

Amidst this boom, the country's real estate market expanded beyond every expectation, but nowhere more so than in New York. In 1928, real-estate agent Joseph P. Day forecast that Manhattan's building expansion would end, "Never . . . It would be difficult for any man to put his finger on a single piece of real estate in the City of New York that is not worth more today than it was ten years ago, and that will not be worth more ten years hence than it is today." Vacancy rates in office buildings hovered at a low five percent from 1925 through 1929. Developers like Charles Noyes, Fred French, and Abraham Lefcourt poured borrowed money into projects across the city, adding millions of feet of office space into a market that promised not to crash—and each made fortunes for their effort. The rise in demand for space sent land values upwards of $350 to $400 per square foot in prime locations. To earn back the investment on such values, buildings had to rise higher so that more floor area could be leased, thereby reducing the cost of the land underneath. Skyscrapers were a self-fulfilling prophecy of the heated real-estate market.

To make way for the hundreds of new developments, no building, no matter how historic, was safe from the swing of the wrecking ball. The *New York Times* wrote: "American vision, daring, restlessness, engineering skill have all been properly read into this marvelous transformation from brownstone into Babylon . . . As for building for eternity, the need does not exist. Thirty years from now they will be tearing up the city once more." The demolition crews had their way with McKim, Mead & White's Madison Square Garden and Richard Morris Hunt's Vanderbilt mansion on Fifty-second Street, but no event served notice to a changing of the guard as much as the sale of the Waldorf-Astoria on Thirty-fourth Street and Fifth Avenue. After rumors early in 1928 that a French concern would buy the famous hotel for the development of a culture and arts exhibition, the Bethlehem Engineering Corporation announced in December 1928 that it had acquired the site and was planning a fifty-story structure with over two million square feet of rentable space, the most of any building in the city by almost double. Its architect was the firm Shreve & Lamb, and the hotel would suffer the arrival of a demolition crew by springtime, taking with it Peacock Alley and the gathering place for New York society. The march of progress would lay victim to another city landmark, and in its place would be built a grand house for commerce.

At the dawn of 1929, prognosticators declared a future bright as gold. One broker explained, "it is a difficult matter to shake the confidence of the people when they are flush with money." Paper profits were spent on conspicuous luxuries and bacchanalian parties. Speculators suffered few hangovers when the next day brought ten point gains on their stocks. Although they denied participation, the truly rich—including automobile magnates like Raskob, Chrysler, and William Durant, and financiers like James Riordan and the Fisher brothers—manipulated the markets in stock pools, enjoying quick kills by pumping up stocks like Radio Corporation. Meanwhile, the investor in Topeka, Kansas, or Mobile, Alabama, insisted that the "ticker don't lie." After first setting foot in New York, the Englishman Claud Cockburn commented, "If the attitudes of Americans to the stock market boom proved anything, it proved that they believed in miracles . . . that if you try hard enough you can make wonderful things happen."

Wall Street, which was once actually a wall built to defend colonists in New Amsterdam from the threat of Indians and stray beasts, had long since been breached by a more formidable foe: greed. Whether in securities or buildings, speculators flocked downtown to seek the highest returns. The battle to build the tallest building was predicated on this exuberance. What was a few extra million dollars to be crowned the highest at a time when money flowed like water? Market panics and depressions were part of the distant past and not a future possibility— not in this new America—so why not spend some of those paper gains on the romance of a monument in steel and stone. When Ohrstrom pulled the lever on a skyscraper that would tower over all others, some of that romance must have been intoxicating.

———

The young investment banker, Ohrstrom, was the initial motivating force behind the Manhattan Company Building's push to be tallest, having initiated the development and, at every stage of land acquisition, ratcheted up the height of the building. The higher the tower went, the more money there was to be earned, and the acclaim of building the world's tallest made the risk of investing so much in its construction easier to swallow. With the Starrett brothers and Craig Severance at his side, each with their own agenda to have their name attached to the tower that out-topped every other, Ohrstrom had guaranteed himself a serious bid for the crown. He always knew who to surround himself with to achieve his goals, and he put them fast to task.

By March 12, 1929, Severance was given the go-ahead to begin the detailed plans. He set his team to the task. He didn't have much time; the meeting with the directors of the Manhattan Company was five days away. Although he had already studied the site and sketched out preliminary figures for a skyscraper with the bank's land included, he still needed to win over the bankers. Otherwise, they would move ahead with the plans for the forty-seven-story building or scrap the entire affair.

Approximately sixty blocks north, it looked like Van Alen was going to see his skyscraper with Chrysler built. The Lexington Avenue site had been cleared and the foundations set. They would soon begin setting the steel for the sixty-eight-story structure. With the plans for the Chrysler Building announced the previous week, Severance knew that to claim the title of city's tallest his design had to stretch past 809 feet. Often plans for a skyscraper were revised: stories cut or added, towers redesigned. But since Van Alen would have now had the permits issued, blueprints finalized, and steel ordered, future changes would be expensive and, if far enough along in the construction, impossible due to structural concerns. It was not like Severance to consider Van Alen much of a threat to his goal of winning the height crown. Van Alen was a good Beaux-Arts architect, and Chrysler was a good commission for him, but as far as a competitor, able to seriously challenge Severance on any level beyond design, he considered Van Alen woefully inadequate. Building the world's tallest took much more than some well-drafted plans.

Today Severance had other concerns, namely putting together skyscraper plans that made financial sense to the bank. As he later said, "You can build anything in New York City if you have the foundation, but there is a certain maximum and a certain average you can use in putting up tall buildings . . . Is it going to pay?" was the more important question at hand. To help him meet his deadline, the architect Yasuo Matsui was called to his side. Matsui worked closely with Starrett Brothers, and as the builder and key investor in the project, they wanted one of their own men involved. Matsui was born in Japan, educated at MIT, and trained at several of New York's prominent firms including McKim, Mead & White and Warren & Wetmore. The fact that Matsui, an associate architect, was in charge of the design was a testament to Severance's businesslike approach. Severance had enough to do organizing the project; the small matter of designing the skyscraper was something that could easily be delegated.

At fifty-three years old, Matsui was known for his quick design revisions, and as president of the firm F.H. Dewey, he was as busy as any architect in New York or abroad. To his credit, he was the consulting architect on several skyscrapers in the works downtown, and years before he had overseen the building of the three largest offices in Japan for the George Fuller construction company, then run by Paul Starrett. His devotion to architecture was clear.

"What is your hobby, Mr. Matsui?" a *New York Sun* reporter once asked him. "Your favorite pastime—your sport, you know."

"My work," he responded.

On Tuesday, March 12, Matsui started the sketches for the skyscraper under Severance's watch. As a guide, they decided to use a design that Matsui had sketched in 1928 for the Houston Tower on Madison Avenue, a skyscraper that was never built. The tower featured a pyramidal crown topped by a narrow mast. Modernized French Gothic was the style, but to know the general shape said little of the details—economic height, story heights, floor plans, financial returns, lighting, elevator placement, zoning setback requirements, construction costs, column spacings, and hundreds of other considerations. In those, the plan would win or lose, and Severance and Matsui were responsible for the solution.

With tens of millions of dollars in potential construction and leasing costs, the building had to pay. This dominated their thoughts as they roughed out the building's design. They weighed the land's value and shape, potential rental income per square foot, building costs, construction schedules, and space loss due to elevators, corridors, and stairwells. The key was settling on the tower floor plan. It was "the theme of the symphony," said *Fortune* magazine in an article on skyscraper design. For the floor plan, Severance considered how many office units ("cells") he could fit on that floor, plus their position relative to the windows, utilities, and columns. From there the rest of the building took shape, particularly as to how the elevators were placed and the structural steel set.

Once the tower plan was fixed, they then decided on the number of setbacks and planned the ground floors. Zoning regulations put in place in 1916 had created what many called "wedding cake" skyscrapers. To prevent the crowding out of light and air, buildings could only rise straight off the street by so many feet. For instance, downtown a building was allowed to rise in height two and a half times its street width (on a hundred feet of street, two hundred fifty vertical feet or roughly twenty floors) before stepping back. Then every five feet of vertical height, it needed to step back one foot from the street. However, the regulations allowed the tower to stretch as high as the architects wanted as long as its floor plan dimensions equaled a quarter of the lot size.

Knowing all this, they needed to establish how high the tower should rise before calculating how much they would all make on rental income. Later that year economist W. C. Clark published a report that stated sixty-three stories would earn the maximum annual profit for a skyscraper, given zoning regulations and a two-hundred-dollar average square foot cost for the land. If land values were to rise to as much as four hundred dollars, then it was necessary to build to seventy-five stories to obtain the maximum profit. Having financed and constructed more skyscrapers than most outfits in New York City, the team at 40 Wall Street didn't need to be told this was so. They understood the higher the tower rose, the more space taken up by elevators to carry the tenants. At a certain point the costs of extending more floors—elevators, heavier steel, stronger foundations, more utilities, and wind bracing—offset the income from renting them.

If the bank signed off, the skyscraper would rise sixty-three stories. After all, they were perfectly reasonable men of business. As long as occupancy rates remained flush to the ceiling, their investment would return in spades. On Thursday, March 14, when Andrew Mellon of the Federal Reserve urged investors to step back on the speculation spree, the Wall Street bulls turned a deaf ear and sent their hot picks up in a "broad advance." Radio Corp shares rose $33\frac{3}{4}$ points; American Radiator, 10 points; Wright Aero, 9 points; du Pont, $6\frac{3}{4}$. Even with the wrong choices, it was hard not to get rich.

Severance and Matsui worked day and night until the meeting with the bank directors. Sunday March 17 came all too soon. While most in the city were enjoying their day with a stroll through Central Park, a quiet read of Sinclair Lewis's new book *Dodsworth*, or a matinee at the Rivoli to see *The Iron Mask* with Douglas Fairbanks, these men of business had more pressing demands. The exact events of the meeting were not recorded, but Matsui described it as "the first time we led to the point of importance and told what could be done if they would do certain things." One can imagine Ohrstrom and his team spread out along one side of a board table; the patriarch of The Bank of The Manhattan Company family, Stephan Baker, and his associates poised at the other end. No doubt Colonel William Starrett and his older brother, Paul, sat in a place of authority, having built more skyscrapers in their lifetimes than many of these men had visited. Ohrstrom was in his element; he was used to earning the trust of men two or three decades his senior. It was critical he convince them that he could get the money to back the project. Although Severance had only sketched out the broad strokes of the skyscraper, his ease and confidence must have been winning. Board meetings were his forte. Matsui likely had a rendering of the skyscraper for all to admire. It was difficult not to get excited by the prospect of so much steel and stone rising so high. The plans called for the bank to have one hundred thousand square feet of space in the new building, including a basement level for their vaults, ground and mezzanine floors for their banking rooms, and three floors above for their offices.

There were many factors still to overcome. They had to discuss the length and cost of the lease, adjustments to rent over the years, tax burdens, and expenses related to designing the bank's interiors, which alone could run upwards of two million dollars. Then there was the issue of the tenants in the bank's current building: several law and engineering companies leased floors at 40 Wall Street, and they had to surrender their space, not to mention that the bank needed a home once the wrecking balls showed up at their doorstep. Yes, arrangements could be made, potentially rent-free until the new skyscraper was complete. The big question on everyone's mind was for the Starrett brothers to answer: was it possible to have the building ready by May 1, 1930? For the skyscraper to have any chance, given interest charges on leasing the land and taxes, the building had to be completed by May next year when old office leases expired, freeing up potential tenants. Plus, the bank wouldn't want to be housed in temporary quarters for the two years or more it normally took to build a skyscraper of such proportions. Nothing like it had ever been accomplished, but if there was one builder in the country who might have a chance, it was Starrett Brothers.

The Herculean task of constructing such a skyscraper in one year was possible if everyone stuck to the schedule. The Starretts could do it. They were masters of scheduling massive construction projects and finishing them promptly. Severance and Matsui would have to burn the candle from both ends to finalize the plans; the steel needed to be ordered right away. As for the demolition of the buildings now on the site, that required special consideration given the time constraints.

The lawyers still had to hammer out the lease, but by the end of the meeting, Ohrstrom had his land.

CHAPTER SIX

An American Invention

When Americans find themselves a little crowded,
they simply tilt a street on end, and call it a
skyscraper.

—William Archer

This reversal of building methods, this change
about in the function and use of masonry walls, and
the introduction of new conditions in large buildings, is a real revolution the extent of which hardly
can be realized . . . A new idea is tried to a limited
extent in one building; a bolder application is attempted in the next . . . Thus the evolution pro-
ceeds.

—Corydon Purdy

It was only fitting, in an age when New York City reveled in movement,
when music beat a fast rhythm, industry roared, and the pace of a
man's step was as important as the cut of his suit, that the word "skyscraper" found in its name the same call for speed. Coined for the winning horse of the 1789 Epsom Derby, the word went on to refer to
high-standing horses, then later to the triangular sail raised at the top

of a ship's mast to catch a strong wind. By 1889, when tall buildings were first popularly labeled skyscrapers, the way in which they were engineered was largely the same as it would be in the Roaring Twenties. To understand the brief history of who and what drove their invention was to better appreciate the height race as it heated up.

In 1867 New York, only the occasional steeple broke up the mass of four- and five-story mud-brown buildings where most people worked. Life in these offices was cramped and unpleasant. The upper floors rented for cheap, as few elevators existed at the time, and the long climb left most winded. In some buildings, a blindfolded horse was taken to the top floor and used to hoist up goods until he expired after years of thankless servitude. During wintertime, the first arrival in the office saw his breath until he lit a fire in the fireplace. To clean his hands, a washstand and a pitcher of water had to do. Many shared few bathrooms, and the "flush" of the cast-iron bowls used for toilets overstated the actual effect. Kerosene lamps lit the rooms at night, and during the summer, the office dwellers prayed for a breeze that seldom came. Such was the work environment of the unfortunate insurance clerk or lawyer.

Things needed to change. Corporations had grown with the rapidly expanding economy, and their owners wanted headquarters that suited their improved fortunes and could house their increased staff comfortably. They needed large office buildings, but given scarcity of property, large meant tall. Insurance companies, burdened by enormous administrative demands, required these offices more than most.

Growing by leaps and bounds, the Equitable Life Assurance Society of the United States decided to erect a seven-story, 130-foot-tall building on lower Broadway. The company's vice president, Henry Baldwin Hyde, insisted that this tallest of office buildings have a passenger elevator, so that the top stories would rent as easily as the lower floors. New York had been acquainted with the elevator since its inventor, Elisha Graves Otis, exhibited it at the 1853 World's Fair.

Vertical hoists dated back to Nero's Rome and Louis XIV's Versailles, but they were crude, dangerous contraptions. Otis managed to make them safe and efficient. Since his exhibition, they had been installed in the Fifth Avenue Hotel and Haughwout Store, but never in an office building.

Hyde won its inclusion in the Equitable Building, despite the reluctance of the real-estate agents and board of directors to risk the novelty. When the building opened three years later, it was a major event. The *New York Sun* wrote: "Before us is spread the most exciting, wonderful, and instructive view to be had on our continent . . . East and North Rivers and the bay appear as if at our feet, with their myriad flotillas of the navigable world. Suburban Brooklyn, Jersey City, Hoboken, Hudson City, and Harlem are all plainly before us. Certainly not elsewhere in all New York can such another unobstructed bird's eye view be had as from the open pavilions of the Equitable Life Assurance Society's Building." The top floors were rented out immediately, and the building was a financial windfall for the company. Subsequently, their competitors, New York Life and Mutual, put up taller buildings, and elevators began to appear throughout the city. The Manhattan skyline was pushing heavenward.

In 1875, the Western Union Telegraph Company completed its new 230-foot-tall, ten-story office building, which dwarfed the Equitable in both height and size. In the same year, the *New York Tribune* moved into their new headquarters, a 260-foot-tall, nine-story building whose tower fell short of Trinity Church—long the tallest structure in New York—by a mere 26 feet. In the span of a decade, architects had begun to design buildings that stretched four times higher than they once averaged. One editorial writer commented that "one might believe that the chief end of the present crop of buildings is the observation of comets."

For all the excitement, though, the revolution had yet to come. All of these buildings were constructed with load-bearing masonry walls.

Although their architects made advances in the use of iron columns and girders for reinforcement, although they incorporated elevators for the first time and managed improvements in fireproofing, heating, plumbing, and ventilation, these buildings proved that a new method of construction was needed. In order to rise 260 feet high, the *Tribune* building required walls over six feet thick in the basement to support the weight of the building. The higher floors carried less weight from above, but still the walls of the *Tribune*'s eighth floor were over three feet wide. Not only did the thickness of the walls turn some offices into dungeons, given the amount of light that actually came through the deeply set windows, but more important for the owners, these walls ate up space that could have been used for tenants. The walls of the first floor occupied approximately half of the 376.5-square-foot site. In other words, load-bearing masonry cost money, lots of money. The answer to this problem, however, was not to be solved in the city that first dared elevators. Instead, a city reeling from disaster found the solution.

The man who solved the problem was William Le Baron Jenney, the son of a New England whaling captain. After sailing around the Cape Horn of Africa, joining the California gold rush, and serving as General William Tecumseh Sherman's chief of engineers during his destructive sweep from Atlanta to the coast, Jenney settled in Chicago to practice architecture. He arrived in time to witness one of the most devastating conflagrations in history: the Great Chicago Fire of 1871. In the course of two days, a blaze swept through the city, incinerating wooden houses, mansions, barns, sheds, jerry-built tenements and warehouses, factories, grand department stores, and office buildings—old and new ones alike. The *Chicago Tribune* building, heralded as fireproof, collapsed on itself. The courthouse tower tumbled, its bell ringing to the last. By the end, the Board of Public Works noted that "the loss of property was greater than has ever occurred before in the his-

tory of the world, amounting to two hundreds of millions of dollars."
Roughly 18,000 buildings were razed over a stretch of 1,688 acres.

"All lost except wife, children and energy" read one sign, express-
ing the fight Chicagoans planned to make in the face of such devastation. Given the vast swaths of now open space and the need for
thousands of structures, architects and engineers had an opportunity
to construct a new, modern city, one that employed in its buildings the
latest techniques, and demanded original ones as well. In the ensuing
years, they ushered in advances in foundation design, so that their
new, larger buildings wouldn't settle in the loose, wet soil. They began
using hollow tile floor arches instead of brick arches; these reduced the
weight of the floors and also proved more fire-resistant. Steam heating
made fireplaces redundant. Hydraulic elevators became standard, and
electric lights looked to be on their way to adoption. The list of improvements was long, but none of them compared to Jenney's in 1883.

That year the Home Insurance Company hired him to build an office building in the city. He was having trouble settling on the design,
knowing that the ten-story structure would require fortresslike masonry walls, even with the advances that had been made in iron-
framed structures. For centuries, architects had used iron for
reinforcing their masonry buildings. More recently, engineers had
gone to great lengths to calculate the best use of cast iron versus
wrought iron. Cast iron had a composition of iron and carbon. Its high
carbon count gave it the ability to bear tremendous vertical weight, but
it was brittle to horizontal cross-strains. Therefore, it was applied primarily in columns to help carry the load of the building. Wrought iron
had only a small measure of carbon; it was primarily iron and iron sil-
icate, which gave it more elasticity. Therefore, it was better suited to
handle the strains placed on girders and beams to support the floors.
Books and treatises were published explaining how to best use these in
construction. By the time Jenney received his commission, ten-story

buildings with interior iron framing were common. The framing improved a building's stability and reduced the size of the masonry walls, but its use in this manner had limits—most notably in a building's potential height—as long as the walls were the main supporting structure.

Jenney knew all of this. He had studied engineering at Paris's Ecole Centrale des Arts et Manufactures. He had earned his practical training while serving in the Union Army. He had traveled widely, seen curious frame structures built in the Philippines, and was aware of the development in iron structures dating back to New York's Crystal Palace, built in 1853. Still, he was having difficulty with the Home Insurance Company design, wanting to improve on what others had done before him. Historian George Douglas described what followed as Jenney struggled on the project:

> He reached a snag early one afternoon and found himself looking out his office window in frustration. Rather than continue to torture himself he went home for the day. His wife was startled to see him so early and thought he might be ill. Getting up suddenly from her chair where she was reading, she looked around for the most handy place to set down her book, and accordingly laid it on top of a bird cage . . . Jenney jumped with surprise when he noticed that this lightweight bird cage could support a heavy load without the slightest difficulty. Back to the office Jenney went with the clue to the skyscraper—"cage design."

His idea was to build a skeleton structure, one with intersections of columns and beams bolted together with brackets that carried the entire weight of the building. The breakthrough rivaled that of the post-and-lintel or arch. Horizontal beams supported the load of each floor. This load was then transferred to the columns, which extended down to the foundation. Walls no longer had to bear the weight of the floors above; now they were simply curtains.

Although a mere ten stories tall, the Home Insurance Building managed a revolution, not only for its skeleton design—which would have been sufficient—but also because Jenney made another innovative leap: he introduced steel into the structural framework. The Carnegie-Phipps Steel Company sent Jenney a letter as the construction workers finished setting the sixth-floor frame. They wanted to know if he would replace the wrought-iron beams planned for the remaining floors with steel beams they had recently started rolling.

Nearly thirty years had passed since Sir Henry Bessemer had refined the process of steel making to the point that it was commercially viable. Bessemer discovered a way to reduce the carbon content and impurities from cast iron by pushing cold air through the metal in its molten state. The resulting composition, which included small portions of several other ferrous metals, had greater compression and tension strength than both cast and wrought iron, plus it was more immune to fatigue or corrosion. Given these qualities, steel's use would allow architects to design taller, more stable structures. The stronger the columns and beams in a building's frame, the more weight it could bear. Yet until the Home Insurance Building, steel companies hadn't rolled members specifically for building construction, focusing their efforts on bridges instead. Jenney was the maverick willing to include them first (although their presence was more symbolic than structurally important because of their use only in floor beams above the sixth floor).

With the breakthrough of the steel skeleton-frame, height quickly became a question of will and money, rather than engineering. As for Jenney, neither fame nor fortune was to be his; others claimed they deserved credit for originating the idea, most notably architect Leroy Buffington, who applied for a patent in 1882 that detailed a skeleton structure, but who never won a commission to see it built. Regardless of the dispute, the architectural advance was quickly adopted. In 1888, the firm Holabird & Roche improved the design with Chicago's Tacoma Building, constructed by George Fuller. For the first time, pedestrians saw workers setting bricks into a wall halfway up the building while there were none below. This was the essence of the curtain wall. Then Daniel Burnham designed the Rand-McNally Building, the first building to be completely made of steel beams and columns. Before its completion, however, the impetus to brave the sky had shifted back to New York.

In 1888, silk merchant John Noble Stearns commissioned architect Bradford Gilbert to design an office building on a sliver of land on lower Broadway. With dimensions of 21½ feet by 39½ feet, the site provided no room for thick masonry walls, yet Stearns needed a tall building with ample rentable space to offset the land cost. Gilbert decided he would be the first in New York to borrow on Jenney's innovation, simply stating that he meant to stand "a steel bridge structure on end" to meet the height demand without the cumbersome load-bearing walls. The city considered the proposition foolhardy at best. Architects, engineers, and editorial writers set out to discredit him. After the Building Department refused him a permit, Gilbert appealed to the Board of Examiners. Months passed before they granted him approval for the eleven-story structure.

As construction began, a close colleague of Gilbert's wrote directly to Stearns, stating that the idea of putting up a 160-foot-tall structure on such a narrow street front was madness. It would topple. Stearns stormed in on Gilbert, holding the letter. If the building collapsed, the owner—not the architect—would be responsible for the damages. To convince Stearns of the plan's soundness, Gilbert showed him how the diagonal braces between floor beams would counteract the strains of gale force winds. He had incorporated the insights of engineers like Gustave Eiffel into the Tower Building's steel-frame structure. Finally

Gilbert volunteered to move his office to the top two floors. "If the building goes down I will go with it," he said. This appeased Stearns. Meanwhile, the proprietor next door put his property on the market and scooted to safety.

When construction neared completion, the Weather Bureau warned of hurricane gales on their way to hit the city. Gawkers crowded Broadway on Sunday morning to watch the building tumble. After all, many had read and seen photographs of bridges buckling and crumbling apart in such storms. Confident of his wind-strain calculations, Gilbert pressed past the crowd as the eighty-mile-an-hour winds blew:

> I secured a plumb-line and began to climb the ladders that the workmen had left in place when they quit work the previous evening . . . When I reached the [top] story, the gale was so fierce I could not stand upright. I crawled on my hands and knees along the scaffolding and dropped the plumb-line. There was not the slightest vibration. The building stood as steady as a rock in the sea.

After the building survived the storm, Gilbert was showered with praise and credited with advancing the cause of the skeleton frame. Now convinced of the soundness of this structure, New York's architects entered the last decade of the nineteenth century inspired to build higher. They were on their way to mastering the steel frame as well as making further strides in lighting, plumbing, and elevators. Their eagerness to reshape the skyline with this new building form was palpable. In 1899 they stripped Chicago of its height crown with the Park Row Building and never looked back.

Designing and building a skyscraper was akin to God creating the human form, and this kind of power was alluring. It took the removed perspective of a British architect, Alfred Bossom, to state this obvious connection. A skyscraper was "like a human being in its organizations . . . [it] has its skeleton of steel, its arteries through which courses heat; its soil pipes for the elimination of wastes; its veins which supply its water; its tingling electric nerves of sensation and communication . . . which make possible the stream of pulsing life. It has in its outer walls of masonry . . . its clothes, on which are its details of decoration and adornment." Skyscrapers symbolized what a man unburdened by history and tradition, but with unbounded energy, resources, and freedom, could create. Architects, and the owners who financed them, invested their lives in these buildings, knowing their creations would stand long after the builders had gone. In twenties' parlance, skyscrapers were great advertising with staying power.

Nobody knew that better than Walter Chrysler.

CHAPTER SEVEN

The Poet in Overalls

Mr. Chrysler is a big man and would not be content
in any city other than the biggest. Everything Mr.
Chrysler does is done in a big way.

—Parker W. Chase

To me this building is a human thing.

—Walter Chrysler

Most executives who decided to build an office building with their
company's name running over the front entrance left the details of its
construction to the architects and contractors. They approved the
broad strokes and signed off on a watercolor of the exterior, with
painted pedestrians providing a sense of scale. Their interest may have
been piqued by discussion of office location and design, but otherwise
they left matters alone. Walter Chrysler was different.

In his office on Madison Avenue, Chrysler often crawled around
the floor on his hands and knees, studying the latest changes that Van
Alen had sent over. Despite the demands of his expanding automobile
empire, he involved himself in every facet of the building's construction, with the same joy he'd had putting together his first engines, or
the twenty-eight-inch model of his father's locomotive which he said

lived within his "mind so real, so complete that it seemed to have three dimensions there." He had a poet's imagination and the mind of a mechanic. Building a skyscraper required both.

Every week he sat down with the construction team to discuss the progress. He ran the skyscraper with the hands-on approach he applied to his assembly lines, requiring the best materials and the most efficient schedule. By the first week of April, the ordered pandemonium at the corner of Lexington and Forty-second Street was adhering to his schedule because he demanded it that way. The foundation work was finished. Hundreds of men labored in double shifts under the direction of Fred Ley and his subcontractors, and more would soon follow. Steel was already stacked around the site, and the derrick operators were prepared to lift the first column into place. Once this forest of columns was set, the builders would connect horizontal beams to them, beginning the steel frame that would rise floor by floor into the sky. Every stage of the skyscraper's life was mapped out on paper, and the site was already beginning to look more structured with its evenly spaced-out sections—resembling a gridiron—where the steel work would proceed. On the walls surrounding the site, Fred Ley's men had even hung signs for the renting office.

In addition to the construction, Chrysler had the final say in every major move Van Alen made, and he fielded hundreds of questions. Chrysler approved the tower design; he approved the parabolic curves of the dome; he approved the Rouge Flamme marble for the lobby, the heating units, and the steel office partitions. He approved the use of his company's car motifs in the exterior façade; for instance, a copy of the Mercury wings on his radiator caps served as a flagstaff holder above the Lexington Avenue entrance. As with the styling of his automobiles, he trusted his instincts. He knew what was needed to distinguish his cars from his competitors'—from the curves of the fenders to the purr of the engine. It was Chrysler who approved his skyscraper's height of 809 feet, thinking this would win him the title of world's tallest.

On April 8, one month and a day after Chrysler announced his sky-scraper plans, a small article tucked into the back of the *New York Times*—page 47, column 2—said that The Bank of The Manhattan Company was planning a sixty-four story skyscraper on Wall Street that would challenge the proposed height of the Chrysler Building. Perhaps Chrysler missed the inch-and-a-half piece buried in the real-estate section; it was a busy news day with a record-breaking heat wave and a bomb discovered on its way to Governor Roosevelt. Two days later though, Chrysler would have been hard-pressed to miss the headlines: "Banker at 34 to Build Highest Structure Here—Work Is Being Rushed" and "64-Story Bank Building to Rise in Wall Street" and "Wall Street Building to Top All in World—Edifice to have more than 63 stories capped by sparkling finial—Ready May 1, 1930."

The site for the Manhattan Company Building covered nearly an acre of land in one of the city's choicest locations. According to one newspaper, it stopped "in its tracks the rumor that . . . the skyscraper district would move uptown and leave Wall Street and the remainder of the downtown section in silence and desertion." Apparently Ohrstrom had already secured a number of tenants, enough to fill most of the 835,000 square feet of rental space. Granite and marble would dignify the first seven floors. The building's cut-glass pinnacle would be illu-minated at night, visible throughout the city and beyond—"a beacon for airplanes and ships at sea." During the day, it would reflect the sun's rays in a prism of colors. The story spread across the country, ap-pearing in papers like the *Baltimore Sun, Boston Globe, Detroit News*, and *St. Louis Times*, as well as the *Billings (Montana) Gazette, Toledo (Ohio) Times*, and the *Oil City Blizzard*. In the *Shamokin (Pennsylvania) Herald*, the column "Hot Off the Griddle" read: "The newest skyscraper will cost more than $20 million and will have 63 stories. There will be 40 elevators. When fully tenanted, its population will be equal to that of an average sized town. Taking some of these statistics into consideration, you will begin to understand why the Seven Wonders of the World inspire only a yawn in these progressive days."

No hamlet was too small, or too distant from New York, to run a piece on the "kid" George Ohrstrom, who meant to build the tallest building in the world. This was the stuff of legends: Danish immigrant's son, wartime aviator, and bank president at thirty-one years old. "This young man calls himself 'lucky' in seeing opportunity," wrote B. C. Forbes in his widely syndicated column. "But is seeing and seizing opportunity wholly a matter of luck?" An *Associated Press* article recounted how Ohrstrom labored in railroad yards to pay for his education, then heroically abandoned it to serve his country. Now, "Twentieth century pyramid builders, who are trying to pierce clouds over Manhattan with massive monuments to themselves and their achievements, have a new competitor."

Not only was Ohrstrom's skyscraper taller at 840 feet, but it would also cost five million dollars more than Chrysler's building, and amazingly be ready at the same time as his own, which was already well under construction. The Starrett brothers planned on setting the foundations for the new building before beginning the demolition. One had to question if that was even possible, let alone getting the steelwork up at such a pace. Nobody had ever built a skyscraper of such height, so quickly.

Chrysler had to have a talk with his architect. Something needed to be done, and soon. After all, he was building a "monument" to himself, his company, and American ingenuity—and wanted it to be the tallest in the sky no matter the cost to change the plans or the work required. This time they would keep secret their intentions and final height.

Walter Chrysler needed the world's tallest skyscraper to house his ambition—and pride. He was *Time*'s Man of the Year. He was taking on Ford and General Motors, having acquired Dodge, debuted the

Plymouth and Desoto models, and constructed the Lynch Road plant. He was, according to *Time*, "prodigious," "fabulous," and "a torpedo-headed dynamo from Detroit with the smile like Walter Hagen's and the sensitive sophistication in oriental rugs." The symbolism of his skyscraper towering over the twenty-six-story General Motors Building and every other building in New York was not lost on him. Chrysler simply explained, "I like to build things. I like to do things."

––––––––

Such was the story of his life. On April 2, 1875, he was born in a Kansas railroad town. His father, Hank, ran trains across Western Kansas as a locomotive engineer for Union Pacific. He relocated his family from Wamego to Brookfield and finally to Ellis, Kansas, when Walter was five years old. Like many towns across the Midwest plains, Ellis began as a patch of dirt scuffed up by the railroad men, then welcomed homesteaders, cowboys, buffalo hunters, merchants, saloonkeepers, and a "lady" or two. A blacksmith's shop was the first building to stand. Then came a roundhouse to work on the locomotives. A man had to know how to use a gun in towns such as Ellis. Whisky-induced brawls were common. People living above the local saloon put steel plates under their beds to keep from being shot in the middle of the night by the cowboys below.

"You had to be a tough kid. Out there . . . if you were soft, all the other kids would beat the daylights out of you," said Chrysler. His family lived in a small house with no plumbing. During winter nights, snow sometimes accumulated an inch high on the plank floors. The windows never fit too well. Before sunrise his mother clanked the lids on her iron pots to wake Chrysler and his two siblings. On banner days, he walked to the trains beside his father, who always carried a six-shooter hidden underneath his coat. He let Walter ride in the cab and yank on the whistle cord as the engine chugged across the dark prairie.

When he graduated from high school, he abandoned his father's plan—that he would go to college—and went straight to the Union Pacific roundhouse to sweep floors and clean boiler flues for ten cents an hour. He wanted to study machines, not books. After six months, he convinced the master mechanic to let him apprentice, even if it meant losing half his current wage. With grease-stained hands and a face blackened with soot, he spent his time tinkering underneath the loco-motives, seeing how the parts worked together to generate motion. If there was a new piece of equipment on a locomotive, whether steam heat, air brakes, or electric signals, he was the first to know how it op-erated.

When away from the roundhouse, he played baseball, practiced the tuba, and courted the Ellis belle, Della Forker, who lived in the town's finest house. Mostly, he worked. He made his own set of tools, starting with a pair of calipers, and etched his initials on them with acid. What he couldn't learn from other mechanics, he read about in *Scientific American*. If the articles failed to satisfy his curiosity, he wrote the ed-itor to discover more information.

After four years as an apprentice, he graduated to journeyman me-chanic, a title people looked up to in those days. Chrysler set valves and laid out shoes and wedges for locomotives across the West: Wellington, Denver, Cheyenne, Ogden, Pocatello, Salt Lake City, and a long list of other towns—too many to name. "I wasn't willing to stick around a shop to prove that I was good. If they didn't appreciate me, if any foreman dressed me down, I'd get my time, pack up my bag, forward my tuba and head for the next shop." Looking for work, he traveled by freight train with machinists, boilermakers, and vagrants. When he chose a direction to travel, he carved his name on the nearest water-tank post with an arrow underneath so those looking for him knew which way he had gone.

Finally in 1901, after years of jumping on the next train to nowhere, a lonesome Chrysler married Della and took a job in Salt

Lake City. That autumn he got his break when a blown-out cylinder head hobbled a train bound for Denver. The railroad called their best mechanic, and Chrysler ran out to fix the train, doing so in less than three hours and allowing the train to leave on time. "You can take her away, she's ready," Chrysler said. Three months later he was foreman of the roundhouse in Trinidad, Colorado, with the nickname that stayed with him the rest of his life: Old Man. He was twenty-six and the boss of over ninety men. From there other railroads called and by thirty-two he was Superintendent of Motive Power for the Chicago & Great Western railroad, the youngest in the railroad's history.

Still he was restless. One afternoon in Oelwien, Iowa, he followed his men as they filed out of their shops. The men lived in small brick houses and grew old repairing the same locomotives over and over. Chrysler stopped in the center of the yard. There had to be more in this world than being the best mechanic on the line. He wanted to do more than center valves and ensure the trains ran on time. He should be the one building and selling these engines. It was time to wash the grease from his hands and move to the other side of the desk.

In 1908 he found his ticket, on a Chicago automobile show floor, when he saw the Locomobile touring car. Three decades later he re-called the scene as if it were his first romance. "It was painted ivory white and the cushions and trim were red. The top was khaki, sup-ported on wood bows. On the running board there was a handsome tool box that my fingers itched to open. Beside it was a tank of gas to feed the front head lamps; just behind the hood on either side of the cowl-ing was an oil lamp, shaped quite like those on horse drawn carriages." He visited the car four days straight and then harangued two friends until they loaned him five thousand dollars. "Just ask yourself what this country will be like when every individual has his private car and is able to travel anywhere." He emptied out his barn, rolled the car in-side, disassembled it, spread the parts on newspapers, drew sketches, studied schematics, and put it all back together again. His wife was short with him, sometimes closing the door behind her with a slam. They were in hock for a car that never left the garage.

Three months later he drove the Locomobile for the first time, and sent it headlong into a ditch. A team of horses pulled him clear. He had seen his future.

After a blow-out with the head of the Chicago & Great Western, he took a job manufacturing trains with the American Locomotive Company (ALCO). He turned the plant around and then made his second leap by joining the automobile business. The president of Buick, Charles Nash, had been told to hire Chrysler by GM board member James Storrow. Storrow, who also sat on ALCO's board, was impressed with Chrysler's ability to manage efficient production lines. When the thirty-six-year-old Chrysler took a tour of the Buick plant, he saw the men making the bodies of the cars out of wood and said to himself, "What a job I could do here, if I were boss." Not wanting one of Storrow's boys in his company, Nash offered Chrysler half his current salary in hopes he would pass on the job. Chrysler turned to him and said, "I accept it, Mr. Nash."

In his eight years at Buick, Chrysler economized and streamlined almost every stage of production. He upped output from 40 cars per day to 550, improved quality, and raised profits at this linchpin division of General Motors to $50 million per year. Although he had no part in the invention of the automobile, he spent every effort in modernizing and perfecting its motion—a relationship not unlike his with Van Alen on the Chrysler Building's design.

The men on the line loved him, for if there was one thing bigger than his pride, it was his fear of that pride showing. After skipping out of the office one day to watch a baseball game, he saw several of his workers in the bleachers. They twisted uneasily in their seats. He ordered popcorn for himself and another executive, and then spun around to ask, "Fred, what would you fellows like?" He insisted on never forgetting what it was like to be out in the cold, forced to knock on strangers' doors for a bite to eat before continuing his search for work. Of course, by July 1916 when he became president of Buick and a member of the General Motors board, making five hundred thousand dollars a year in salary and stock, he never had to worry about that again.

Developments at General Motors, however, had him running on a collision course. Before accepting the top job at Buick he demanded the freedom to run the division without interference and to report directly to GM's president, William Durant, whom he admired. He didn't have to wait long before both conditions were violated. First, Durant meddled in his operations. Then, the company's power structure began to shift, loosening Durant's control over GM—and Buick. Pierre du Pont, urged by his erstwhile stenographer, John J. Raskob, had been acquiring blocks of GM stock. Because of du Pont's windfall in selling munitions during the war, he had money to spare. In 1917 he purchased twenty-four percent of the outstanding shares. During a visit to Durant in November of that year, Chrysler looked through the open door to see his boss, "staring at the wall as if in a daze. He seemed completely unaware of me and just stood staring blankly, as rigid as if he had been turned to ice." Chrysler entered and shut the door behind him. In the office were Pierre du Pont and Raskob. "I seemed to be in a room full of Napoleons at various stages of Napoleonic careers. I decided to vanish from the scene . . . There was nothing I could do." By 1919, du Pont and Raskob essentially ran the show. Soon thereafter, Chrysler quit, was talked into coming back, and then quit again for good, irked at his bosses and their expansion into everything from refrigerators to tractors and airplanes. He left the Napoleons to their own devices.

Chrysler departed before GM's stock collapsed, his millions secure. He traveled to Europe, entertained, played golf, once again grew restless, and came back to take two jobs, one at Willys-Overland for a million dollars a year and another at the Maxwell Corporation, one of the first automobile manufacturers. At Willys he met a trio of engineers—Zeder, Shelton, and Breer—who would design his first car over the next four years. The job at Willys ended when the board insisted he was being paid too much, though he had saved the company his salary several times over by cutting costs. With his usual subtlety, Chrysler said, "If that's the way you feel about it, you can stick that job up your ass."

He then focused on modernizing Maxwell's plants and eliminating their crippling debts. In only three years he put the company into the black. He stole his weekends away at a stripped-down factory in Newark where his engineering trio put their careers on the line to design his first car. Chrysler financed much of their work out of his own pocket, determined to produce his own line of cars. On his visits he inspected their latest modifications and then test drove the high-compression engine hidden under the hood of an old beat-up Maxwell.

When the first prototype was finally ready in July 1923, he arranged for Maxwell to take over the ownership of the plans and he premiered the car, dubbed the Chrysler Six, at a New York automobile show in January 1924. He paced the lobby of the Hotel Commodore where the car was showing, anxious to see what the industry executives and dealers thought. If the car failed to impress, the bankers wouldn't extend the money he needed to produce it. They had already backed out once on the financing. All his effort in corralling people over to his cars, slapping backs, and shaking hands was not needed: the Chrysler Six stopped the show on its merits alone. The engine was powerful, the look was sleek and modern, and the price hit the mark. The bankers opened up their checkbooks, the dealers clamored to sell the car, and the plant fired up its line. Although it took some maneuvering before the Maxwell Motor Company took his name, the cornerstone of his empire was put in place in 1924—the same year he decided he needed to build a skyscraper in New York.

Right across the street from the Hotel Commodore, where Chrysler proudly displayed his new car, lay the site on which he would build that skyscraper.

———

Van Alen was buried in revisions when Chrysler asked to meet. In the first two weeks of April, the architect delivered a ream of design changes to every floor, from the cellar to the sixty-seventh floor, altering column dimensions, floor levels, elevators, windows, stairs, vaults, elevations, and entrance details, among many other things. Van Alen first discussed changes with Chrysler and his builder-architect-carpenter, Frank Rogers, then he returned to his office. He and his draftsmen placed tracing paper over the previous blueprints and drew out the new lines, one after another. The specification writers followed. If new materials were needed, representatives from the manufacturers brought in samples to inspect. When the changes were complete, blueprint copies were sent to Fred Ley, his subcontractors, and Rogers.

The Chrysler job was not, however, a building by committee. There was one boss: Chrysler. He had his opinions, and when he wanted a new idea to be explored, he didn't worry about time or expense. After the announcement of the Manhattan Company Building, Van Alen must have known the meeting with Chrysler wasn't going to be about elevator designs.

More details had been published about Severance's plans, or more likely those drawn by his associate architect Matsui. Rather than the sixty-three or sixty-four stories first announced, the 40 Wall Street skyscraper was set to rise sixty-seven stories, the same number as the Chrysler Building. Severance himself had cleared up the misunderstanding to the press. The tower would rise to sixty stories, then three penthouse floors for executive offices and perhaps a club. The remaining four housed fire tanks, mechanical equipment, and an observation floor. A steel pinnacle of sixteen feet promised a maximum elevation of 857 feet, fifty feet taller than the Chrysler Building.

Van Alen shouldn't have been surprised that his former partner had talked his way into building the world's tallest skyscraper. This was a character who went to the Plaza Hotel with his Pekinese in tow; if and when the waiter strode over to his table and instructed him that under no circumstances were dogs allowed, Severance leaned back and debated the merits, and lack thereof, of the policy, all the while chewing on his sandwich and finishing off his plate. When finished, he put his napkin on the table, and said, "I'm done with lunch anyway." Ten years of partnership had acquainted Van Alen with the fact that there was little Severance couldn't talk himself into getting. Their friendship had long since passed into the kind of bitterness one reserved for an enemy whose betrayal had yet to be revenged.

Now the chance presented itself. The meeting with Chrysler was quick and certain. There was nothing unclear about what he wanted from the architect: not only did he want the world's tallest building, but he wanted that building to be the world's tallest structure. "Make this building higher than the Eiffel Tower," he instructed Van Alen. No real-estate developers downtown were going to best him. Kenneth Murchison characterized the meeting with a bit more drama, but the point was the same:

> "Van," said Walter Chrysler. "Van, you've just got to get up and do something. It looks as if we're not going to be the highest after all. Think up something. Your valves need grinding. There's a knock in you somewhere. Speed up your carburetor. Go to it!"

Van Alen was given a signed blank check to make his skyscraper rise above his former partner's. For an architect who had spent his life participating in design competitions ridden with restrictions and parameters, this was an unprecedented offer. He had a free hand. The only caveat was that the entire plan had to be carried out in secret. The few who had to know were sworn to silence. As far as Van Alen was concerned, the surprise would provide an even sweeter victory. This was one competition he needed to win.

———

Returning to his drafting table with his marching orders, Van Alen understood that the paper plans to stretch higher came at the risk of the men hired to follow them. On April 20, as the first columns cast their shadows on the building's foundation floor, some of their brethren on another site were about to pay the ultimate price.

In addition to working on the Chrysler Building, Post & McCord was in charge of the downtown construction site of the Western Union Building, heralded as the "largest telegraph building in the world." The foreman, Frank Richards, had worked steel on buildings for the last thirty-two years, two decades' worth with Post & McCord. He began carrying water buckets, then passing rivets with a pair of tongs to the men who drove them into the beams. Now he could be found on the site leading his men with a cigarette stuck in the corner of his mouth. His face was weatherbeaten and wise. Once he had to dance on a beam hundreds of feet in the air to prove to the men on a job in Central America that the steel was safe from collapse. In French Guinea, he ran a crew of convicts from Devil's Island. His men were tough, as they had to be to do their jobs well.

"Running up a building's like playing baseball," said Richards. "You've got to have a team. There isn't any more place in a steel gang for the individual star than there is on a baseball team. I pick my own men, and I pick 'em to work together. Sure, to the fellow who never put up a thirty-story building it looks like a simple matter of putting one steel beam against another and riveting 'em together. That's all it is. But you can't rivet a cross-beam unless your two end supports are up to the same height at the same time. That's where the organization and the teamwork comes in. My men know their business."

Many knew each other better than they did their own families, often traveling together to find work.

At the corner of Thomas and Hudson Streets, a patrolman was trying to settle a fight between a truck driver and the pedestrian he almost hit. The rivet guns echoed in the canyons of the tall buildings. The bricklayers were already up to the ninth floor, and Richards was busy with the coordination of the steel being placed on the twenty-second floor. On the Thomas Street side of the construction site, a derrick was lifting a three-and-a-half-ton bundle of steel to the top floor. The derrick engine had a fifteen-ton capacity, plenty of strength to raise the girders dangled above the workers like guillotine blades. When the bundle reached level with the twenty-first floor, the signalman, Emil Simonson, shielding his eyes from the sun, relayed "Boom up" to the stationary engineer, Edgar Harper. The beams swayed in toward the building as the boom rose several feet. Then something went wrong.

The main power on the building site blew a fuse. A derrick lifting girders on the Worth Street side of the site stopped and the steel hung mid-air, the hoisting machine's brake locking. On the Thomas Street derrick, however, the automatic brakes failed and the cable lifting the girders paid out too fast. Harper pressed on the manual footbrake, but that failed as well. He closed his eyes, knowing there was nothing to do. The boom swung downward and struck the steel on the twentieth floor. The lead cable continued to pay out. The eight steel girders jackknifed down, slicing through the ninth-floor scaffolding where several brick-layers were sealing up the black-and-red steel skeleton. Then the girders shot through a canopy on the second floor. Four men—

Salvatore Cardoni, Antonio Corio, Samuel Jones, and Sam Rowning—never had a chance to leap away and were swallowed up in the crash, buried under tons of girders, cables, bricks, wooden planks, and blocks of stone. The patrolman sprinted to a call box to get help as some of the workers wailed out in Italian and Polish. Others stood absolutely motionless, their faces covered in dust.

Overhead some hoisting equipment dangled over the twenty-second floor and several men were dispatched to remove it. Crowds circled around, and the police and fire departments hurried to save those buried underneath the rubble. The girders lay twisted on the street. Eleven men suffered contusions, severe cuts, and shock from the accident. Richards and several others were arrested by the police commissioner, charged with manslaughter. Corio left a young boy fatherless; Jones a family of five; Rowning three children. Although Richards was the easiest to blame, the accident was not his fault.

Steel work was dangerous business: some reports suggested that one death should be expected for every floor erected above the fifteenth floor on a skyscraper. Chrysler wanted to better those fatality odds, hoping to avoid a similar incident by the Post & McCord workers on his own site. He pushed Rogers and the builder Fred Ley to employ every effort to guarantee the safety of the men. Still any solution Van Alen proposed to win the skyscraper race would test the skills of foremen like Richards, who for all their experience and attention to safety, remained vulnerable to the potential errors of machine and man on a construction site that employed so many of both, higher above the ground than any other crew had ever gone.

CHAPTER EIGHT

To Scrape the Sky

Let's speed—speed—speed!
Out to where the whistles plead,
Wailing at their toiling mob,
Laughing at the lives they rob,
Sneering at the biggest job,
There's work to do. Let's GO!
> —*Excerpt from "Whistles" by C. D. Chamberlain,*
> *the favorite poem of William Starrett*

The idea is my own and I have copied from nothing.
> —*Frank Lloyd Wright*

When settlers crossed the Atlantic into New York's harbor, they discovered an island of rolling meadows and dense forests. Porpoises and seals frolicked in the harbor and birds sang from nearly every tree. The Lenape Indians moved from camp to camp, following the seasons. The retreat of the glaciers thousands of years before had carved out the surrounding rivers, peninsulas, and tidal marshes. Ponds fed by underground springs dotted the island, and streams trailed throughout the land. A hill in what is now called Staten Island claimed the highest point in the area at 410 feet.

Severance faced a much more hectic island than the one inhabited by the first Dutch settlers. By 1929, half a million commuters a day stepped into the Wall Street district alone to work at one of the eighty banks, nineteen trust companies, one hundred railroad corporations, four hundred insurance companies, twelve safe deposit companies, fourteen cable and telegraph companies, and the hundreds of coal, iron, steel, copper, and steamship companies—among many others. Exchanges traded everything from stocks and bonds to sugar, coffee, rubber, and leather. The rattle of ticker tapes and elevated trains had long since replaced the blackbird's song. Shoeshine boys lined the corners and chauffeurs and taxicab drivers crowded the streets waiting for their customers. It was a long way from the whipping posts that once populated the area and the old Buttonwood Tree underneath which merchants traded the first stocks.

Severance and the Starrett Brothers entered this melee, charged with the job of demolishing buildings of heavy masonry, setting foundations seventy feet deep into bedrock, delivering seventeen thousand tons of steel, and managing the legions to do the work. It was May 1929. They had less than a year and the shoeshine boys, taxi drivers, and bank clerks couldn't exactly be told to take a holiday until the building reached hundreds of feet in the air. To reduce the carrying charges of the land, speed was important, but another reason to move quickly hung in the minds of the architects and builders as well as the bank's directors, which they revealed in their monthly magazine: "The proposed building may later be exceeded in height, for two are projected in Chicago of loftier measure, and a 100-story building has been planned for New York, but none of these buildings seems possible of completion before the time estimated to finish the Manhattan Company Building. Until any of them or some other not now projected skyscraper outstrips the Wall Street structure, its preeminence among skyscrapers must go unchallenged." They already considered trumping the Chrysler tower a foregone conclusion and were more concerned with the seventy-five-story Chicago Apparel Mart, the 1,022-foot Crane Tower, and the Larkin tower in New York, none of which ultimately proved competitors.

On April 11, 1929, Severance filed the finished plans for the skyscraper with the Manhattan Bureau of Buildings. The steel erectors, Levering & Garrigues, were already making schedules with the bridge shops, having received preliminary sketches from Severance before the official filing. Severance had also added to his "board" the architectural firm Shreve & Lamb, who were known for their efficient, precise approach to their work. Lamb designed. Shreve operated the gears of their architectural practice, perfecting schedules, setting out workflow diagrams, and trimming the fat from the construction process. He equated the building of a skyscraper to "a parade in which each marcher kept pace and the parade marched out of the top of the building, still in perfect step." Lamb studied architecture at Columbia, then at the Ecole des Beaux-Arts; Shreve started his career with an architect for New York State, left to earn a degree at Cornell, and was hired by Carrère & Hastings after he supervised their construction of Goldwin Smith Hall on Cornell's campus. There he met Lamb as well as Severance. Shreve and Severance shared an understanding of architecture as business, not to mention a passion for fishing, which made their involvement as consulting architects a welcome addition to the board. Their experience in designing office buildings for Standard Oil, Reynolds Tobacco, and General Motors was a factor as well.

Of the May 1, 1930, completion date, some said they were dreaming. It was an impossible deadline and useful only as a publicity stunt. Nonetheless, the 40 Wall Street team meant to finish first. Under Severance's direction, the engineers Spencer, White & Prentis investigated how to save time with the demolition and foundation work, which often took as many days as the raising of the structural steel. They decided to raze and excavate at the same time. The idea was to finish the foundation work just as the demolition and removal of the buildings overhead were completed—a tricky proposition that had never been attempted on a building so large. The first steel was scheduled to arrive on June 24, giving them only a month and a half to get everything done. First, the tenants in the buildings on the site needed to be relocated. Arrangements were made for the bank to move to 27–29 Pine Street, which was not incorporated into the skyscraper site until much later. The new owners promised the building's other tenants that they had a spot in the new skyscraper, but needed to vacate immediately.

On most jobs, the demolition crew arrived with the buildings already clear of people. They posted a sign, "Building Coming Down," before knocking the glass out of the first window. Only after the razing was completed would excavators with their steam shovels dig for the foundations. At 40 Wall Street, while clerks continued to type and file in their offices above, foundation workers streamed into the fourteen-story Manhattan Company Building basement and chipped at the floor, the first step on their journey to bedrock. After two and a half weeks, the last of the bankers and other tenants moved out, and the razing of the buildings moved into high gear. Totaling twelve hundred men working three shifts, seven days a week, the separate demolition and foundation teams hurried to finish at the same time. The demolition crew needed eleven thousand truckloads to carry away the seventy thousand cubic yards of old building. It was a filthy job and dangerous as well, but the foundation men must have envied them for it. While the buildings above them were being demolished, they had to work under cramped, low basement ceilings and slog through boiling quicksand in half-darkness. Hydraulic jacks boomed like cannon fire as they struck the steel cylinders. Sweat soaked their shirts and overalls, and half the time they sloshed around in ankle-deep water.

A skyscraper depends on the soundness of the foundations placed underneath the steel. If weakened, the building might shift under the crushing weight of steel and stone, and possibly topple. The engineers on 40 Wall Street first consulted the Viele Map that showed the positions of the streams and ponds that once existed when the Lenapes ruled the land. Then they drilled holes into the ground underneath the site to see how many layers of clay, gravel, dry sand, loose rock, and quicksand they needed to go through before reaching bedrock. The column foundations stood on Manhattan schist, the key to New York's skyscrapers. The rock was 450 million years old, rough textured and very solid. In some spots of Manhattan, one had to dig a mere five feet to hit bedrock, in others as much as two hundred feet; but its strength was consistent throughout the island. The bedrock surfaced from fifty-eight to one hundred feet below Ohrstrom's site. Given the height of the building, the foundation engineers needed to sink seventy-six tower and exterior caissons to carry the tower columns, the heaviest of which had a load of 2,300 tons. Plus, they had to underpin the surrounding buildings lest they settle.

With minimal space, a tight schedule, and round-the-clock destruction overhead, the Starretts had to use the open-caisson method to carry the caissons to bedrock. Pits were dug underneath the basements and excavated to water level. The walls, footings, and piers of the old buildings interfered at every turn, and the foundation engineers often simply went underneath them. Using the weight of the buildings above for bracing, hydraulic rams jacked down steel cylinders—ranging from forty-four to fifty-two inches in diameter—into the ground.

Men excavated these cylinders by hand, scooping up the soil of clay and fine sand and then placing it into buckets that were hoisted out by electric winches. Once they cleared eight feet of a cylinder, it was jacked farther down. They were careful not to excavate too close to the cylinder bottom; otherwise quicksand could boil up. Steam siphons were used to extract water. Finally when they reached hardpan (typically forty-nine feet below the street), which was packed tightly enough not to seep water, the cylinders were jacked down three feet to prevent any leakage. The foundation men then dug through the hardpan in open shafts down to bedrock. From street level, some of these shafts ran as deep as a hundred feet, though the average was sixty-four feet. The hard rock was benched so that it would have a level bearing, and then concrete was poured onto it. Once the shaft and cylinder was concreted, a steel billet was placed atop the caisson. This procedure had to be executed for the sixty tower and wall columns needed to carry the sixty-seven-story Manhattan Company Building.

The true ingeniousness of the foundation plan—whose purpose was to shave off construction time to what Severance called the "irreducible minimum"—centered on its use of lighter footings to bear the weight of the first twenty stories of the skyscraper. On June 15, when the riveting gangs were scheduled to replace the wrecking crews, the foundations would be able to support the structure to that level. As steel erectors went about their work, the foundation men would sink additional steel-sheeted caissons around the "temporary" lighter footings to bear the full weight of the 857-foot skyscraper. In comparison, the Chrysler Building crews began their demolitions in October 1928 and set their first columns nearly six months later. If Severance managed the same in a remarkable seven weeks, 40 Wall Street would only need to make up two months of steel erection to catch the Chrysler Building and ensure that its claim on the title of world's tallest was short-lived at best.

The structural steel had long since begun its journey to the shipyards of New Jersey, where it would then be brought across the river. This journey testified to the great economic machine that made skyscrapers possible in the first place. Much of the iron ore mined to produce steel in America came from the Mesabi Range northwest of Lake Superior. Outside mining towns like Hibbing, Minnesota, men dug chasms in the earth, sometimes 4,000 feet in length and 320 feet deep. Steam shovels scooped sixteen tons of iron ore at a time out of the open-pit mines and deposited them in fifty-foot rail cars. Then the ore made its thousand-mile journey by barge across the Great Lakes to the mills of western Pennsylvania and Gary, Indiana. The captains of these barges logged forty thousand miles of lake-faring during the eight-month transport season, rarely coming to shore. Meanwhile, coal miners, some as young as eight years old, labored deep into gassy tunnel recesses, suffering black lung and cave-ins, to retrieve bituminous coal that was then baked for forty-eight hours to produce coke, the less volatile fuel that powered the mill furnaces. The steel plants ran twenty-four hours a day. Thousands of men worked twelve-hour shifts in the terrestrial equivalent of the seventh ring of hell. The heat—a rabid, penetrating, constant, insufferable heat—seared their faces. Mill men bore their scars from "bad heats" with silent resignation.

Orders from New York, Chicago, and across America called for more steel and the furnaces needed to be fed. First the iron ore was layered into the furnaces with coke, manganese, and limestone, and set afire. Blasts of air into the furnace raised the temperature to 3,500 degrees Fahrenheit, purifying the ore of excess carbon, sulphur, manganese, and other substances. The resulting pig iron was then moved into the open-hearth furnaces, purified again, and then mixed by metallurgists with silica and other ingredients to produce steel with the right tensile strength. A spout channeled the metal from the furnace into a ladle; the ladle poured the molten metal into ingot molds; these molds then soaked in gas-flamed pits and then repeatedly passed through rolls that stretched the metal like baker's dough until it formed the shape specified by the structural engineers. Blades cut off the ends, the metal cooled and was straightened, and then trains brought the finished steel to bridge shops. There, riveters put together the hundreds of girders and columns needed for the skyscraper, with holes already punched for their rivet connections. Builders sometimes boasted that their operations were so efficient that the steel was still hot when it arrived in Manhattan.

Severance and the Starretts needed every such economy of motion to meet their schedule.

As the Manhattan Company Building neared completion of its foundation and demolition plans at the end of May, the steelwork on the Chrysler Building had risen to the fourteenth floor. The first setback and the light court above the fifth floor on the western side were taking shape. A tall fence and covered walkway surrounded the site, as well as a constant stream of flatbed trucks. Derricks were perched atop the steel frame, ready to take the next column or beam to its connection. Wooden planks were laid over the frame to serve as floors. Later, concrete would be poured in their place. Along the lower floors, bricklayers feverishly set the façade while standing upon scaffolding. They worked in long rows, sometimes fourteen men at a time, their bricks stacked up behind them.

The skyscraper was being constructed to the same design depicted in a large rendering by Van Alen that the Architectural League featured in a member exhibit at the Grand Central Palace. The papers prominently reported on the exhibit, carrying Van Alen's rendering, not those of Ely Jacques Kahn, Ralph Walker, or Raymond Hood. He was the star of the show. This rendering, however, didn't reflect the final design, for Van Alen hadn't yet drawn it. He wrote: "When it was decided that the topmost part of this building should out-top every other existing structure, it was necessary to resort to the unusual because of its after-consideration nature. Such problems are the especial joy of engineers and constructors." And architects, Van Alen should have added, because it was his revised design they would ultimately erect. It was less an issue of whether he would find the right solution to Chrysler's late demand to be the tallest, as much as *when* the design would come to him. The sand in the hourglass ran quickly. He needed the solution before the steel work was finished.

An architect of firsts, Van Alen was certain of his design solutions.

Innovation required it. He was the first to design elliptical show windows, one for the Lucky Strike cigarette shop, and the other for the Delman shoe store where those on the sidewalk could watch the cobblers making shoes on the second floor. Some called him the Ziegfeld of his profession for these kinds of ideas.

At the Standard Arcade, Van Alen was the first to introduce windows with shallow reveals. Before this, windows were always set back into the masonry wall just as they had been since the days when masonry actually carried the weight of the floors above. For the Childs restaurant chain, he employed curved windows at the corners of the six-story building. It was the first time corner columns were discarded for the use of a cantilever. At the Albemarle Building, he designed the building without a heavy cornice; another novel idea. If other architects continued to clothe buildings as they had for centuries, that was their problem.

Once asked if he read many of the popular architectural magazines, Van Alen replied, "I am not particularly interested in what my fellow men are doing. I wish to do things original and not be misled by a lot of things that are being done by somebody else."

"And you don't pay attention to anybody's work but your own?"

"That is my general policy."

This was the man Chrysler charged with his after-consideration decision to go higher than the original plans, the ones used by structural engineer Ralph Squire to figure the column loads, wind bracing, and positions for the steel that had already been ordered, rolled, and, in part, constructed. Inspiration was a reluctant mistress, and Van Alen had spent the last two years wooing her to envision how a skyscraper should rise over the street and terminate in the sky.

It was not a question of cost because from the beginning Chrysler told Van Alen to spend what he needed. The architect obliged, hiring the noted painter Edward Trumbell to design a mural for the lobby ceiling; ordering expensive slabs of marble and black Shastone granite for the walls; creating elaborate brick friezes and gargoyles to honor the automobile giant; handcrafting the elevator cabs so that no two looked alike; and sheathing the dome with a new German steel, an alloy called Nirosta, consisting of eight percent nickel and eighteen percent chromium combined with iron. It gave the appearance of steel suffused with starlight, and Chrysler experimented with the alloy in his laboratories to make certain its silverlike finish wouldn't dull from exposure.

The question was how to be faithful to the building's expression of height. Finally, in the last days of May, Van Alen set upon the first element in his redesign to win the skyscraper race. He planned to add floors to the dome, bringing the building up to seventy-seven stories, ten more than originally announced. Rather than wedge floors into the middle of the tower, he added an arch to the six already drawn in the original design released in May 1929. More important, he stretched the crown to make the additional height about more than the number of feet it added to the total. Instead of six staid semicircular arches, the seven arches looked to almost point to the sky. The redesign spoke to the vertical movement of the skyscraper: its appearance of height, rather than height alone. From the first moment he brought pencil to paper for his design of a structure on Forty-second Street, the movement of the lines was everything to him.

Chesley Bonestell, who before assisting Van Alen had worked for many of New York's finest architects, including Cass Gilbert and Thomas Hastings, said "To my mind, Van Alen was the best of the modern architects of the period, and the Chrysler Building expresses New York of the time better than any other building." He was there when Van Alen retrieved a pencil, straightened out his paper, and drew the tower that would rise over Forty-second Street, creating the design as it came to him. It was the first and only time Bonestell had ever witnessed another architect do so on a building of such scale. The sloping dome of seven arches covered in gleaming metal and punctured by tri-

angular windows was completely original and it was a brave masterstroke.

Despite these breakthroughs and many hours since spent at the
drafting table, by the first of June, Van Alen hadn't yet lived up to
Chrysler's demand to design a structure taller than any ever built by
man. The changes to the dome brought the skyscraper a few feet above
Severance's design of 857 feet, but the French landmark topped out at
984 feet, still a long way to go.

Instead Van Alen toiled away at the detail work. He and his draftsmen made some minor alterations to the façade between the seventeenth and thirty-third floors, primarily dealing with the windows.
They fine-tuned the contours and curves of the dome. They drew floor
layouts for the additional stories above the sixty-seventh, including
the observation room, and made changes to the steel and elevators on
these upper floors as well. The focus was most definitely upon the skyscraper's crown, but the daily stacks of plans sent off for approval from
Frank Roger, or Chrysler himself, didn't reveal the bold architectural
element that would carry the building higher still. One had the sense
from studying the schedule of plans drawn and delivered that Van Alen
was approaching this element but had yet to reach it. He needed that
breakthrough moment.

Architects, like any artists, found their inspiration in different
ways. Some scoured old plates. Others crossed the Atlantic to walk
among ruins—as Chrysler had urged Van Alen to do. A few copied
everyday objects, realizing their design by the straightness of a pencil.
Frank Lloyd Wright drew the plans for his famous house Fallingwater
in the time it took his client Edgar Kaufman to drive the 140 miles to
see the designs. Regardless of not yet having drawn them, Wright
replied, "Your house is finished," when Kaufman called and welcomed
him to come. The next thing his assistants knew, "He's in the studio,"
then "He's sitting down!" As one assistant recounted, they scrambled
to find Wright at ease, working out the plans that he had up to then only

envisioned in his head. Wright "took three sheets of tracing paper in different colors, one for the basement, another for the first floor, and a third for the second floor and sketched it to a scale of one-eighth inch equals one foot. We were all standing around him. I'd say it took two hours." Pencils ran dull and snapped. Wright drew the elevation and details, talking all the time: "The rock on which E.J. sits will be the hearth, coming right out of the floor, the fire burning just behind it. The warming kettle will fit into the wall here . . . Steam will permeate the atmosphere. You'll hear the hiss . . ." Pressure from his client helped spur on his work.

After visiting the site for the famous Wainwright Building, architect Louis Sullivan came back to Chicago still unable to sketch his solution. He was stuck. Leaving the office, he took a stroll up Michigan Avenue, "far away from paper and pencil," to ruminate. Not long after, he sprinted back to his office, and the lines of his design poured out of him in less than five minutes. "This was Louis Sullivan's greatest moment—his greatest effort," recalled Wright who was working for him at the time. "The 'skyscraper' as a new thing under the sun, an entity with . . . beauty all its own, was born."

When Van Alen left his office, he had many opportunities—some voyeuristic, others cultural—to draw his inspiration. The modern, topsy-turvy world came at him from every corner. New hotels and restaurants appeared by the day. Two avenues west the latest in theater, musicals, comedies, moving pictures, and dance drew a quarter of a million revelers to the Great White Way every night. The lights burned bright and the action was never so loud as on Forty-second Street and Broadway, acclaimed the "liveliest spot on Earth." Electric signs above Times Square competed against one another in size and brightness. On the roofs of the Astor and Commodore Hotels, eleven-piece bands played underneath the stars. Revues hosted sharp wits, gags, and scantily clad dancers. Odette Keun described the scene: "As soon as the dusk falls, Broadway bursts into a scintillation which has no equal in the world. [It] is the apotheosis of electricity. It makes your head reel; it flares, flows, writhes, rolls, blinks, winks, flickers, changes color, vanishes and sparkles again. Red, white, green, yellow, blue, orange, purple, they urge, solicit, press, command you to go somewhere and buy something . . . Mountains, towns, lamaseries, men with top hats, nude women with teeth, spring into existence and are wiped off into oblivion."

"Culture follows money," said F. Scott Fitzgerald, and with all the fortunes being made in New York, it abounded. The Architectural League hosted studios for members to work on their new designs, experiment with textures, glass, and lighting, and display photographs from their latest sojourns abroad—North Africa, the Far East, wherever. Science fiction, like H. G. Wells's book *Men Like Gods*, and Fritz Lang's film *Metropolis*, stirred thoughts of the future to come. Art galleries now featured those modern artists who first took New York by storm at the Armory Show—Pablo Picasso and Henri Matisse, among others. "Fuck Literature," said a young Hemingway, disdaining the past, as he and his fellow writers—William Faulkner, Langston Hughes, Sherwood Anderson, Willa Cather, W. E. B. Du Bois, Eugene O'Neill, and Maxwell Anderson—gave new strength to books and plays. Broadway shows and the dawn of moving pictures revolutionized the draw of entertainment. And of course there was jazz. From the moment George Gershwin played *Rhapsody in Blue* at Aeolian Hall, sound was never the same. Musicians came together to mingle, riff off one another, and popularize the first true American music. The Cotton Club and Connie's Inn drew thousands to Harlem to listen to the likes of Duke Ellington and Louis Armstrong. The loose beat, ragged rhythm, and lone thrust of a single note gave voice to the voiceless.

Van Alen's designs of the Chrysler Building—its theaterlike lighting, zigzag metal work, soaring gargoyles, and parabolic dome, evoked all of this spirit. But the inspiration of how to win the height crown for Chrysler came from the very word used to describe the building he was designing: "If this is to be a skyscraper," Van Alen decided, "why not make it scrape the sky." He set to design a great spire, one to pierce the clouds above as never before. He called on his engineers and builder to help him devise the plan, for it was no easy task to erect such a structure in secret. On June 5, Chrysler received the plans. They were as hot and expressive as the jazz playing on the streets.

CHAPTER NINE

Equivalent to War

Therefore, when we build, let us think that we build forever. Let it not be for present delight, nor for present use alone, let it be such work as our descendants will thank us for, and let us think, as we lay stone on stone, that a time is to come when these stones will be held sacred, because our hands have touched them, and that men will say as they look upon the labor and the wrought substance of them— "See! This, our fathers did for us."

—*John Ruskin*

Cold hard numbers often measure the scale and danger of war: how many divisions fought, the number of men lost, how many of each kind of soldier saw action, and how many weapons were on the battlefield. In the construction of skyscrapers, the builder was the four-star general in this "nearest peace-time equivalent to war," as William Starrett called it. At best, the architect served as an advisor. Men fell and lost their lives; ground tactics and speed won minor skirmishes; but ultimately, strategy steeled with determination carried the day. Still, the numbers told much of the drama of this war now being waged solely between the Chrysler and Manhattan Company buildings.

On the construction of the former—which by August had reached the forty-fifth floor—the builder Fred Ley employed:

400 masons and common laborers	8 glaziers
130 electrical workers	256 plumbers
150 steelworkers	100 carpenters
6 riggers	100 ventilation workers
4 roofers	20 workers on door bucks
14 waterproof workers	4 marble/stone cutters
10 asbestos insulators	3 stone cutters
60 tile layers	40 hoisting workers
25 iron workers	35 window workers
35 workers on sidewalk bridges	15 sprinkler system installers
	6 steel expediters
	4 mail chute installers

Plus, there were hundreds of other workers, from structural engineers to bricklayers, blacksmiths, master plumbers, concrete workers, derrickmen, sawyers, plasterers, and watchmen. In the end, Chrysler paid for the labor of 2,400 men, 21,000 tons of structural steel, 3,826,000 bricks, 391,881 heated rivets, 794,000 partition blocks, 446,000 tiles, 3,750 plate glass windows, 200 sets of stairs, aluminum railings running two-fifths of a mile, 15 miles of brass strip, 35 miles of pipe, and 750 miles of electric conductor wire. The heaviest columns carried loads of up to seven million pounds.

On the lot of 40 Wall Street, the numbers of material and men under the Starrett brothers' watch roughly equaled that of the Chrysler Building, but these numbers were all the more staggering because of how rapidly the construction was executed. By the middle of June the wrecking gangs began to pack up their gear. The first steel billet was placed on June 20; the first column set up on June 27, and by July the workers poured the first cinder concrete arches on the lower floors. By

August 8, the steel had reached the twentieth floor. The builders aimed to finish the skyscraper in thirty weeks, short of the necessary tenant changes. The general of the Manhattan Company Building, William Starrett, commanded with an iron-fist and clockwork precision. He planned every move and had "expediters" watch that his orders were carried out to the letter—and second. They knew the art of this war better than anyone.

There were actually five Starrett brothers. Raised in Lawrence, Kansas, they came from a family of carpenters and stonemasons. Building was in their blood. Their father, a minister who survived Quantrell's raids on the town, designed and constructed the local Presbyterian church and the stone house where they lived. Their mother, a Quaker schoolteacher, instilled a work ethic that bordered on the masochistic. The family moved to Chicago when the city was "a young giant bursting [its] clothes," in the words of Paul Starrett. The oldest son, Theodore, cut a path for his younger brothers to follow, joining the office of Burnham & Root as a draftsman. Paul left school early as well, going first to a ranch in New Mexico to fend off tuberculosis, then moving back to Chicago for a stenographer's job that Theodore arranged with "Uncle Dan" Burnham. Not skilled at drawing—"lousy," Paul said of himself—he focused on overseeing the construction of the firm's commissions; he liked figuring the strength of the columns and beams, setting foundations, and learning everything there was to know about brickwork, plumbing, hoists, elevators, flooring, and how they came together on a site. He considered becoming an engineer until Burnham stopped him. "You can hire any number of engineers who will be content spending their whole lives doing routine," he said. "You Starrett boys are different. You have a genius for organization and leadership." At Burnham & Root, he superintended the construction of two pavilions at the 1893 Columbia Exposition, among a number of other major projects, before moving on to New York, where he rose to be president of the Fuller Company, which was the first construction company to organize itself into a large-scale business. At this position, he oversaw the building of landmarks including Pennsylvania Station; the Plaza, Commodore, and Biltmore Hotels; the Lincoln Memorial; and a multitude of office buildings.

The third and fourth brothers, Ralph and Goldwin, also went into the business. The youngest, William, was saved from the grocery trade when hired as an office boy at the Fuller Company. In New York, he was the timekeeper on the Flatiron Building's construction (1902), ensuring the scheduled flow of material and men. Before turning thirty years old, he superintended the erection of Washington, D.C.'s Union Station (1907), managing hundreds of men and millions of dollars in costs. His understanding of how each of the trades worked off one another, despite their separate paces, and how the timely delivery of steel and stone fueled this motion, gave him a reputation for efficiency. During World War I, he ran a division of the War Industries Board responsible for the war effort's domestic construction, including barracks, hospitals, airfields, roads, electricity, and other facilities needed to house and train 1.8 million soldiers. He oversaw roughly $150 million worth of construction in the summer of 1917, the speed of his work contributing significantly to the mobilization of trained draftees to the Western Front. At the time of the Armistice signing, he had been promoted to colonel.

In 1922, Paul and William joined forces and added a partner, Andrew Eken, a Fuller Company vice president, to build one of the largest construction companies in the country. They were widely praised for their speed and well-organized management of projects. Their principal role, as detailed by William Starrett in his famous volume, *Skyscrapers and the Men Who Build Them*, was "not to erect steel, brick, or concrete, but to provide a skillful, centralized management for coordinating the various trades, timing their installations and synchronizing their work according to a predetermined plan, a highly specialized function."

If you stopped at the 40 Wall Street site and peered through a gap in the ten-foot-high protecting wall, you would have seen only chaos. In the morning, men kicked about in lines to receive a nod from their foreman that they had a job for the day. An endless flow of Mack trucks brought wood, wire, aluminum, plaster, brick, and stone up the Pine Street ramps, unloaded, and drove away. Just as quickly the material was hoisted through wooden chutes and up the sides of the building. In this beehive, spare space was a luxury. Derricks swung their booms. Rivets shot through the air. Pneumatic hammers went rat-tat-tat. Electric saws cut through wood. Wheelbarrows careened through the traffic of men and machine. Donkey engines whined, and bell signals rang and rang, as if a nervous child was at the helm in the foreman's office. Men with notebooks spun through the maze of a dozen trades, spying here, looking there, ducking past men carrying sacks, scribbling on their pads, and then hurrying away to another corner of the site. Timekeepers filed in and out of the constructor's field office. Mixers clattered and spun their viscous dough. Cables and pipes snaked through the lower floors, sharing space with terra-cotta workers and the sweepers who tried to fight back the swell of debris.

Steel gangs scrambled up the columns to receive the beam connections, no mesh net or rope to stop a fall. They moved about like spiders on the web they spun. With the high summer sun beating relentlessly on their backs, the men dripped with sweat, but no more so than those charged with heating rivets in their small cauldrons up two hundred feet high. On the cable scaffolds below, bricklayers shouted for more mortar, their bodies twisting up-left-and-down-right to fix the eighth-floor wall with hand and trowel. Concrete was slathered onto steel. Hoists brought more hoppers of brick. Winches clattered. Temporary mine-cage elevators carried the men from floor to floor. The derricks lifted another tier of columns. Debris shot down the chutes and crashed into a bin, shooting up a cloud of dirt and dust. Two thousand men heaved, shoved, cut, climbed, hammered, groaned, smoked, ate, drank, signaled, lifted, mixed, threw, dodged, and spent muscle and sweat in a flurry of motion.

To glean any order from the chaos, one needed only to step into the field office, a shedlike structure placed strategically at the edge of the action at 40 Wall Street. There, a heavy-built man with mallet hands, Mr. Adams, stood among a crew of timekeepers and auditors. As job superintendent, the former carpenter oversaw every worker on the construction site. He took his marching orders from central command, a thirteenth-floor office on Fortieth Street and Park Avenue which was Starrett Brothers & Eken headquarters. Paul and William Starrett sat behind solid, plain desks. There was no fine artwork on the walls or fancy ornamentation, the sparse furnishings belied the fact that at the moment they ran over $40 million in construction projects. Behind their soft features, spectacles, and bald pates stirred a passion for building and leadership that distinguished them as more than worthy competitors to Chrysler and any others hoping to erect the world's tallest skyscraper. At sixty-two years old, Paul Starrett, and his younger brother, William, had witnessed the birth of skyscrapers in Chicago and had written much of their history since. They brought that vast pool of experience to 40 Wall Street.

On the site, Mr. Adams had stacks of plans to execute for the Starretts. Like a battalion leader, he changed the location of his command quarters every six weeks or so, and his team of ninety packed up and shifted across the field to be better placed amid the action. Beyond the schedules for steel deliveries and erection dates, the progress of each trade was charted out by odd-numbered days and even-numbered story levels. The lines looked to be chasing one another across the page: steel, pouring arches, brick, floor fill, elevators, plaster, electric work, tile, marble, plumbing fixtures, and terrazzo. This said nothing of the thousands of drawings (architectural, structural, mechanical) blueprinted, filed, and indexed on cards. The construction site was orchestrated down to the lowliest laborer.

According to William Starrett, building skyscrapers "is a fascinating game . . . and to those of us who stay in it year after year it's like strong drink; we get so that we just cannot do without the strenuous activity of it all. And it is a compelling thing, too; a man gets his pride up over it, pride of accomplishment, pride in making good on prediction and forecast. 'It can't be done' carries a challenge that the dyed-in-the-wool builder sometimes too eagerly accepts." Naysayers were frequent casualties of the Starrett brothers and their schedules.

Every morning before 8 A.M., the foreman of each trade hired his crew for the day. At the gate, they were issued a hiring ticket detailing name, class of worker, and pay rate. The timekeeper then gave each a number and a brass coin that he returned at shift's end. Twice daily, thirteen timekeepers moved around the site to inspect what the men were doing and whether or not they had slipped out for a drink at the nearest speakeasy. At week's end, each worker was issued an aluminum check with his number that he then handed in to the paymaster. The job runner on the site acted like a field commander, scrambling between architect and subcontractor with drawings, verifying that each revision in the plan was checked and counterchecked. His team of seven expediters ensured the on-time delivery of materials, tracking shipments such as stone from the quarries to the construction site. The chief foreman then managed the eight hoists that carried these materials to the workmen on each floor. They followed orders from the construction department, who managed each of the fifty subcontractors. Every system was so well traced that the Starrett brothers, who owned the hoists, charged the subcontractor's use of them by the hour: $5 per. A daily job diary, much like a battlefield report, detailed the number of men employed by the Starrett brothers and their subcontractors. In shorthand, it listed the activities of the men, including even the number of water boys, who given the sweltering August heat, were in sharp demand. While the Starrett brothers ran fifteen other construction jobs simultaneously with 40 Wall Street, they knew what costs they "had in the building as of August 18, just how far each item of construction had been carried, and whether or not (barring acts of God and the public enemy) the building would be finished on the following May 1."

The most important factor in the schedule was the delivery and erection of the steel. If the iron workers and derrick gangs ran even one afternoon behind schedule, then the other trades were forced to slow down. In a rare show of faith, Starrett Brothers entrusted the structural engineering, fabrication, and erection of the seventeen thousand tons of steel to the fabricator Levering & Garrigues of New York. Given the tight schedule, fabrication of the steel was split between three plants, one run by Levering & Garrigues and two contracted out to Bethlehem Steel Company. On Monday morning the men in charge of fabrication, erection, purchasing, and shop drawings planned out the steel needed that week and what days it should be delivered. Despite experts harping that the demand for speed was simply too harsh for the steel fabricators, the president of Bethlehem promised the Starretts, "We will make our deliveries on time. Work twenty-four hours a day, Saturday, Sundays and holidays if necessary." They never disappointed, having the tiers of steel ready as needed. The expediters then contacted the foreman two days prior to delivery to learn the exact hour the derrick and riveting gangs required the steel.

Railcars brought the steel to the New Jersey shore, a fact always confirmed by the expediters, who contacted the railroad yards. The boat captains who navigated the steel across the river were informed of the weight of that day's steel. The expediter also contacted the New York City dockmaster, who would arrange for a berth for the lighter, and the trucks knew when to arrive to pick up the steel from the Old Slip. Every rolled column and beam was tattooed with a number and other markings, specifying the truck to carry it to the site and the derrick to lift it out. The truck matched its color code with that of a derrick at 40 Wall Street. After maneuvering through the congested downtown streets, the drivers idled south of William Street and waited for their colored flag to be raised, and then drove forward for the steel to be hoisted from the truck bed. Military precision.

By middle August 1929, they had already completed the complicated truss work for the banking rooms and the setbacks on the eighth, twelfth, and nineteenth floors. Soon the steel erection would move into high gear. The tower only had 33 columns to carry each floor, a sharp reduction from the 103 needed for the fourth floor. The weight of each of these columns fell as dramatically because the higher they were placed, the less of a load they needed to carry. Of course, all of this was charted out in scores of diagrams, each steel member calculated to its exact load, then numbered and punched with slots for its connections. The engineers forecasted potential wind loads and designed kneebraces to secure the tower's rigidity. Every energy—from the members of the 40 Wall Street board, from Levering & Garrigues and Starrett Brothers, to consulting structural engineers Purdy & Henderson, to Craig Severance, Yasuo Matsui, and consulting architects Shreve & Lamb—had been directed toward the soundness and efficiency of the design.

Then Severance discovered that the steel and architectural plans, as drawn, didn't carry the tower higher than the Chrysler Building. Their uptown rival was set on going higher than the announced 808 feet. This was unacceptable for the 40 Wall Street team, even as derrick #5 lowered its boom to hoist the bundle of steel from truck #7D, and the surefooted Ed Radigan readied to heat another rivet. It was the first of many surprises to come in the days ahead.

CHAPTER TEN

A Three-way Race

My name is Ozymandias, King of kings:
Look on my works, ye Mighty, and despair!

—*Percy Bysshe Shelley*

The better the secret, the harder it is to keep. Chrysler took a leap of faith in thinking word of his going higher would remain a secret. With each person in the know, the possibility of a slip grew tenfold: a draftsman in Van Alen's office might have glanced at one of his finial drawings and had a friend who worked for Severance; the structural engineer Ralph Squire might have dictated a letter to the wrong stenographer about a change in the shop drawings; a foreman at the steel fabrication shops might have told the Starretts since they brought so much business; or perhaps someone simply spoke too loudly over dinner. In the small New York construction community, it was only a matter of time before Severance learned of Chrysler's plan. He never confessed who told him, nor would one expect him to tell. At least Van Alen and Chrysler managed to keep the specifics of their plan from leaking. By August, Severance only knew that Van Alen meant to beat out the Manhattan Company Building in the height race.

The summer should have been a good one for Severance. He was the lead architect on what he thought would be the tallest skyscraper ever built in New York. He had recently won the commission from Julius Nelson to build a forty-five-story skyscraper at Thirty-fourth Street and Seventh Avenue that he promoted as a "modern interpretation of the ancient Greek architecture." The building boom continued, and business was good. A legion of draftsmen and specification writers toiled away in the huge open space of his twelfth floor office on Forty-fourth Street. His two lead designers, Langfour and Lazinsk, drew most of the original sketches and plans, working together so effortlessly that they seemed almost one person. While Severance met with clients in his private office fitted with a gold Tiffany desk set and a horsehair couch, his secretary, Charlie Gross, a tall unsightly man, made sure the boss's orders were followed and tracked every dollar that went in and out of the office. Severance had job captains leading teams of draftsmen on different projects and engineers for them to consult with on structural or mechanical questions. The speed of construction on the Manhattan Company Building was proof of the kind of architect that excelled in this modern world.

But forces beyond his control, namely the press, were out for him. In June, the same critic that lambasted his design of the Delmonico Building struck again with a review of the Ohrstrom-backed office building at 400 Madison Avenue. "Distressingly pretentious," said T-Square. The crown "breaks out in a riot of battlements and machicolations that seem entirely unnecessary. And oh, the unevenness of the stone jointing." Severance couldn't have taken this well, but there was nothing to do. When he had previously sued the *New Yorker* because of a bad review, the attention drawn to the suit only brought more notice to the embarrassing remarks. Then in August *Pencil Points* published a flattering profile of Van Alen that depicted Severance as a "suffocated poet," one who had sacrificed his imagination and passion for the sake of business success. The article concluded that since Van Alen had severed their partnership, "his most strikingly original and interesting things have been produced." To worsen matters, the *New Yorker* subsequently published reports of a race between two New York skyscrapers, first saying that Van Alen was designing both and, second, mistaking the Manhattan Company Building with One Wall Street.

> Never, so far as [Van Alen] knew, had an architect been placed in such an awkward position before. Things have been going along in his office strangely—staff divided into two, each side commanded to secrecy, secret codes, two kinds of hog-Latin employed, secret passageways, workmen pledged. All most complicated. What will happen to Mr. Van Alen nobody knows, but observers think it likely that when both buildings are done Mr. Chrysler will probably release a ten-thousand-ton, collapsible, unfolding, one-man top on his building and be countered by No. 1 Wall Street with a semi-floating Zeppelin superstructure, and that the duel will then begin all over again.

Humiliatingly for Severance, the correction two weeks later failed to name him as the architect on the Manhattan Company Building. Not only was Van Alen aiming to go higher, but the press continued to treat him as some kind of hero while Severance suffered its scorn, or worse, absence of mention. Severance was not one to turn the other cheek, especially to the likes of his former partner. He had a reputation to maintain, and there were few able to hold his will at bay.

Van Alen was now decidedly in his path and had much to fear in placing himself there. George Ohrstrom was just as stalwart a competitor, having proven his mettle in war and by amassing an empire in terrain thick with those who prey on the unfit. He needed weekend fox hunts (golf was too slow) and the five-mile walk from his office each night to burn off all the fight he had left in him by the end of each day. This was a man who said that his career was not motivated by money, but rather "the game" of outwitting those who dared go up against him. As for the Starrett brothers, it took only so many of their allusions to the equivalence of war and construction to see what they had at stake. A change in the schedule and the additional costs of revising the height was a small price to pay for a building that would "last as long as the pyramids," said their partner Andrew Eken.

The winner of this race had much more at stake than a trophy on a shelf or a line in a record book. His victory would stand tall in the skyline long after his days had ended. To win was to secure one's place in history with the most visible of landmarks. Yet as the skyscraper race in New York came to a boil, expressions of pride at stake were muted at best. The architects and their clients talked about achieving the maximum levels of return in rentable area. "Economic height" was the phrase of choice. Meetings discussing plans to go higher were kept quiet, and the reasons for such even quieter. Publicly they maintained that every decision about height was based on the bottom line.

Yet these were men of Homeric levels of hubris in an age when anything and everything was possible. Having attained the pinnacles of success in their chosen professions, they each were looking to crown their careers. As for a challenge of egos, well, that was left to anonymous statements like the one *National Geographic* published after the close of the twenties:

"Why did you make it so high?" the journalist Fred Simpich asked the owner of a "cloud tickler" on Forty-second Street.

The man discoursed on land values, zoning regulations, leases, cubic foots, square foots, and crowding.

"Yet Egypt couldn't have been so crowded," Simpich pressed. He promised not to use any names in the article. "When Cheops piled up his Great Pyramid; nor Babylonia when its people raised their tower . . . But there was Nebuchadnezzar . . ."

"Of course; pride, too," the owner confessed, moving to his office window. He stared out at the city below him as drifts of fog passed across the sky.

The Manhattan Company Building, like most skyscrapers in New York, had a return to make and was planned to achieve this end. To win the crown of the tallest, however, the architects and their backers made decisions that had little to do with anything as rational as economic height. Their actions spoke for themselves.

"Don't tell me how it can't be done. Tell me how to do it," Ohrstrom often told his people, and he must have been in such a mood when he brought the Starretts and Severance together and decided to change the plans. It would wreak some havoc with the schedule, but by the third week in October, one way or another, they would surpass the Chrysler Building.

The architects began the redesign. Although Matsui was not as motivated as Severance to beat Van Alen, the Japanese architect understood the "lure of having the highest and largest structure" and proved instrumental in their efforts to attain it. By August 18, they had settled on adding five "penthouse" floors on top of the sixty-seven stories as previously announced, bringing the total height of the Manhattan Company Building to 900 feet. By increasing the pitch of the pyramid crown, they fit the additional stories. It was a simple solution that didn't require any major adjustments to the structural steel design in the lower floors. Some builders later commented that the foundations and structural steel were planned from the beginning to support a heavier load, if necessary, in order to "whipsaw" Chrysler's skyscraper into second place. Known for certain, however, was that the additional height (and costs encumbered) added a nominal amount of additional rental space for potential tenants and was excluded from investment return calculations. "Economic height" was not an issue in the 40 Wall Street team's decision.

Now they needed to keep this secret from reaching Van Alen, or they would have to push even higher. As for a "Zeppelin superstructure," as predicted by the *New Yorker*, such a plan was never floated, at least not on Severance's skyscraper.

In August of 1929, a rumor floated in real-estate circles that a new developer would soon take over the Waldorf-Astoria site at Thirty-fourth Street and Fifth Avenue from the Bethlehem Engineering Company. Its president, Floyd Brown, had failed to deliver the final payment due Chatham Phenix National Bank and Trust Company, and the bankers promptly took the lease away from him. The head of Chatham Phenix, Louis G. Kaufman, put together a syndicate of the who's who of New York business to finance the project, promising a monumental office building instead of loft-space for light manufacturing and storage as previously designed by Shreve & Lamb. By August the site had yet to be cleared and there were no further announcements from Kaufman's office.

Who would swoop in and take over the project? Given the steep rise in land values, the two-acre site would need a tall skyscraper to see any return on the lease's purchase. More important, this was the Waldorf-Astoria: the epicenter of New York society for nearly four decades. The eight private dining rooms and ballroom had seen extravaganzas and fêtes for kings and queens. If anything replaced it, it would have to be grand.

Three months before, the hotel had received guests for the final time. People wept. The city mourned. The event had all the trappings of a public funeral: baked meats, sober speeches, an American flag at half-staff, and people soaking their sorrows in too much wine. Some lamented the passing of a great landmark, one that hosted royalty, noble statesmen (including every United States president since its opening) and returning soldiers from World War I. Others already missed Oscar, who ran the place with the kind of old-world service that was disappearing in this hectic, hard-driving city. William Pendergrast, chairman of the Public Service Commission, gave the hotel's eulogy to the five hundred prominent New Yorkers invited to the final ballroom dinner, saying, "Instead of having the feeling that something near and dear is dying, another interpretation is that something very much like a great personality . . . is retiring after many years to a peace to which it is entitled."

In more genteel times, the night may have ended with that, but this was 1929. In the roof garden, Benjamin Wise, a famous auctioneer, stood behind a podium and called forth a glass-topped mahogany dresser.

"The first item of the sale, ladies and gentleman, and a gorgeous thing it is. Solid mahogany. Beautiful lines. Please do not say anything less than fifty."

"Ten," came a cry. Wise began listing all the celebrities who had touched the dresser's mahogany. The bids surged to twenty dollars. A woman shouted, "Twenty dollars and fifty cents."

"Who said fifty cents?" Wise asked. "There is no such thing as fifty cents, madame. This is the Waldorf. Please don't forget. This is the Waldorf."

It went on for hours—rugs, tapestries, paintings, tables, and Louis XIV chairs.

"Who starts it at $20?" Wise yelled. "Seven, seven, seven, Eight! Ten—twelve and a half. Fifteen! Seventeen! Waldorf rugs. No dollar-a-yard sale stuff here! My, what a bargain! Going at nineteen! Sold to this lady. Show your number, lady. Sixty-nine. Sold!"

Another landmark was reduced to what the market would bear in dollars (the Waldorf-Astoria Hotel would later relocate to Park Avenue and Forty-ninth Street). Yet for all the New York glitterati at the farewell evening, two men were conspicuously absent from the evening's list of attendees: John Jakob Raskob and the former Governor of New York Alfred E. Smith. The press had hounded the two for months, demanding to know what they planned to do now that Smith's bid for the presidency, backed by Raskob as the Democratic National Chairman, had ended in defeat. It was heard that Raskob, having left General Motors to run the 1928 campaign, would join the Chrysler Corporation to help the automobile man gain on his rivals. But when General Motors reelected Raskob to the Finance Committee, these rumors ended. If Chrysler snubbed him, neither spoke to the press about it, but relations between the two definitely cooled. Raskob also floated the idea of an investment company where those less fortunate than he could invest two hundred dollars but receive five hundred in stock, the difference made up by a loan granted by a subsidiary company. "There would be no limit to the capital of the company," said Raskob, nor the possible returns to the investor, particularly in these heady stock market days.

As for Smith, he took a position on the Metropolitan Life Insurance Company board while local Democrats continued to urge him to reenter politics. Most stories, however, featured an idle Smith training his parrots to say, "Hello, Al," and playing the organ grinder for guests at his fourteenth-floor apartment at the Hotel Biltmore on Madison Avenue near Grand Central Terminal. He joked, "Now, if only I had one of those monkeys from my old Albany zoo, I could go out and make a good living." Sarcasm and investment plans aside, many waited for the real announcement of what these two men, who held so much political and financial power between them, would embark on next.

Masters of the art of spin, Smith and Raskob had plans, but they waited to reveal them until all the pieces moved into place. Known to only a select few, letters and conversations passed back and forth between Raskob and Chatham Phenix's Kaufman about developing the Waldorf-Astoria site. The two had been close for years and had the kind of relationship where business was done first by handshake, contracts later. Quietly, Raskob gathered information about building operations. He ran figures, lots of figures. "Please do not trouble to acknowledge receipt of this," he ended one letter to Kaufman, as if closing the loop as tightly as possible. He had two of his men prepare a report on the cost and returns of the General Motors Building in

Detroit and the du Pont Building, in Wilmington, Delaware. Kaufman returned with letters that detailed estimates he had run for the Waldorf-Astoria property. Reference was made to the "enormous size of the building," that Raskob proposed. Indeed. He had big plans, ones to challenge the Chrysler and Manhattan Company towers leaping into the sky. Though at the moment they were battling each other to be the tallest skyscraper ever erected—their builders executing lightning-fast plans—they risked defeat from another front, one that was still only an idea and some profit-loss estimates. Raskob seldom failed to carry through on his plans, and he had already promised Smith could come along with him for the fight.

———

The caged green parrot in the corner belted out a "Hello, Al!" as the ruddy former Governor of New York eased back into his chair, shirt-sleeves rolled up, at the Biltmore Hotel suite where he had lived since leaving Albany. The room was fitted with trophies from Smith's political life, including a Tammany tiger, photographs with various presidents, and the blue-and-gold Governor's flag furled in one corner. The whiff of a cigar was constant in the air. It was August 29, 1929. The morning's headlines would pale in comparison to the next day's. In the nearly ten months since Hoover beat Smith in a landslide election in which the governor lost his own state, there hadn't been much news to report on Smith. He had retreated from the spotlight because of a long campaign of taking it on the chin for being a Roman Catholic, a New Yorker, an anti-prohibitionist, a man who pronounced radio "raddio" and hospital "horspital." The electorate had spoken: they cared more for the business of business than the people who slaved away in shops and factories. It made him even question his faith in the Emma Lazarus sonnet carved on the Statue of Liberty's pedestal: "Give me your tired, your poor . . . Your huddled masses yearning to breathe free . . . Send these, the homeless, tempest-tossed, to me . . . I lift my lamp beside the golden door."

Smith was raised at 174 South Street in Manhattan, a poor immigrant neighborhood considered the "Wickedest Ward in New York." At night, prostitutes and petty criminals ruled the tenement-lined streets. Smith's father was an Irish immigrant in a time when bias against them ran deep. Still he managed to carve out an existence for his family. He drove horses and worked as a part-time guard. There were happy days, like the ones playing on the docks or crossing the Brooklyn Bridge on a rope-and-board walkway before the bridge officially opened. Unfortunately, his father died before Al Smith turned fourteen. His family left destitute, Smith dropped out of Catholic school two years later to support his mother, taking odd jobs as a fishmonger, plumbing supply salesman, and subpoena server. He entered politics to level the playing field for those like him. He fought heroically, won the sobriquet "The Happy Warrior," and became an institution in New York politics. Now his hold on the levers of power had been wrenched loose.

His six-week vacation in Florida and Cuba—courtesy of his political backers, a litter of Irish-American fat cats including James Riordan, William Kenny, and John J. Raskob—had helped a little. The board positions at Metropolitan Life Insurance Company and Riordan's County Trust Company eased some of the financial pressure of losing his salary, grand residence, staff, and the only job he had known for the last decade. Still, he was a career politician without an office to hold, and his supporters, some of whom were among the reporters crowded in his living room, wanted Al Smith to have a mission, much as he had in fighting for the rights of the underclass, most famously in the wake of the Triangle Shirtwaist Company fire that claimed 146 lives, the majority teenage immigrant girls. In the eight months since his defeat, he refused to comment much on the mayoral election slated for that fall, nor on how Hoover was faring in the White House.

Today, he was surrounded by reporters for the first time in months, brushing off their incessant questions: Would he reenter politics? When? In what capacity? Taking a puff on his cigar on that late August afternoon, Smith drew in his audience of reporters. The fifty-five-year-old former actor was a master of anticipation. His short, wiry frame bristled with energy.

"I'm to be an Irish landlord," Al Smith said with a smile. His bodyguard and the last of his staff from Albany, Sergeant Roy, was ready if any in the room rushed him, demanding to know more. Few dared mess with the big Irish former bouncer.

Smith had a statement to read, but he rarely glanced at prepared scripts. His keen memory held on to facts and names learned years before, and he fascinated friends by attending plays and later repeating dialogues from memory. He could have delivered his prepared speeches verbatim without notes, but he preferred to ad lib. Once during a floor debate in the state legislature, a group of Republican assemblymen tried to humiliate him because of his rough-and-tumble upbringing. Interrupting Smith, one of the men called out, "Mr. Speaker, I have just heard that Cornell won the boat race." Across the aisle someone shouted, "That doesn't mean anything to me. I'm a Yale man." Another returned. "It doesn't mean anything to me. I'm a Harvard man." After yet another said, "It doesn't mean anything to me, I'm a U. of M. man." Smith spun around and retorted, "It doesn't mean anything to me . . . I am an F.F.M. man." One of his Tammany colleagues yelled, "What is that, Al?" Smith responded, "Fulton Fish Market. Let's proceed with the debate." They had to quiet the laughter down in the assembly first.

That afternoon in his apartment, he put on the same showman's hat. First he made it clear that he was living up to his promise to tell them of his future plans as soon as he had learned of them. Two hours before their arrival, he had accepted a job as the president of a new corporation that would soon begin demolition of the Waldorf-Astoria

Hotel to build an eighty-story skyscraper called the Empire State Building (hereinafter referred to as the Empire State). The development would cost $60 million, cover two acres of land, and boast a tower that ascended toward the heavens. The job was his main business, and they planned on finishing the construction in eighteen months.

"There are no pikers in this organization. I'm in good company on this deal," Smith said, detailing his board of directors—some of the wealthiest men in New York, including John J. Raskob; Pierre du Pont, head of General Motors; and Louis Kaufman, president of Chatham Phenix. When asked about the complicated history of the site, how it was that Bethlehem Engineering Company lost their hold on the lease to Chatham Phenix and how Smith and Raskob became involved, the politician simply answered that they had bought the property "from the present owners." That was the end of that line of questioning.

"But this building we're going to put up," he enthused, "will be wonderful. It's going to be the largest office building in the world and the largest single real estate undertaking in the history of the country."

He then turned to the written statement, as if duty bound by Raskob. "The building will be close to 1,000 feet high, the equivalent of the length of five city blocks. It can house at one time more than 60,000 people, which is half the population of the city of Syracuse . . . It will tower over the busiest section probably in the world. It will contain 3,000,000 square feet and 64,000,000 cubic feet. From the roof of the building on a clear day looking to the south you can see Sandy Hook, to the north the hills of Westchester Country, to the west the Orange Mountains of New Jersey and to the east a large part of Long Island."

Not able to help himself, the showman put down the paper. "Why when you get to the tower of that building, nobody will be able to build within 300 feet of us north and south . . . Wouldn't that be a dandy place for a broadcast station?"

"Do you plan to put one there?" a reporter asked.

"Not that I know of—yet. It just occurred to me what a dandy place it would be for one." He said that he didn't even know what he was to be paid, nor had the architects for the skyscraper been chosen.

"Does this mean you are leaving politics?" another reporter pressed.

"No, indeed. I'm not retiring from politics either city, state or national. But I haven't any political plans at the moment." He promised to be busy on the construction of the skyscraper, commencing three weeks hence, and later running its operation.

As he finally led the reporters from his suite, one asked when he was moving to his Fifth Avenue penthouse. "Not until after the election, I think," the former governor replied. "Although the architect was here just before you came and said it would be ready October 1. Do you know one of the things I'm most interested in are these goldfish here?" Underneath the parrot's cage was a glass bowl of goldfish. "It's a terrible job," Smith said, "having to change the water for those fish and the architect is trying to make me a self-filling bowl so I'll not be bothered with it."

The next day this blend of underplay, showmanship, wit, and substance had its desired effect: the announcement was carried in the headlines of papers across the country: "80-Story Tower Will Rise Soon" and "Smith to Direct Tallest Building." Only the Graf Zeppelin's round-the-world flight and Palestinian riots won out in terms of coverage. Smith "The Happy Warrior" indeed had big plans. The question remained whether the new competitor for the world's tallest building, whose height promised to be the first to surpass the Eiffel Tower, would be constructed. If bookies posted odds, they set them on no more than a guess. The superskyscrapers of John Larkin and Mussolini remained unbuilt, as did a number of other promised thousand-footers. The leaseholders of Empire State, Inc., could be looking to turn a quick buck. The only one truly able to answer this question was not Al Smith but, rather, John Raskob, who pulled the development's strings. However, he rarely offered the press an opportunity to court such speculation.

The 40 Wall Street team decided to move ahead with their new plans, more concerned with Van Alen's redesigns than a paper tiger like the Empire State Building. The question was how to implement those plans in secret. The Manhattan Bureau of Buildings required the filing of all plans and alterations for a building, whether it was seventy-story skyscraper or three-family house, an addition of ten floors or the installation of a bathroom on a tenement's third floor. The forms needed to be filled out in triplicate, notarized, and approved by the superintendent's office. Failure to do so resulted in a stop on construction or severe fines. The law was clear, and all these filings were available to the public—and then often published by the press. Somehow they needed to keep their revisions from dockets that detailed the most minor of alterations in the city.

The city no longer reeked of corruption; Teddy Roosevelt no longer stormed the streets as police commissioner, finding crooked dealings at every level of city government. Nonetheless, New York remained a metropolis where influence greased the wheels, and between the Starrett brothers, George Ohrstrom, and Craig Severance, they had plenty of influence at the Bureau of Buildings, given the tens of millions in construction projects they controlled. Not surprisingly, none of them admitted using their influence to keep the plans secret while the steelworkers rigged another column higher (nor did anyone from the Chrysler Building team on their changes). But on or about September 1 revised plans were filed for 40 Wall Street, and nothing showed up on the dockets for public consumption. Paul Starrett said there were attempts "made to learn the closely guarded secret" of their skyscraper's height, but they managed to keep it quiet, at least for the moment. One can imagine Severance slipping the plans to Charles Brady, the bureau superintendent, over a drink at the Metropolitan Club. Or perhaps Brady knew nothing of it. Perhaps Severance's trusted lieutenant, Charles Gross, went down to the Municipal Building, the bureau's headquarters, to pass the revisions to one of Brady's minions who had been convinced to aid their little deception. What was the harm, really? If confronted, the clerk could confess that the plans were lost in the shuffle of the hundreds of forms that landed on his desk every month. After all, the plans eventually found their way into the building's file.

These were the chances Severance willingly took to stamp his mark on history. His favorite expression was borrowed from Rudyard Kipling's *The Palace*: "Carven deep in the timber . . . Chiseled deep in the stone . . . After me cometh the builder . . . Tell him that I too have known."

Oxygen to the Fire

If a man saves fifteen dollars a week and invests it
in good common stocks, and allows the dividends
and rights to accumulate, at the end of twenty years
he will have at least eighty thousand dollars and an
income from investments of around four hundred
dollars a month. He will be rich. And because income can do that I am firm in my belief that anyone
not only can be rich but ought to be rich.

—*John Jakob Raskob*

Labor Day weekend offered a brief respite from the mad crucible of
New York, but by Monday evening, September 2, 1929, the crowds returned to suffer the heat. A line of cars ran five miles long to enter the
Holland Tunnel into Manhattan. Some families abandoned their boxy
Fords, the wait for the tunnel pointless, and carried their suitcases to
the nearest train station. There they found little relief as hordes of
sunburnt beachgoers packed the trains and buses. Even the piers were
overcome with nearly ten thousand passengers just off the liners from
Europe, their sea legs not yet adjusted to solid ground. The record
temperatures only fell a few degrees as midnight approached. The
streets gave off heat like coils on a radiator.

By dawn the next day, cars continued to pour from the tunnel at a rate of two thousand per hour. The clear morning sky promised an afternoon sauna. Although another day with sand between the toes would have been nice, the brokers and bankers heading into Wall Street couldn't resist the call of the opening bell. Some were charged by yesterday's radio announcement from astrologist–turned–stock picker Evangeline Adams that "the Dow Jones could climb to Heaven." Little did most commuters know that on this day they would reach a market high not to be surmounted again for a quarter of a century. "Wall Street was pandemonium," said Philip Gibb of the downtown scene that fall. "The outside brokers—the curb men—were bidding against one another for stocks not quoted on the New York Exchange, and their hoarse cries mingled in a raucous chorus. I stood outside a madhouse staring at lunatics." The stock market bubble—once tethered on a long, thin string to reality far below—had come loose. At the closing bell, the Dow Jones Industrial Average was 381, compared to 104 five years earlier. In the last three months alone, average values had risen twenty-five percent.

For all the decade's marvels and activity—the speed records, dancing contests, political ballyhoo, speakeasy raids, airplane crashes, and talking picture premieres—nothing captured the country's attention like the market that day. Yes, some cared about Bobby Jones winning another golf championship. A few preferred finishing *All Quiet on the Western Front*, the best-selling book in America, to studying the latest newsletters that predicted stock runs down to the hour of the day. But let there be no question, the market loomed like a giant on everyone's horizon, whether they speculated on stocks or not. It determined the mood of men and women on the street. There was no better antidote to the heat than a double-digit gain on U.S. Steel or General Electric hitting 395. Seeing Oscar Hammerstein's *Sweet Adeline* in the "artificially cooled" theater on Broadway was, at best, a distant second. As one British observer said: "You could talk about Prohibition, or

Hemingway, or air conditioning, or music, or horses, but in the end you had to talk about the stock market, and that was when the conversation became serious."

Throughout the summer the bull market brought record highs in both trading volume and market averages (up seventy-six percent from 1928). Some high-profile stocks traded at thirty times earnings and increased by ten or twenty points in a single day of trading. Although a substantial number of stocks had stalled or were suffering downtrends, few speculators saw the forest from the trees. Without hesitation, the bulls shrugged off attempts by the Federal Reserve to rein in margin loans. They muzzled the bears who dared predict doom, calling them "destructionists" of America. Investment trusts, like Riordan's County Trust, opened at a rate of several per week and were leveraged to the hilt. Readers rushed newsstands to read John J. Raskob's article "Everybody Ought to Be Rich." One paper called his plan "a practical Utopia"; another said it was the "greatest vision of Wall Street's greatest mind." Advice on how to win a fortune on Wall Street became a business in its own right, publishers printing thousands of "morning letters" every day to show how to beat the market. The quick kill outpaced the investor's interest in something as mundane as a dividend yield. In August Walter Chrysler announced in an article entitled "Here Comes Prosperity" that "a new era of prosperity which will sweep the world and revolutionize modes of living is rapidly approaching."

Talk of the market was hard to escape. Neighbors shared tips over a barbeque. Waitresses, chauffeurs, and shoeshine boys eavesdropped on their Wall Street customers for stocks on the run. Policemen and the gangsters they arrested found they shared more than an interest in crime. Cowboys, bookkeepers, ladies-who-lunched, train attendants, and lawyers were united by their attraction to public utilities. Buying on margin spoke to one's ambition, not foolhardiness. Investors jammed brokerage offices during lunch breaks. Families shortened

holidays to get back to the market. Tales of hastily won fortunes rico-
cheted about office hallways, subway cars, and automats. As Frederick
Lewis Allen described, "a young banker had put every dollar of his
small capital into Niles-Bement-Pond and now was fixed for life; a
widow had been able to buy a large country house with her winnings in
Kennecott. Thousands speculated—and won, too—without the slightest
knowledge of the nature of the company on whose fortunes they were
relying, like the people who bought Seaboard Air Line under the impression that it was an aviation stock." Actually, Seaboard turned out to
be a railroad company. People quit their jobs to track stocks full-time
and gambled their life savings to beat the market. Ocean liners boasted
facilities where passengers traded by shortwave radio. The wealthy in
London, Paris, Brussels, and Amsterdam invested as well. Even small
children wanted in on the game. The *New York Times* ran a story about a
southern girl who wrote to Standard Oil about sinking the four dollars
she earned in the tobacco fields to buy "as little an intrest or shear in
your Oil Wells as $4.00 four dollars [sic] to start with and then take
what it makes for me and add to the four dollars until it amounts to a
fifty dollar share for me." She wanted to have them tell her when she
might "start drawing money off of it. I am a poor girl and I work on a
farm with my home people." Despite the small percentage of
Americans actually speculating in the market, every story of sudden
wealth spread the obsession.

At noon a preacher mounted a box in the shadow of Trinity Church
to warn of greed's charm. His cries fell on ears deaf to any sound other
than "Buy. Sell. Hold." The oracles of the day were men like Billy
Durant, who had traded his automobile executive's hat to become a
player in the market. When he called to meet the President, Hoover
made time in his schedule. Money ruled. People cheered the market
with the enthusiasm of parents celebrating their child's success.
Investors made decisions on rumors rather than studied calculation.
Chances were what one took if he let his eye stray from the ticker tape.

Throughout the summer, brokers lent $400 million a month to investors.

The crowds packed Wall Street on September 3, needing to be near the action, to feel the pulse of the market. The ninety-four-degree temperature did little to dampen their enthusiasm. Gossip about which stock would soon break muffled the sound of the riveter's gun. Trading volume reached another record high. The tape ran twenty minutes behind, not able to match the pace of trading. Those reading the *Evening Post* on the subway home marveled at the advances: "The summer holiday is now over and the speculative element back on the job, invigorated by long-weekend recess."

The battle to build the world's tallest skyscraper fed off this enthusiasm, like oxygen to a fire. It was in periods like these, when a nation and its leaders were flush with prosperity and pride, that they erected their most ambitious monuments. The ancient wonders of the world—the Great Pyramid, Temple of Artemis, Hanging Gardens of Babylon, Statue of Zeus in Olympia, Colossus of Rhodes, Lighthouse of Alexandria, and the Mausoleum of Halicarnassus—were built at such times. It was this same spirit that drove the men behind the Empire State, Chrysler, and Manhattan Company buildings to go higher, ever higher.

Part Two

CHAPTER ELEVEN

Call It a "Vertex"

What figure the poet might employ to describe the
skyscraper, dwarfing the church, outpointing the
cathedral spire . . . There is an epic implication in
man's defiance of the laws of gravity and beauty in
the naked uplift of steel.

—*Sheldon Cheney*

Every time William Van Alen stopped at the Chrysler Building construction site, he was watching a line of his design being realized, whether by the men putting up the brickwork or those connecting another story of the skyscraper's frame to the one below. It was a slow, deliberate process, advanced one day at a time. He must have been anxious to speed the construction, to see the dome rise in a web of steel. Still he had much to appreciate by September 4. Workers had finished the four setbacks flanking the north and south ends of the skyscraper. To the west and east, the tower rose from the fifth story clear toward the sky. His many months of paper designs had finally taken form in steel and stone.

Below the first setback at the seventeenth floor, the gridiron of windows, along with the basket-weave pattern of white brick and Georgia marble, gave, as Van Alen had hoped, an expression of "an absence of motion . . . where a sense of stability [was] to be desired," in the lower masses of the building. Before the second setback at the twenty-fourth floor, the vertical movement of the skyscraper began. The windows flowed upward in a seamless line, the result of his use of aluminum spandrels between the windows on each floor. The surrounding white brick drew the eye toward this vertical movement. Between the third and fourth setback, the three stories of brick punctuated by windows had more horizontal lines, again to express the firm base before the tower rose from all four sides. At the thirty-first floor, gargoyles in the shape of the Chrysler radiator cap would cap the corners of this setback. Van Alen had designed their wingspans to spread fifteen feet. More than ornaments, they served to break the optical illusion of the tower bulging at the top. Between the thirtieth and thirty-first floors, a black-and-white brickwork mosaic of cars raced around the skyscraper. Van Alen had drawn these mosaics, and much of the building's surface treatment, during his rush of design work the preceding February. While Chrysler had his cars and Mercury wings, Van Alen put his mark on the building with a series of inverted V figures patterned in the brickwork between the windows on the twenty-sixth floor. The chevrons were a symbol from the Van Alen family shield.

Above these setbacks, the tower rose unobstructed. In the center of each tower face, the windows drew the eye upwards in one great sweep. He managed this by designing the spandrels between the windows of each floor with dark tones, so they matched the look of the windows from a distance. Then to the sides of the tower face he highlighted the horizontal lines of each floor by specifying black glazed brick to be set in the piers between the windows. Black brick, stretching from the edge of the windows to the corners of the tower, further tied together these horizontal bands.

On September 4, Post & McCord was putting together the sixty-fourth floor, while the bricklayers hurried below them. A derrick perched on the twenty-sixth floor brought up another bundle of beams from the street and rested them on the landing platform. Another derrick station on the fifty-ninth-floor stepback relayed the steel higher. Since the setback was only nine feet wide, a special cantilever platform had been constructed to widen the space by twelve feet for the derrick. Other derricks then carried the steel to the connectors now putting up the next frame of steel. It wouldn't be long before the builders would begin the erection of the dome, a complicated web of curved and angled steel whose members were shaped in a shipbuilding shop and would require painstaking exactness to assemble. Unlike the floors below, the dome was not a matter of repetition; rather each steel member demanded a close look at the blueprints to see where it went. Plus, the men would have to work from pipe scaffolding since the interior framing at these levels was too complicated to stage the steel erection.

Despite these difficulties, this work was nothing compared to what would be constructed within the dome's fire tower at the sixty-fifth floor. Only those who had to know of this "vertex"—as Van Alen called his secret weapon to win the skyscraper race—were informed. Not even the steelworkers selected to build the tall spire would know fully what they were constructing. Since Van Alen came up with the idea earlier that summer, he had sketched and revised the vertex numerous times. With Ralph Squire, the structural engineer, Van Alen settled on the design of the twenty-seven-ton steel structure. Nothing had ever been built like it, but Van Alen knew it would serve as the perfect finishing point to his skyscraper.

"The tower should grow out of the lower masses surrounding it," he said of skyscraper design, "and it should terminate in a crowning feature that is a natural and logical development of the tower itself, not merely an ornament placed on the top of the tower. All parts of the design should be tied together in a closely knit composition, each part not only belonging to the whole but accentuating the effectiveness of the other parts."

Theory aside, Chrysler hoped the radical design would win him the skyscraper race, particularly after Van Alen revised its height upward after Al Smith's Labor Day weekend announcement. No contender, particularly the skyscraper to rise eight blocks south of his own, would trump his ambition to claim the height crown.

Although it was called the Empire State, to Chrysler, it might as well have carried the General Motors name. He was in direct battle with his former company in the automobile business, and now its two lead men, who had largely caused him to leave Buick years ago, had announced intentions to build a skyscraper higher than his own. Although they had once exchanged letters of kind wishes and good-natured ribbing, Chrysler and Raskob were now set against one another in a competition of ego measured in stories of steel. It was proof of how little human nature had changed in the seven hundred years since rival Italian merchants erected competing towers to prove their prowess in the marketplace.

The brilliance of Van Alen's spire was that, if they managed to keep it secret, it would stun Raskob and the 40 Wall Street team. But their ability to keep their plans under wraps would be tested soon enough.

———

"This is not a building for investment primarily, but is to carry the ideals of Mr. Chrysler," explained Frank Rogers at the September 10 craftsmanship award ceremony for the skyscraper's workers. The event should have been a quiet one, not worthy of much coverage, if any, in the newspapers. Periodically the New York Building Congress handed out certificates and gold buttons to the workmen who had distinguished themselves on a particular site. Typically, representatives from the Building Congress, workmen, and the skyscraper's architects and builders congregated for some speeches about a job-well-done and the presentation of awards, yet this afternoon several journalists crowded into the fourth floor of the Chrysler Building for the event.

Reports of a skyscraper race were increasingly circulating, and the newspapermen were there to see if it was true.

Neither Chrysler nor Van Alen showed at the ceremony, perhaps not wanting to answer the press's questions. Standing in for Van Alen, C. B. Deer offered his congratulations to the men and told them how Chrysler had been intimately involved in all of the building's plans. The contractor Fred Ley stood up to tell the men that "the better you do your work, the more we can do for you." And after apologizing for Chrysler's absence due to an urgent meeting in Detroit, Rogers praised his boss as a "super-craftsman" and credited the workmen for their craftsmanship and interest in helping make the skyscraper a unique addition to the New York skyline. As a symbol of their great efforts, Chrysler planned on placing in the building's lobby the mechanic's tools that he had created many years before.

Then a *New York Sun* journalist stood up and posed the question: were the rumors true that Chrysler had plans for his skyscraper to surpass its stated height of 808 feet and sixty-eight stories? He wanted to know if Chrysler planned on allowing the Manhattan Company Building, and the recently announced Empire State, to rule the skyline. In a devious play of telling as little of the truth as possible without lying, Rogers answered that the skyscraper consisted of "sixty-eight usable floors." That evening, the *New York Sun* carried a single column article recounting Rogers's response and then mentioned the names of the awarded workmen. Soon enough the articles would command more space and make their way to the front page, above the fold.

A race between skyscrapers suited the "jazz journalism" of the decade perfectly. Interest in politics lost out to business, and business to a good story, mostly those that had a good dose of sex, crime, and outlandishness: Al Capone and speakeasy raids, Babe Ruth's home-run bonanza, Commander Byrd's Arctic expeditions, or a Jack Dempsey fight. As an old-fashioned contest of wills, a skyscraper race would provide great material for the full-page photograph sections now popular in the tabloids. Aside from the two thousand daily newspapers, the newly founded NBC and CBS networks were eager to fill the round-the-clock radio airtime with juicy tales. This demand for stories spawned the cult of celebrity, and like the race to fly solo across the Atlantic, the height contest was about men using the advances of the modern era to soar into the clouds.

————

Safe from the spotlight, the men who actually built these skyscrapers with their sweat and labor worked backstage to the architects and owners eager to settle old scores. They were not dissimilar to the Florentine *uomini senza nome e famiglia* ("men without name or family") who built Filippo Brunelleschi's dome at the cathedral Santa Maria del Fiore. They worked long days, reported to a foreman who timed their labor by the hour, climbed hundreds of feet by ladder, ate their meals high above the ground, and if hurt on the site, were often left destitute. In their job a careless slip meant a gruesome death, and there were many such accidents. Under the guidance of Rogers, the Chrysler Building site protected the workers better than Brunelleschi could have hoped for his own men, yet for all the watchmen, temporary railings, elevator shaft barricades, tubular scaffolding, and around-the-clock medical aid, only skill and luck prevented a strong gale of wind from unbalancing a riveter and pitching him headlong from the sixty-fourth story. The reward for their work, tallest building or not, arrived on payday.

The steelworker's premium rate, $15.40 a day, and high insurance premiums was proof of the peril involved. One insurance company recorded two thousand deaths among the fifteen thousand men they provided coverage in the preceding twenty years. Of course, a look at the men on the Chrysler job demonstrated the risk: the foreman was missing a pair of fingers; a rigger walked with a staggered step, his left leg shorter than the right despite the aid of an artificial heel; a sweeper had a shoulder that sloped at an awkward angle.

Every steelworker had a dozen stories to tell. There was the Frenchman who became unbalanced on a beam ten floors high and saved himself from the long drop by catching his foot on the steel as he fell. He swung himself down to the ninth floor. There was the Irishman who slipped and tumbled down through the interior of a skyscraper before catching his hand on a plank. Then there was the "Prince of Wales of the Girders," Paul Rockhold for short, who was thirty years old, had started working on steel at fifteen "as a kid on the loose," and recently won a gold button on the Manhattan Company Building job for his exceptional work. Several years before he had fractured his leg in ten places after a fall from a site off Riverside Drive. When asked "why weren't you killed in that fall?" Rockhold responded, "The devil wasn't out that day." Another time he skipped the stairs and took a ride down on a hoist; the cable slipped and the engineer saved him in the nick of time, stopping the hoist at two hundred feet from the street. The shock of the stop was nearly as bad as the crash would have been.

"Anyone hurt?" a reporter asked him.

"We got our hair rumpled a little. Nerves too perhaps," Rockhold said.

"Ever been really scared up at the top?"

"Yes, and scared plenty. But when that happens you've got to beat the scare."

"How?"

"Get fighting mad."

Rogers could post as many safety bulletins as he liked, but it was men like Rockhold whose sweat and willingness to take risks was what made these buildings rise. On a suspended duck-walk, the bricklayers moved to a tireless rhythm: grab brick from pile, set in place, spread mortar, rotate, grab next brick. A few stories up, the concrete workers poured the floor while the carpenters prepared the walls and elevator shafts. To pass boards up, men stood at the building's edge and relayed them one at a time. The first man swung the plank in an arc to the man on the floor above, who in turn grabbed the end and swung it in another arc to the third man, and so on up the side of the skyscraper. These workers suffered accidents and the occasional deadly mishap, but the steelworkers stood closest to the reaper's blade. Of course, those "roughnecks up above yuh," were puffed up with so much pride, some of the "brickies" thought they deserved what they got.

When the derrick brought up the next tier of steel, the connectors scaled the top of the column below, lined up the holes, and stuck in temporary bolts. They had the most dangerous jobs and as one derrickman put it, "wore out the most clothes." Another gang scampered up the column after them and dangled a plumb-line down to make sure the steel was set straight. Then he secured the connection with more bolts. The four-man riveting gang followed. They moved to their own timing, one developed over years together. A riveter's skill rested not only in his own ability but also in the way he worked with the three others in his gang. And there were always four: the heater, catcher, bucker-up, and gun-man. They developed as a gang and won or lost their jobs as a gang. If a riveter fell ill, the entire gang missed out on the day's pay and another four took over. When one member found himself on the wrong end of the pneumatic hammer or surrendered to a safer job, then the gang brought in another fellow, passed on their skill, and developed a new rhythm that balanced itself with the old. More often than not, they came from the same town or country. The best gangs usually came from Newfoundland, where their fathers and grandfathers, former sailors, passed on the skill of working up high. Some were Irish, others Mohawk Indians who spoke to one another with hand signals and seemed least affected by the hundreds of feet of empty space below their feet.

A new member worth keeping was one who learned how to do the job well—and *quickly*. He learned when and how to toss a red-hot rivet to the catcher thirty feet away, whether he was on the same floor or not. He grew skilled in catching the rivet in a tin can ("the cup") without losing his balance or letting it fall on the unsuspecting public below. If he missed and it hit someone down below, that cheap lump of steel suddenly could cost the builders ten thousand dollars in damages. He learned how long he could drive rivets before his arms went numb and it was time to switch with the bucker-up. Holding the dolly bar on the other end was an easier job than managing the pneumatic hammer that weighed thirty-five pounds, drove a thousand blows per minute, and shook the steel for a good ten stories.

The new guy learned how to avoid the snaking coils of pneumatic tubing under his feet, and why it was not such a good idea to drink at the local Irish bar past midnight the night before. Most of all, he learned to take care in bad weather. Said one riveter, it was "the most dangerous part of the work. We see quite a lot of the weather. When it rains, everything gets slippery. And when it gets cold, sometimes your hands get so stiff that you can't hang on to anything. That's bad."

In spite of all these lessons, a man still needed to master his fears to take the elevator as high as it would go and then ascend a series of wooden ladders to the topmost part of the skeleton skyscraper. It was not uncommon, said one grizzled foreman, for new steelworkers to "find themselves on a narrow beam with no handhold, fall flat on their stomach, clutch the beam, wrap themselves round it, shut their eyes and gasp as though drowning." Unlike the thousands forced to construct the pyramids of Egypt, these steelworkers chose this line of work, despite the risks. "You don't retire from this job," said one heater on the Manhattan Company Building who had a scar on the side of his head from rivet he failed to catch. Older men, deaf from the concussion of the riveter's gun, continued steeplejacking until their bodies gave out. Some were thrill-seekers and simply liked the view; others started in the trade as a rivet-jack, running errands for the gang, and knew of no other life than the one up on the narrow beams.

Most loved the freedom of knowing that if their boss rode their backs too hard, they needed only collect their pay and move on. There was always another frame of steel going up across the street or in another city. Their allegiance to the owners of the skyscraper was tenuous at best. Described one steelworker: "We have an old axiom: when working on something that may fail and leave us behind, we work one hand for ourselves and one hand for the company."

At 4:30 when the whistle blew, the cacophony on the site ended abruptly, as if the curtain had been drawn on a great show. Tools were set away; the coke furnace used to heat the rivets was extinguished. The steelworkers threw on coats and grabbed their lunch pails. Some slid down columns. Others moved quickly to the ladders, then the elevators. They settled with the timekeepers and scattered in a hundred different directions, some to sit down with their families for dinner, others to clean up for a date with the new gal, and many to put back a whisky at the nearest speakeasy and call it a day's job done.

Did they care about the height race? Probably not, unless they had bet a few days' wages on who would win. "When a steel man gets through with a skyscraper," said journalist William Bridges after profiling several in the *New York Sun*, "it isn't a part of him. It's a good job, or a tough job, or maybe he almost got bumped off while he was working on it, so he remembers it for that reason. As a thing that artists paint and writers strive mightily to describe, he doesn't see a skyscraper. His part of it doesn't show, anyway. The brick masons come along at his heels and cover up the skeleton as fast as he runs it up. It isn't his building when he gets through."

They were like the sailors of the great expeditions of old. They enjoyed their freedom, bore the perils, and took pride in their skill. As Paul Rockhold said, "You get to love it and can't quit it. Life down on the street's too slow. Who wants to be a pencil pusher after he's worked with steel . . . It's nice to point to a mighty suspension bridge or a towering building and say, 'I helped erect that.' " But the glory went to those whose orders they executed. In building skyscrapers, this glory, and the concern in obtaining it, was reserved for the likes of Walter Chrysler and the others who wore suits instead of brown denim overalls, rubber-soled shoes, and caps drawn tight over their heads.

Paul Starrett had long since traded in his scuffed-up clothes for attire befitting the board room. In the second week of September as the Manhattan Company Building speeded toward its completion, he and his brother, William, arrived at the Biltmore Hotel to meet with Al Smith and bid on the Empire State job. Had they been gamblers, they would have referred to this as covering their bets in the skyscraper race. Four other builders had already met with the owners. The Starretts, always ones to take advantage of an edge, knew Robert Brown, a vice president of Chatham Phenix and the man charged with setting up these presentations. They were "old friends," said Paul Starrett, who told Brown that he wanted to be the last builder to make his proposal. This way he could play off and against the promises made by the others. In a call before the meeting, Brown also let him address a concern that Raskob and his team had about the 40 Wall Street construction job.

During the call, Brown said to Paul Starrett, "A rival of yours just told me that you spent money like drunken sailors down there on overtime."

Paul admitted the overtime expense. It was "justified" and "worth $2,000,000" to have the skyscraper ready by May 1930.

"I am glad to hear that, Paul," Brown said. The builder's word was enough to end the matter.

The two brothers rode the elevator to the fourteenth floor and the secretary told them to wait. The competition filed in and out of Smith's office. Paul was anxious, an emotion foreign to him when bidding on a job. After all, the Starretts had built this very hotel. He had mastered these meetings long ago, knowing what to say and when. His confidence in his craft went unquestioned, still Paul felt the same unease of a kid pacing before his first interview. He wanted this job more than any other; he sensed its importance before knowing much about the design or whether Raskob would come through with the financing.

Finally the fourth builder headed out of Smith's office, and the secretary ushered the Starretts inside. The former Governor greeted them. "Well, what have you got to say for yourself?"

Raskob was there, no doubt drumming his fingers on the table, which he often did when in the process of making a decision. Even at fifty years old, he had the look of an eager student, perched at the edge of his chair, listening intently, in command of all the facts. Smith sat at the table's head. Pierre du Pont, Louis Kaufman, and the other members of the syndicate also attended. The wealth in the room and its hold on the city's levers of power awed architect Richmond Shreve, whose firm Raskob had unofficially chosen to design the skyscraper. The architect provided another edge for the Starretts in this meeting. As a consultant on the Manhattan Company Building, Shreve had seen the builders in action. He could testify to their efficient command on site. Plus, if the Starretts won the job, nobody was better to work with than Shreve and his partners.

The mild-mannered Shreve had the presence of an accountant and often took to scribbling numbers in his notebook. He wore conservative suits, glasses, and had the thinning hair of a man who constantly ran his hands through it while trying to solve a problem. There were few architects with more vigor and understanding of the complexities of building the modern skyscraper. Every morning, Shreve worked two hours at home before having breakfast and leaving for the office at eight o'clock. In the evening, he hiked a mile uphill to reach the house he had designed overlooking the Hudson River. In between, he directed an architectural practice with over thirty draftsmen, oversaw commissions worth millions of dollars, and demanded that his office and construction projects run on or ahead of time—no compromises. Shreve was an immigrant from Nova Scotia, had run his own paper route growing up in Albany, New York, and possessed a keen dislike for wasted effort. One architect who had spent time with Shreve on the various architectural and building committees he led said that if the polite Shreve "thought his idea in danger or accomplishment delayed or obstructed, his natural instincts of a fighter were roused; people were of secondary importance and he could be quite ruthless." Raskob had chosen his architect well. Hopefully, he had the same good taste in builders.

Paul began his pitch with a little truth-twisting, saying that they were the only builders who first trained as architects. He recounted their jobs with New York Life and Metropolitan Life (Paul knew the latter's money would be useful to the Empire State Company in winning a loan to finance the $50 million skyscraper). As for speed, the rate of four floors erected per week on the 40 Wall Street site spoke for itself. Paul told the group that they were the ideal candidates to build the Empire State and that construction speed was paramount.

"Our fee is insignificant compared with the amount we will save you by shortening the time of construction," the builder said, deflecting early the criticism that Brown warned him about.

"How much is your fee?" Smith asked.

"Six hundred thousand."

"That's your asking price."

"No, that's our real price!"

"But you fellows will get a lot of advertising out of this," Smith countered. "Think of it, the biggest building in the world, and your name down there on the fence! Advertising is a wonderful thing, Starrett! Look at Dobbs. Dobbs gives me all my hats, and when I go out and make a speech I hold up the hat so that people can see the name Dobbs on it! That shows what value Dobbs puts on advertising!"

Raskob and the others laughed. Paul's nerves had settled enough for him to respond, "I know it would be a wonderful thing to build this building, but I'm through with building buildings to advertise myself. I've been in the business forty years, Governor, I don't need that kind of advertising."

"How much equipment have you got on hand?" Smith asked.

"Not even a pick and shovel." He needed to prove why they were worth the fee, not argue the number, not yet. Paul realized another builder had promoted their command of all the equipment needed for the job. "Gentleman, this building of yours is going to present unusual problems. Ordinary building equipment won't be worth a damn on it. We'll buy the new stuff, fitted for the job, and at the end sell it and credit you with the difference. That's what we do on every big job. It costs less than renting second-hand stuff, and it's more efficient!"

"How much of the work will you do yourselves and how much will you let out?"

Again Paul Starrett saw right through the question: another builder promised their firm would execute much of the work themselves. "We won't do anything that we can sublet to advantage!" He surprised those in the room. It was important to differentiate themselves from the other builders, and by hiring subcontractors for most aspects of the construction, they would ultimately save time and money.

"How long will it take you to do the job? It took five years to build the New York State Capitol and not so big a building either."

Paul and his brother had run the numbers, using their experience on the Manhattan Company Building to study the schedule for a skyscraper nearly three times its size. "Well, Governor, we'll show you the difference between building for the government and building for a private company."

At the end of the interview, they exchanged the usual pleasantries and Smith thanked the Starrett brothers for their time. Paul and William left the room and hoped their bold answers had won the board's favor. Back in Smith's office, Raskob knew he had just met the men who would build his skyscraper. As usual he had let his front man run the conversation, while Raskob held the final word. The decision to choose Starrett Brothers & Eken, who now battled Chrysler with the 40 Wall Street skyscraper, was a quick one. Smith and Shreve were dispatched to the builder's office on 101 Park Avenue to settle on the price. It was a minor expense compared to the $16 million for the land and nearly double that in labor and material costs. By September 13, they had a letter agreement with the Starretts, and an announcement was made soon after.

All that remained to be done was to settle on the design and begin knocking down the old Waldorf-Astoria's walls.

CHAPTER TWELVE

A Monument to the Future

Men are only as great as the monuments they leave
behind.

—Napoleon

On October 2, 1929, John Raskob invited nine men to lunch in his
book-lined suite in Carlton House. They were a disparate group, connected only by their friendship with Raskob and the billions of dollars
all but one of them represented in the stock market.

At the table sat Billy Durant, whose diminutive size and shock of
white hair belied the influence he had among traders. He had won and
lost fortunes several times over and was now heavily leveraged in the
market. Alongside him was the former grain trader Arthur Cutten, who
had recently deemed himself "a bull on stocks—a bull on the United
States." Born penniless in Canada, the speculator had managed to put
together a fortune by dominating the Chicago Board of Trade. Oris and
Mantis van Sweringen were invited as well; the two only had eighth-
grade educations, but through grit and common sense, these brothers
from Wooster, Ohio, found success in Cleveland real-estate, then in
railroads. That they reportedly slept in side-by-side twin beds in a
colossal mansion was not Raskob's concern. They had financial mus-

cle. Percy Rockefeller and the du Pont brothers stood in for the social top end of the scale.

Before the others arrived, Raskob told James Riordan the purpose of the meeting: to rally confidence in the market, which had stumbled since its record high on September 3. Riordan, a former truck driver who went on to start the United States Trucking Corporation and the County Trust bank, also had a significant interest in seeing the market remain strong. The two were fast friends and closely linked with Al Smith, who served as a director at County Trust.

The only one at the lunch without a fortune was William Lamb, whom few of the others knew. There was something both formal and nervous about the architect. Everyone except his wife addressed him as "Mr. Lamb," and she could never bring herself to refer to him as anything but "William." His nervousness came out in his incessant smoking and the rapid movement of his eyes. Although he had no influence on the market itself, Raskob invited him for a reason that his guests would soon learn.

Raskob wore one of his signature colorful shirts, the collar tight around his tanned neck. Although he had personally pulled back on some of his investments, he pointed out to each of his guests that he believed in the bull market, that it still had much strength and potential. His orchestrated speech was given in a slow, steady voice; he watched each of the men's faces as he said that the forces gathering to speak unfavorably about the market must be silenced; it was essential for all of them to project optimism in the market, much as Cutten had a few days before when he said that the amount of brokers' loans was not unnecessarily large. Those around the table agreed.

More must be done. Investors needed to listen to someone other than financial advisor Roger Babson, who early last month announced "that sooner or later a crash is coming, and it may be terrific . . . factories will shut down . . . men will be thrown out of work . . . the vicious circle will get in full swing and the result will be a serious business depression." His comments had caused such a decline in stock prices that editorial writers called the event the Babson Break. Since then there had been an uneasy feeling on the street. Many considered a crash to be a real possibility. The *Wall Street Journal* published a Mark Twain quote as its September 11 "Thought of the Day": "Don't part with your illusions; when they are gone you may still exist, but you have ceased to live." The *New York Times* financial editor Alexander Noyes compared the present market circumstances to those of the panic in 1907 and warned of catastrophic consequences. The market had continued a slow downward spiral until September 24, when another serious break in share prices further darkened the mood. Investors by the thousands were selling off their portfolios. Gangsters in Chicago threatened their brokers if they dared make a margin call. The president of the New York Yankees, Ed Barrow, even held a special meeting to tell his players to abandon the market.

Raskob understood the danger of this mood. He stared into the eyes of each of his lunch guests as he slowly walked around the table. One of his guests grumbled that bankers were becoming too cautious. Another said that the previous day's brief rally, led by U.S. Steel, was evidence that Wall Street still thought the economy had legs. Raskob disagreed; he thought the rally meaningless because it was used as another opportunity for investors to cash in on their holdings. Until he and his guests—and their powerful friends—gave the market some "snap and buoyancy," the declines would continue. They must spread the message that stocks were destined to trade at "ten times their present price, and brokers' loans will be billions more than they are now." Raskob believed in this future, despite the current feeling in Wall Street.

"In a healthy market we prosper," he said. "In a sick market we suffer."

Stepping away from the table, he told William Lamb to follow him

out of the dining room. Lamb trailed behind his client, limping no-
ticeably. The architect had lost a leg while motorcycling through Italy
after graduation from the Ecole des Beaux-Arts and now used an arti-
ficial leg. Riordan knew what Raskob was about to reveal; his friend had
told him his strategy in advance. His final move was to express his vision of America's greatness; a vision born out of poverty, but powerful
in its effect.

―――――

"John Jakob Raskob, capitalist"—so he signed one of the many documents in the purchase of the two-acre plot west of Fifth Avenue between Thirty-third and Thirty-fourth Streets. Of the many who had
won fortunes from the explosion of share prices on Wall Street, few had
profited as handsomely as Raskob. His claim on the land underneath
the Waldorf-Astoria Hotel signaled a sea change. Gone now were the
blue-blood families from their mansions along Fifth Avenue, once
deemed "the most elegant street in the city" where all the "great
people" live. Gone were Mrs. Astor, her black wig, diamond brooches,
rope of fake pearls, and her social yardstick, Ward McAllister, who explained, "There are only about four hundred people in fashionable
New York society, don't you know. If you go outside the number, don't
you see, you strike people who are either not at ease in a ballroom or
else make other people not at ease. See the point."

It was doubtful that Raskob, a former stenographer for the
Worthington Pump Company in upstate New York, the great-grandson
of an Alsatian immigrant, the son of a cigar-man, measured up to
McAllister's grade. He often talked of business and as a young man he
used to scribble notes on the cuffs of his shirt when he ran short of
paper.

Raskob came from squalor, born in the industrial town of
Lockport, New York, in 1879. His mother was Irish and a devout

Catholic. His parents had little money to spare on their four children. There were no private schools and summers in Europe. A roof overhead and a warm meal at night were luxury enough. After his father died when Raskob was nineteen, he needed to care for his mother, younger brother, and two sisters. Running his newspaper route and taking on boarders was not enough. It was once said by a distinguished judge that "the best education you can give a boy of fifteen to twenty is to put his widowed mother on his hands to support. If there is anything in that boy, it will come out, and education consists in bringing things out, not pouring them in." This burden brought out in Raskob an intense, sometimes Machiavellian drive, but one bolstered by good intentions.

Only days after his father passed away, he went to his mother and asked her to tally up the family's assets and liabilities. A week later she came back to her son and said that once they paid off their debts, they would have only twenty-five dollars left in the bank. Raskob gathered the family together, told them the situation, and then made one promise: "We are never going to be in this position again."

He made true on his word, starting with a $7.50-a-week position as a stenographer for the chief engineer of a Worthington Pump Company subsidiary. After his boss denied Raskob a raise, he wrote a friend in Lorain, Ohio, to see if he knew of any better jobs. His friend told him about Pierre Samuel du Pont, who was serving as the president of a street railway company, and needed a secretary. The great-grandson of the E. I. du Pont de Nemours & Company's founder offered pretty good coattails to ride. Raskob wrote du Pont for the job and asked for a thousand dollars a year salary, two and a half times his current income. Pierre du Pont appreciated this boldness and hired him, the first of two "fortunate accidents" that shaped Raskob's life.

Although his ambition sometimes got him in hot water, like the time he tried to renegotiate a deal that du Pont had already consummated, the young secretary worked his way into his boss's confidence.

A young William Van Alen
Courtesy of Christopher Gray

H. Craig Severance
Courtesy of George C.S. Hackl

Richmond Shreve, William Lamb, and Arthur Loomis Harmon in
their architectural office   *Courtesy of the Shreve family*

Early sketches of the Reynolds Building by William Van Alen

General Research Division, The New York Public Library, Astor, Lennox, and Tilden Foundations

Stages in the design of the Chrysler Building by William Van Alen

General Research Division, The New York Public Library, Astor, Lennox, and Tilden Foundations

Walter Chrysler
Baldwin H. Ward and
Kathryn C. Ward/
CORBIS

George Ohrstrom   *Courtesy*
of Maggie Ohrstrom Bryant

John Jakob Raskob   *Hulton-*
Deutsch Collection/ CORBIS

Foundation work on the Chrysler Building (March 13, 1929)   *Photograph*
by Peyser & Patzig. Courtesy of Princeton Architectural Press / David Stravitz

Bucker-up and Gunman *Courtesy of Avery Architectural and Fine Arts Library, Columbia University in the City of New York*

The steelwork underneath the Manhattan Company Building.
Courtesy of Avery Architectural and Fine Arts Library, Columbia University in the City of New York

Riding the Ball *Courtesy of Avery Architectural and Fine Arts Library, Columbia University in the City of New York*

Paul Starrett *General Research Division, The New York Public Library, Astor, Lennox, and Tilden Foundations*

William Starrett *General Research Division, The New York Public Library, Astor, Lennox, and Tilden Foundations*

Jack Reilly, intrepid photographer, perched from the 72nd story of the Manhattan Company Building on the day after the steel work was completed on November 13, 1929 *Bettmann / CORBIS*

Derrick raising one of the five sections of the vertex up the side of the Chrysler Building   *Robert F. Wagner Labor Archives, New York University (Charles River Collection)*

The day the vertex was raised atop the Chrysler Building to win the skyscraper race—temporarily   *Photograph by Peyser & Patzig. Courtesy of Princeton Architectural Press/ David Stravitz*

William Van Alen, dressed as the Chrysler Building, and his wife at the Beaux Arts Ball in 1931   *Bettmann / CORBIS*

Top of the Chrysler
Building's Nirosta-sheathed
dome *Photograph by Margaret
Bourke-White (January 1, 1931)
Margaret Bourke-White/TimePix*

Life magazine photographer
Margaret Bourke-White
focusing her camera from
her perch atop the eagle
gargoyle on the Chrysler
Building (January 1, 1935)
Oscar Graubner/TimePix

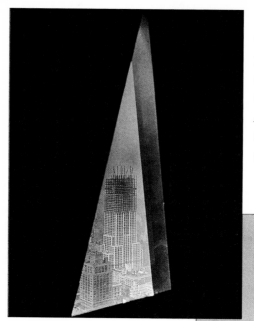

View of the Empire State
Building in mid-construction
through the window of the
Chrysler Building *Courtesy of
Avery Architectural and Fine Arts
Library, Columbia University in the
City of New York*

The Empire State on
November 18, 1930, nearing
completion *Courtesy of Avery
Architectural and Fine Arts Library,
Columbia University in the City of
New York*

Alfred Smith and
his grandchildren
at the opening of
the Empire State
Building (May 1,
1931) *Bettmann/
CORBIS*

In many ways, du Pont became a surrogate father for Raskob, and in private he even referred to him as "Pop." After two years, Raskob tripled his salary to three thousand dollars, and when Eugene du Pont died and Pierre and his two cousins purchased the gunpowder manufacturer outright, Raskob was on track to become the company's treasurer. Despite never attending college, he mastered the nuances of finance and outplayed many an Ivy League graduate.

The second "fortunate accident" befell him when he decided that General Motors, which Durant was making into an automotive powerhouse, was a good investment. He persuaded du Pont of the company's merits, and together they bought three thousand shares, a small position yet one that placed them in a decisive role between two conflicting groups on the General Motors board: Durant and his bankers. With Raskob's guidance, du Pont maneuvered his way into the chairman's seat and the stenographer-turned-secretary became a director. After World War I, he urged Pierre and the du Pont company's thirty directors to invest an additional $50 million. Despite their hesitation, they agreed, having plenty of free cash from munitions sales. Then late in 1920, Raskob and du Pont negotiated with GM's board for the reorganization of the company, and after a meeting that lasted through to the morning, they forced Durant out and took control.

By 1928 their investment was worth $800 million. The reserved, unassuming Raskob, who chewed on his cheek when nervous, now ran the finances of a company that employed three hundred thousand people and was valued at more than $3 billion. In the process, he managed to amass a personal fortune reported at $100 million. When Raskob boarded a liner to Europe in March 1928 and told a reporter that GM's stock was underpriced—that it should be trading at fifteen times, not ten times, its earnings—the market listened, sending GM's share price skyrocketing. Suddenly people no longer asked "What's a Raskob?"

Although he loved his wife and children, donated a fortune to the

Catholic Church, and was welcomed by the pope in Rome, he was no saint. He liked power, was known to run everything he undertook, held fast to his opinions, and remembered those who crossed him. He enjoyed the environs of the Tiger Club, an establishment run by the construction tycoon William Kenny on the top floor of a Twenty-third Street office building. There the rich and influential drank together, played poker (Raskob always donated his winnings to charity), and discussed politics amidst tiger statues and motifs. He met Al Smith at the club and fell under his considerable charms. When Democrats nominated Smith for president, Raskob decided to bankroll the four-term governor's campaign. Soon thereafter he was named Democratic National Chairman, and General Motors forced him to resign from the board.

Some said that he was shooting to become the Secretary of Treasury, a position of great influence, by the end of the twenties. For the first time, he stepped into center stage and suffered its glare. Hooverites coined the term "Raskobism," a slur that *Time* magazine said "contains the following ingredients: one part Roman Catholicism, one part wetness, one part political irregularity (Mr. Raskob used to be a Republican), one part big business." The bid, and his commitment to it, was a risk and one that ended in failure. Like Smith, he retreated from New York after the defeat to salve his wounds. Since his rise had begun, Raskob had never endured such a loss of influence or direction in his career. The death of his nineteen-year-old son, William, in a car crash in Centreville, Maryland, in July that same year cast an even darker shadow over him. His friends rallied around him, Governor Smith included, but there was little they could offer except their condolences as Raskob buried William in the family mausoleum in Wilmington, Delaware.

As the Empire State development came together, he found a way to reinvent himself and renew his conviction that "there is a divinity which shapes our ends." The day before the skyscraper's official announcement, Raskob sent a letter to Louis Kaufman about the sky-scraper's financing. After he detailed his substantial personal invest-ment in the project, he concluded the letter, thanking the banker for the opportunity of doing "something big and really worthwhile. I am sure it will be the most outstanding thing in New York and a credit to the city and state as well as to those associated with it."

Raskob had long harbored the idea of building an epic skyscraper, but he shared this vision with very few. Although it was in his nature never to make a public move until the private dealings were finished, he revealed his dream to Eddie Dowling, an actor and close friend, who explained that it was "a small town boy's idea. [Raskob] told me that the first time he came to New York, he wanted to see the Woolworth Building, and the Statue of Liberty. The Washington Monument had al-ways impressed him, and pictures he had seen of the Eiffel Tower. When he became affluent, got to be head of General Motors and all of that, he went up in the Eiffel Tower. It burned him up to think that the French had built something, by hand, higher than anything we had in this great country of ours."

Dowling said he was there when Raskob first told Smith about his plans. It was a few days after Smith's loss to Hoover. A small group of Democratic supporters, twenty-eight in number, met for dinner at the Lotus Club in New York to celebrate Franklin Roosevelt's victory in the governor's race. Present were many of Smith's friends, and the evening had a bittersweet air to it. They cheered Roosevelt, yet knew what his own loss meant to Smith, who sat up on the dais with Roosevelt. As the dinner trailed toward its end, Smith escaped to the men's room. Dowling followed him inside.

"Eddie, I could cry," Smith said.

Dowling tried to raise his spirits. "What about, Governor? You've had a wonderful career. You came up out of the sidewalks of New York . . . You're the greatest Governor New York ever had. Most of the social legislation that our city and state are enjoying, you were father

of. Your successors will pick up where you left off, Governor. You will
be in the hearts of your people forever. Don't worry about this."

"I haven't got a five-cent piece. But I've got children. I'm a poor
man. My God!"

While Smith continued his rant, saying how "there's nothing as
dead as a defeated politician, not even yesterday's newspaper," Raskob
came into the bathroom.

He stopped Smith and said, "Governor, I've got some news for you.
I hope this will please you. I can understand your feeling the way you
do. Some friends of yours and myself have assembled a plot at the corner of Thirty-fourth and Fifth Avenue. There we are going to build the
tallest building in the world—You're going to be the president—and it's
your job for life."

Raskob and Smith never indicated that Dowling's story was true,
never gave their own version of events, and never admitted their involvement in securing the Waldorf-Astoria site prior to summer 1929.
But there are reasons to believe Dowling's story is true. Floyd Brown of
Bethlehem Engineering Company was the one who secured the lease
for the land, and Raskob was a close associate of several of the men in
the syndicate that helped Brown get that lease. To sketch the site's
plans, Brown chose Shreve & Lamb, architects whom Raskob knew well
from their design of the General Motors Building in New York. And Al
Smith's daughter revealed that her father knew of Raskob's role in the
skyscraper long before its announcement and that many of the plans
had already been drawn before the "official" hiring of Shreve & Lamb
in September. One account had Raskob showing a scale model of the
building to James Riordan in April 1929, long before any written
record of his involvement. After a toast that recalled both of their pau-
per upbringings—"The Past—May it never be repeated"—they raised
glasses of champagne to the skyscraper's future success.

Regardless of the exact moment Raskob devoted himself to the
idea and brought Smith into the fold, he bore many risks to see it rise.

The Empire State Building was to be a symbol of "what the poor are able to achieve in America," and nobody—not George Ohrstrom, Walter Chrysler, a roomful of nervous investors, or anyone else—was going to get in the way of his making this symbol the greatest, tallest, most awe-inspiring structure ever built.

That early October afternoon in his apartment, Raskob was ready to reveal his vision to the city's power brokers, who remained waiting around the dining table in the other room. No doubt they were curious to know why their host had excused himself during the height of his pitch, let alone brought an architect to a meeting ostensibly about the market. Finally, there was the sound of footsteps, and Raskob and Lamb returned, carrying with them a large model of the Empire State Building. They carefully set in on a nearby table.

"Gentlemen, this is part of what I have at stake. A monument to the future," Raskob said proudly, returning to his seat to watch their reaction.

It was one he expected. A Van Sweringen brother called the skyscraper a "powerful piece of work." Others nodded and murmured in agreement, amazed at what they saw, the sheer massiveness of the design.

Raskob told his guests that the planned structure represented the United States, "a land which reached for the sky with its feet on the ground." Despite the millions needed to construct the Empire State, he expected to see it built because of a "faith in the future reflected in the stock market."

He then turned the presentation over to William Lamb, who chronicled the enormity of the project, the amount of steel, limestone, brick, telephone cable, and windows needed to build such a skyscraper. It required millions of dollars and thousands of people working together in unison, toward one goal, to see it rise. The scale of the project was unlike anything the guests had known.

Pushing back his chair, Raskob moved toward the model. "Gentleman, a country which can provide the vision, the resources, the money and the people to build such an edifice as this, surely cannot be allowed to crash through lack of support from the likes of you and me."

His guests left impressed with this symbol and motivated to bolster confidence in the market, but for Raskob, who had a fortune of his own on the line with the Empire State, there was much to be concerned about if stock prices fell through the floor. Numbers could be run by the finest of financial minds (of which his was one), but in the best of locations in the best of times, building a record-breaking skyscraper entailed tremendous risk. The location of the proposed Empire State at Thirty-fourth Street and Fifth Avenue was not even considered an office district by most building experts and managers. Stores and boutique shops dominated the area. Some feared the skyscraper would exist in the no-man's-land between the Grand Central district on Forty-second Street and the financial heart of New York's downtown.

If his lunch guests failed to prop up investor sentiment and the market crashed, then Babson's doomsday warning might come to pass. Raskob's hope of finding tenants for his skyscraper would fade if the economy busted, businesses failed, and unemployment rose. He'd be better hiding his millions in a large mattress.

Yet the skyscraper was already moving ahead. The demolition of the Waldorf-Astoria Hotel had officially begun two days before, when Al Smith stood in front of a crew of photographers and warned, "Gentleman, stand back while I start the real work of demolition." He pulled a cable, bringing down a ten-foot section of copper ornament on the roof. "The northward march of progress has reached the heart of the city," Smith said. "I feel sorry to see this historic old building torn down, but progress demands that it must go . . . On this site will rise the largest office building in the world—eighty stories tall." The promise had been made. Raskob hid his reaction from the press after one of the men sawed into the "marble" column in the famed Peacock Alley and a cloud of plaster dust spit out. If this event augured doom, he either neglected the sign or decided to forge ahead nonetheless.

The Empire State Building project had begun.

CHAPTER THIRTEEN

The Prize of the Race

New York is the San Gimignano of today, its
bankers and wholesalers playing Montecchi and
Capuleti with each other.

—*Karl Lamprecht*

In early October, Severance drove down with his daughter, Faith, to
the Manhattan Company Building to tour the skyscraper. The column
tiers had reached the fiftieth floor and they had to maneuver around
the trucks bringing the next bundle of steel. Speed and height were the
two measures of this race, and the 40 Wall Street team led in the first,
and as far as the press and Severance knew, they were slated to win the
second.

Leaving the chauffer to park the Rolls-Royce, Severance and his
seven-months-pregnant daughter entered the site. She didn't have to
sign the usual waiver required by visitors. They stepped through the
site and into the mine-cage elevator, which was simply a caged wooden
platform operated by one of workmen. One writer called it a "vertical
coffin." Faith was not afraid as the gate closed and the bell rang, sig-
naling the platform's rise. It jarred and ratcheted upwards, gathering
speed with each floor. While holding to the side of the cage, Faith ob-
served in quick succession the various stages of construction. In the

basement engineers installed the three massive vaults. Four enormous trusses allowed the second floor banking room to run its length without columns. On the seventh floor, workers laid the granite and limestone walls. The bricklayers had completed the walls from the eighth floor to the thirtieth floor and were fast at work on the next. Over two hundred workers moved about these floors lathing and plastering the inside. Derricks on the twenty-sixth-floor setback lifted steel up the side of the building and mixers turned the concrete before laborers poured it on the wooden-framed floor arches. Two thousand men—carpenters placing hoist rails, pipefitters attending to the steam siphons, asbestos helpers covering water risers, electricians wiring outlets, glaziers putting in windows, heating contractors installing radiators, laborers pushing buggies full of debris—moved about to the Starretts' orders, and Severance pointed out to Faith what some of the men were doing. He spared her details on the importance of column loads and wind braces, unless she asked.

On several floors, Severance introduced his daughter to the men. He knew many by name and was as comfortable around them as he was the businessmen and financiers he met with at the Metropolitan Club. Regardless, the popular game of craps played by some of the workers on the higher floors was likely shelved until he departed.

The elevator didn't yet extend to the fiftieth floor. Severance and his daughter would have had to scale a series of ladders to reach that high, but several floors below, Faith watched the riveting gangs securing another connection of steel. White-hot rivets passed between the heaters and catchers. The din of pneumatic hammers drowned out the taxicab horns and whistles of the boats passing in the harbor below. The fall winds would soon make the erection of the tower, rising from the last setback on the thirty-sixth floor, a more dangerous and numbing experience. Even now the wind rattled the scaffolds and blew the men's shirts out behind them like sails. Crews worked day and night on the skyscraper, and they were catching up with the steel on the

Chrysler Building, which had slowed as the first two arches of the dome were erected. The gangs on each building measured each other's progress from their perches in the sky. Even the steel fabricators on each site were so uncertain as to which building would rise tallest that they wagered against one another as to the outcome.

Severance kept the exact details of the height race from his daughter, including the secret changing of plans and that he had promised to go higher than the Chrysler Building, regardless of how many stories Van Alen added. She knew this kind of promise was typical of him and that his desire to win the height race was only equaled by his wish to see Van Alen defeated. As they stood on a narrow section of scaffolding, no walls to any side, Severance and his daughter watched in silence as another rivet arced through the air, and the catcher, after receiving it, tapped the rivet against the column to shed any flakes from the coke fire. The pride Severance felt to have his daughter standing with him hundreds of feet in the air was matched by the swell of feeling Faith had for him, for designing this skyscraper and having achieved so much from the pure exercise of his will.

In October 1929, there was no absence of will—or some said, hubris—being exercised. Far to the west, sculptor Gutzon Borglum was shaping George Washington's face in the granite side of Mount Rushmore. He and his miners dynamited, drilled, and chiseled his features, the first of four presidents to be memorialized in stone 5,700 feet over South Dakota's Black Hills. Of his work, Borglum said he wanted "a few feet of stone that bears witness, carries the likenesses, the dates, a word or two of the great things we accomplished as a Nation, placed so high it won't pay to pull down for lesser purposes. Hence, let us place there, carved high, as close to heaven as we can, the words of our leaders, their faces, to show posterity what manner of men they were. Then breathe a prayer that these records will endure until the wind and the rain alone shall wear them away."

If Americans felt they needed monuments to symbolize their presence in history, they only had to look toward their cities, where every year they added yet another batch of skyscrapers, hundreds of feet tall. Few cities were immune to the fever of building higher. Earlier that year the *New York Sun* began a series of daily photographs of these towers under captions like: "A Building Like This in Winston, Salem." They had an abundant supply of city skyscrapers to choose from: Boston's Custom House Tower (twenty-nine stories), Philadelphia's Fidelity Trust Company Building (thirty-four stories), Cleveland's Terminal Tower (fifty-two stories), Detroit's Penobscot Tower (forty-six stories), San Francisco's Russ Building (thirty stories), Seattle's Smith Building (thirty-eight stories), Chicago's Board of Trade (forty-five stories), and Houston's Gulf Building (thirty-five stories), among nearly four hundred other skyscrapers higher than twenty stories in major and minor cities across the country.

In October 1929, in spite of the restless nights of many Wall Street investors, "world's tallest" announcements sparked more imaginations than Borglum hoped to with his sixty-foot presidential busts. People argued about what prompted this rush of super-skyscrapers— some said they were the result of rising land values or a last gasp attempt to sell a plot of land by drawing attention to it; others thought that one-upmanship had finally become an art form. Whatever the reason, skyscrapers hit the headlines day after day.

The first came on October 2: The City Bank–Farmers Trust Building would rise seventy-one stories and 925 feet, only a few blocks from 40 Wall Street. Demolition was already underway in the construction of this "King of Skyscrapers." Two days later, the architect Harvey Wiley Corbett slipped word to the press that the Metropolitan

Life Insurance Company had plans for a hundred-story skyscraper, final height not yet determined. "Desire for height supremacy has no part in the plans," said one bank official, presumably with a straight face. "The most efficient height consistent with the size of the plot is the aim." Hired as the builders, the Starrett brothers had their hand in this challenger for the title as well. Unfortunately for Metropolitan Life, it shared headlines with the developer A. E. Lefcourt, who claimed he was adding another skyscraper to his collection of twenty: this one one hundred and five stories, 1,050 feet high, and so slender in its upper stories that renting space there would be all but impossible. At least Lefcourt suggested that if a skyscraper taller than his was announced, he would abandon his plans.

He didn't have to wait long. On October 6, the *Herald-Tribune* broke the story of a one-hundred-and-fifty-story structure, a "pile of steel, granite, brick and marble—a quarter of a mile high and two blocks square," to be erected in the old dry goods district north of City Hall by Charles Noyes, who "always accomplished what he set out to do." The sixteen-hundred-foot tower would cost $100 million, but real-estate experts assured Noyes the building would pay. New York architects weighed in on the developer's plan; Raymond Hood said, "Some time ago I got our engineers to figure up just what would be the theoretical maximum height for a skyscraper. It is 7,000 feet. The affair is very simple . . . I proposed a tower 2,500 feet high and nobody batted an eye."

Skyscrapers had plenty of detractors. New York's Health Commissioner, Dr. Wynne, deemed skyscrapers seventy stories high a "menace to health," and must have had a fit after hearing the news of a building more than twice that height. Henry James likened skyscrapers to "youth on the run and with the prize of the race in sight." For this traditionalist, these new buildings crushed "the old quite as violent children stamp on snails and caterpillars." Russians explained these lofty structures as capitalist greed, needing to squeeze the most profit from the smallest plot of land. The Swiss-born architect Le Corbusier characterized the world's-tallest competition as a clear sign of American megalomania. Propagandists railed against the construction of ever taller buildings, calling them sky-scratchers, fly-scrappers, monstrosities, constrictors, engulfers, crowd-breeders, and dinosaurs. One lambasted New York's skyline as a "dentillated jawbone."

Noyes countered the critics by saying that he had received letters and phone calls from people across the country inspired by his grand plan. Financing the project, he assured, presented only opportunities for investors. International sportsman Major Kennelly said that he "feared for the angels in flight through the heavens at night if Noyes didn't put signal beacons on the tip of his building," but otherwise it was likely to prove a success. A few days later the announcement of an eighty-story building in the theater district barely deserved mention. In the *Architect*, Kenneth Murchison took a swipe at this New York obsession with height: "They seem to be springing up like asparagus tips all over the city, these high ones. We don't mind them at all. It gives the town an excitable, nervous look that appeals to us . . . And it's a great publicity-getter, too. All a man has to do is to announce, mysteriously, that he is going to erect a hundred-story building and presto! He gets on the front page. Remember Mr. Larkin with his hundred-story Lick telescope on West 42nd Street? It never got any higher than a linotype."

In Los Angeles, plans were under consideration to construct an airport to serve one hundred planes an hour on the roof of a skyscraper. There appeared no limit in sight to what builders dared propose as the twenties spun to a close. "How long will it be before office workers look down from their windows upon cloud banks . . . The helicopter and the gyroscope will enable a man to land and start from a shelf outside his dwelling window," read a *New York Times* editorial in 1929. "No dream is too steep for America."

Van Alen refused to tilt his sword at every new skyscraper; the Manhattan Company and Empire State buildings were formidable enough. In the first two weeks of October Van Alen drew only one new design, for the lobby's information booth. He had other concerns, like the construction of the vertex. Despite the fact that the vertex wasn't finished, Chrysler's press flaks were already telling newspapers that the steelwork was complete. This made the Chrysler Building "the tallest building in the world," as the *New York Times* put it on October 16 (the Eiffel Tower was not considered a building because it didn't lease space to tenants), "surpassing the 792-foot elevation of the Woolworth Building by 16 feet. This greatest height distinction, however, is not likely to be held very long, as the Manhattan Company Building on Wall Street is rapidly ascending to its maximum height."

These articles showed how easily newspaper journalists and others were tricked. Van Alen knew the "last beam" on the Chrysler Building had yet to be set, and the skyscraper stood over 850 feet when the *Times* published its article. Of course, it was difficult to measure a sky-scraper's height by simply looking at it from the street or atop the Manhattan Company Building four miles downtown. The riveting gangs there could see that the Chrysler Building had finished the steel on the third of the seven receding arches, but that told them little of its exact height. If a journalist had managed to figure its precise height through the use of some surveying equipment, it was not reported, nor could any outsider know what had yet to be constructed.

Only Van Alen, Chrysler, and a few others knew the final height. The vertex was brought up to the dome in five sections. The difficulties in the structural design and erection necessitated an original ap-proach. As Van Alen said, "It was manifestly impossible to assemble this structure and hoist it as a unit from the ground, and equally im-possible to hoist it in sections and place them as such in their final po-sitions." A derrick perched on the seventy-fourth floor relayed the

first section of Van Alen's spire up the side of the building above the
fifty-ninth-floor setback. Once the steel cleared the dome, the derrick
then lowered the section into the fire-tower court, resting its square
base on two 12-by-12 boards, 20 feet long, on the sixty-fifth floor. The
vertex was hidden within the higher floors, and some of the floor framing had to be temporarily eliminated so that the vertex could fit.

Each section was made up of stacks of four corner angles, with light
angle struts and V-type bracing. A cross-sectional view of the steel design made the vertex look like a stack of ever smaller pyramids. The
second section was riveted onto the first, the third on the second, and
so on. Later, the vertex would be covered in chromium nickel steel
called Nirosta, the same finish that Van Alen selected to use on the
dome. To attach the finish beforehand added too much weight to what
Van Alen knew would already be a dangerous raising operation.

Setting the vertex into place was a tricky proposition, but Van Alen
had an engineer's mind and he was certain of his insight into how
things worked. Once on an ocean liner in the Atlantic, he and a cadre
of fellow architects debated the strength and direction of the Gulf
Stream. The debate turned contentious. Van Alen grabbed a menu,
took out a pen, and jotted down his address and a note: "$5 reward if
returned to William Van Alen." He slipped the menu into a bottle,
corked the top, and tossed the bottle overboard. He promised its return from a faraway shore. Nine months later the bottle arrived at his
office doorstep, sent by Colin Campbell of Scotland, who found it on a
beach two thousand miles from where Van Alen had tossed it. Another
example of Van Alen's engineering insight was his invention of the
Pentz compass, which he thought up while using an airplane to scout
sites for his clients and asking the pilot about the workings of a plane's
navigation. The compass was used on the first airmail routes between
Chicago and New York.

Van Alen had closely studied the problem of raising the vertex, and
understood how the mechanics of lifting it would work. But he knew

that his engineering insight had its limits, and he called on his structural engineer, William Edwin Squire, to ensure that his plan wouldn't
end in disaster. Squire, Van Alen's younger cousin, ran a successful
engineering practice with his father, who had designed the steelwork
on Ebbitts Field. William Edwin moved a slide rule so fast that one
could barely follow his hands. Squire checked and double-checked the
vertex's load and wind stresses; he inspected the steel when it arrived
on the site, carrying around a hammer that he hit the steel with and listened to the sound before announcing, "Pretty solid." For additional
consultation, Van Alen hired Homer Balcom, an expert in wind vibra-
tions who had cut his teeth at the American Bridge Company and built
ships during World War I.

On October 17, the vertex was a week away from being ready.
Engineering complications aside, Van Alen must have wondered what
people would think of this last-minute addition. The early reviews of
his design were favorable. The previous week in the *New Yorker*,
T-Square had written that Van Alen's "great tower . . . improves
steadily as it progresses. The outlines of the soaring parabolic-dome
treatment which will crown its peak are distinctly interesting, as is the
modern use of contrasting dark and light material throughout, and the
employment of metal panels at various floor levels." In *Pencil Points*,
Francis Swales praised that his design "seems to me better than nearly
anything I have seen in the design of office buildings during the past
several years."

He had to believe the critics would also appreciate his terminating
flourish.

CHAPTER FOURTEEN

The Butterfly and Its Cocoon

The architect examined his plans. Right in the center of the tower he found a fire tower which, to the
untutored mind, is nothing more or less than a
large hole in a building. "I will build," mused Bill,
"something in that fire tower."

—*Kenneth Murchison, on the Chrysler Building*

Severance was sure he had Van Alen dead to rights. In the third week
of October, the Manhattan Company Building surpassed the height of
the Woolworth Tower. The high winds slowed the erection of intricate
truss work in the pyramid crown, but the schedule had the steelworkers topping out the steel on November 12. Meanwhile, the four sides of
the Chrysler Building's dome were closing in on one another at an angle,
preventing it from rising much higher. Van Alen had shown his cards
first: His skyscraper would be 840 feet tall, maybe 850 at best—that was
without the sixty-foot flagpole Severance had learned about earlier in
the week. Announcements from the Chrysler Building Corporation that
they had finished their steel work didn't fool him. The derrick poised
above the dome was there to raise this flagpole. Severance knew what to
do. "When you get a guy down, don't let him up."

The 40 Wall Street team decided to go higher again. Ohrstrom set out to build the tallest and wouldn't be beat out by less than ten feet. The builders agreed. Paul Starrett had an aphorism about these kind of changes: "Even in building a dog house . . . you find you have to make it larger because the dog's tail is longer than you thought it was." No doubt the bondholders who financed this skyscraper thought that every dollar they had invested was used to produce the most efficient income-producing office building, but ultimately some of that money was spent on satisfying pride—for all involved.

Back at the drafting table, Severance and Matsui designed a lantern story and lengthened the top of the structure with a flagpole of their own, one twenty-five feet tall. By mid-November when the work-ers raised the flag, it would snap in the wind over the Manhattan Company Building at 925 feet. Chrysler and Van Alen would only boast the world's tallest building for a short month, only long enough to be of minor note in the years ahead.

The 40 Wall Street team tried to keep these revised plans quiet. Not even The Bank of The Manhattan Company's directors knew the final height. Their vice president, Raymond Jones, had to admit to his employees that he didn't know the elevation of the last set of plans, saying the skyscraper "will rise to a height of——, well, the builder won't tell us now, but they admit it will be at least 900 feet high."

At week's end, however, he had his answer when a journalist broke the story. "New Skyscraper Race is Won by Bank of Manhattan Building—Plans Altered Twice to Beat Out Chrysler," read the *Evening Telegram* headline on Saturday, October 18. Albeit premature, it was great press for Severance and the building's owners: "[The Manhattan Company Building], unlike the Chrysler Building, was little heralded at first and possibly by virtue of this fact was able to come through in a Garrison finish to win the title of the tallest . . . The Chrysler con-struction is so far advanced that further changes are impossible." The article featured photographs of the towers taken on Thursday and an illustration of their future height marks: 905 feet for the Chrysler Building and 925 feet for the Manhattan Company Building.

Severance had much to celebrate at his weekend house in Point Pleasant, New Jersey. One could hardly begrudge him if he toasted his success with a highball or two, Prohibition be damned. Plans for his design of the Nelson Building, a 525-foot-tall skyscraper on Thirty-fourth Street and Seventh Avenue, were published on the same day as the *Evening Telegram* article. The real-estate firm, Brown, Wheelock, Harris, Vought & Company, had an army of agents out soliciting tenants for the Manhattan Company Building and were making good progress, particularly with its promise of world's tallest. And now that a reporter had revealed his and Van Alen's secret moves, his former partner knew the final score. The race was settled between them and, in only a few weeks, would be punctuated in steel.

Meanwhile, the press had a good story in their teeth with this race, and they had no intention of letting the team behind the Manhattan Company Building relax. A *New York Times* journalist called Paul Starrett at his Greenwich, Connecticut, home over the weekend, wanting to know if he was willing to confirm or deny the *Evening Telegram* reports that Severance had altered the Manhattan Company Building's plans twice to carry the height of his skyscraper to 925 feet. "Because of pyramiding in the upper floors of a skyscraper," Starrett responded, "it is difficult to define building heights in terms of floors, especially after the sixty-second floor has been passed." It was the answer of a seasoned politician—the nonanswer—but one only had to know Paul Starrett, knowing how he planned every movement of labor and material on his construction sites, to see through his claiming ignorance of the height of his own skyscraper. After all, he had ordered the steel to exact measurements, even factoring in the slight compression of the columns, particularly on the lower floors, due to the load they had to bear. On his buildings, an eighth of an inch in height discrepancy was considered "the very limit of allowable error."

Starrett held his ground. The reports were accurate, but he didn't want to reveal their plans. The journalist then suggested that Ohrstrom and the Starretts were set against Walter Chrysler in a race to erect the world's tallest building. Starrett balked: he was not involved in any such race. The original plans, as filed with the Bureau of Buildings, were the ones they intended to implement. Furthermore, in his opinion, the Manhattan Company Building stood "too high now." Despite his protestations, the article concluded that the Starretts' fast progress would soon bring the height crown back downtown in a few weeks, as the *Evening Telegram* had reported.

Yet for all the close coverage of the race, not one journalist had connected the fact that the two architects who designed these competing skyscrapers were former partners in a practice that ended badly, nor had journalists uncovered the final height of Chrysler's plans. In truth, a sixty-foot flagpole told only part of the story.

———

On October 23, the executive committee of the Empire State—the owners, architects, and builders—came together for their weekly Tuesday meeting. The day before, another article in the *New York American* had detailed where the skyscraper race stood. Paul Starrett "definitely established" the Manhattan Company Building's final height at 840 feet. Sitting at the table with Raskob, Smith, Kaufman, and the architects, Shreve, Lamb & Harmon, Starrett knew that was a blatant lie. As for the Chrysler Building, the *American*'s real-estate editor, J. P. Lohman, made a call to William Van Alen's office the day before and learned that their skyscraper rose only sixty-eight stories and 805 feet. It looked like the Manhattan Company Building was set to be the new leader at any height greater than 806 feet. At least to the press, the truth was a commodity to be bargained with as freely as a penny stock, and all the race's participants traded it freely.

Down on Wall Street, the ticker tape revealed that Raskob's call to his friends to support the market hadn't worked. Trading was heavy, and despite a few rallies over the previous two weeks, many of the market's leading stocks were trending downward. A few investors had already lost everything, and rather than face their margin calls, they took their own lives. The unease that hung over Wall Street's brokers continued, despite statements from Charles Mitchell, a director of the Federal Reserve Bank in New York, that recent declines were a healthy correction that had played itself out.

Nonetheless, the Empire State, Inc., board pressed ahead with their business. The wreckers had already hauled away tons of the former Waldorf-Astoria, including much of its marble and gold fixtures, and the board needed to resolve the skyscraper's plans in order to arrange for the steel and submit a loan application to the Metropolitan Life Insurance Company. There had been many discussions about the building's height, and now that the Starretts had run the costs for an eighty-story skyscraper, the committee had to make a final decision on the design and put the machine in motion to build it.

Governor Smith presented Starrett Brothers' findings: the skyscraper would cost $50 million, including $27 million for construction and $16 million for the land. The young real-estate agent Hamilton Weber provided the numbers for the potential rental income for the skyscraper that Raskob promised him would be "the biggest and the highest building in the entire world." In an exhaustive report given to Chatham Phenix's Robert Brown, who sat on the skyscraper's executive committee, Weber estimated the yearly income from the roughly 2.3 million square feet of rentable space to be an exact $7,961,580. He broke the numbers down by floor and based them on an occupancy rate of 90 to 100 percent. Given yearly expenses (operating, taxes, interest on loans) of roughly $6 million, the building would spin off at least $1.5 million in dividends for its investors. For "practical purposes," he didn't take into consideration "the character of ownership and certain other features connected with the building." One of those considerations included the most important feature of the skyscraper: its future claim as world's tallest.

For months now the architects and builders had struggled to rein in Raskob's desire to build higher. When they first told him the most economical height was seventy-five stories, Raskob instructed them to come back with plans for eighty-eight stories. It was progress from earlier discussions of one hundred stories and questions like "How high can you make it so it won't fall down." Shreve had explained this number of stories was simply unrealistic: they would require an additional elevator bank and this "utility cone" cut into the number of square feet available for rental.

There were few architectural firms more sober-minded than Shreve, Lamb & Harmon. That was not to say they lacked ambition. In 1921 when Shreve and Lamb joined the letterhead of Carrère & Hastings, the partnership agreement allowed them to profit exclusively on the small jobs they brought in, an arrangement that, Shreve said, "would have been fine if they had stuck to dog houses, garages, and small homes." They quickly won the commission for Standard Oil's new Manhattan office building and the new partners argued with Hastings about how the fee should be split. Shreve and Lamb then decided to set off on their own. They won a number of commissions and created a large practice based out of the same Madison Avenue building where Van Alen worked. In May 1929 they offered the puckish Arthur Loomis Harmon, who had distinguished himself as a AIA Gold Medal–winning designer of the Shelton Hotel, a partnership in their firm after Harmon admitted to Shreve on a train ride that "he was afraid that the day would come when he would design great buildings and be unable to clinch the contract with the client because he had no organization to transform good plans into buildings of steel and stone." Seeing the opportunity, Shreve said, "Loomis, I think you'd better come in with Lamb and me. We can go a long way together." With the design skill of Lamb and Harmon matched with the management acumen of Shreve, the practice proved to be the modern ideal for an architectural firm—an ideal that Severance & Van Alen had given up years ago in a fit of ego.

In this modern ideal, Shreve didn't respect the architect with "heavy black pencil, long hair and temperamental disposition" whom he thought fit better in "those high and far off times when all women were beautiful and the brave deserved the fair." The esprit de corps of Shreve, Lamb & Harmon was cooperation among the members of the boards, and that cooperation had one purpose: to make the building pay. In this spirit Lamb had taken the reins of the Empire State's design. Harmon provided the out-of-box ideas. Shreve made it all work. "The program was short enough," Lamb described the origination of his design: "—a fixed budget, no space more than 28 feet from window to corridor, as many stories of such space as possible, an exterior of limestone, and completion by May 1, 1931, which meant a year and six months from the beginning of sketches. The first three of these requirements produced the mass of the building and the latter two the characteristics of design."

At the beginning, Lamb tried to maintain some of the fifty-story loft building's massing. He cut indentations into the tower's face to provide for light and used the same elevator placement, its banks perpendicular to the building's main axis. Using the thirtieth floor as the master floor plan from which the rest of the skyscraper took shape, he drew several schemes. Shreve then took each and calculated whether it would pay. As the days passed, the skyscraper revealed itself more clearly to Lamb. Raymond Hood, who had vied to be the Empire State's architect, advised his friend, "Well, there's one thing you won't have to struggle with, to make it look tall." Lamb cut away floors, eliminated setbacks, and simplified its mass. Finally he settled on placing the elevators parallel to the building's axis and making the tower floor plan more square in design. Then it was a question of how to maximize the rentals of each floor and provide the most light.

Lamb put away his fifteenth scheme and started anew. He drew his final inspiration from a large pencil held aloft. After the fifth floor, Lamb decided to start the tower sixty feet back from the street. Like the unbroken lines of that pencil, the tower then rose to the eightieth floor with only the slightest of setbacks. The design offered the clean expression that matched his tastes, met the zoning regulations, provided ample light and ventilation, and would earn a pretty dollar from renters. Plus, its simplicity met the demands for construction speed. With his partners, he finished the necessary floor plans, elevation drawings, and perspective rendering. The three congregated in the firm's small library whenever they needed to iron out a certain detail, a scene that reminded Lamb of his *charette* days at the Ecole des Beaux-Arts. Thanks to Shreve, however, these plans came with figures detailing the dollars and cents to be earned in rentable square feet. Raskob had adopted these plans, called "Scheme K."

It had been three weeks since the acceptance of this scheme, yet the question remained: how many stories should the skyscraper rise, particularly in the face of a market on the brink of disaster? Shreve's arguments and those of the builders prevailed on Raskob. At eighty stories the Empire State would be the tallest, unless one of the parade of skyscrapers announced in October went further than a rendering for the press. Just in case, they would leave some wriggle room in the loan application with the Metropolitan Insurance Company, stating the building would contain eighty stories plus an undetermined number of penthouse stories. Similar to the Manhattan Company Building, these additional stories were not included in the estimates for rental income. Soon the Starretts could claim their involvement in the two tallest buildings in the world. Shreve, Lamb & Harmon had their hands in both as well.

As for Raskob, he meant to keep his promise to Weber and others. If eighty stories was enough to be tallest, fine. The committee adjourned, resolved to move ahead with the eighty-story skyscraper. He even forwarded the motion. But if this turned out not to be enough, Raskob would go higher—whatever it took to beat Chrysler and the others. He may not have liked the spotlight, but he never played for second place.

Unbeknownst to the Empire State board as they broke up their meeting, and unbeknownst to Severance, who had already been crowned winner in the skyscraper race despite being three weeks away from topping out, Van Alen was preparing to distance himself from his rivals in one sweeping architectural gesture. No question that Severance's lantern story and flagpole were solid additions, but they were typical of an architect who was praised in the same *Architectural Record* article that said: "It is fortunate that up to this time, no attempt has been made by architectural dilettanti to talk of an 'American Style' in city architecture. It is fortunate in as much as there is *no* such style, never has been and, in all probability, never will be such a style." Severance borrowed French Gothic traditions for his building's crown. Van Alen wanted to prove an American style existed, and that it required putting convention aside and using steel to its fullest potential.

On October 23, 1929, however, revolutions in design took a rear seat to the weather. Van Alen needed the day to be clear of hurricane winds or else raising the giant obelisk-shaped spire would be impossible. The previous day a storm had hit the city from the southwest. Its cutting rain and fifty-two-mile-an-hour winds made steel erection in the Chrysler tower too dangerous. The workers scrambled to lash down wooden planks to the beams on the top floors. Several times throughout the construction, high winds had thrown planks down onto Forty-second Street and Lexington Avenue. Charles River, a steelworker on the Chrysler Building, said that to stand up straight during these storms meant risking being blown off the floor. They crawled instead. Down on the street, people ducked for cover as their umbrellas snapped inside out. Power lines, street signs, and construction fences were blown down. One woman was picked up by a gale of wind and thrown like a stone into the window of Schrafft's candy store on Fifth Avenue. That same day Thomas Hastings, one of the deans of American architecture, passed away at sixty-nine years old, silencing his disdain for those "elongated packing boxes" called skyscrapers that should "be passed ever in haste." It was as if the storm and Hastings's death gave pause to reflect on how much New York's skyline was about to change in the days ahead.

The winds had finally settled. A low drift of clouds crossed the sky like a moving mountain, and the temperature was a cool sixty degrees. Chrysler was about to realize his long-held dream, his "fascinating visions of the fantastically high buildings" that he first saw on coming to New York in 1911. The automobile man had set all the gears in motion to see this happen. He had pushed his lawyer, Nicolas Kelley, to negotiate a deal with Reynolds and Cooper Union. He had bankrolled every extravagance in the design, from the steel-sheathed dome, to the grand marble lobby, to the thirty-two elevator cabs, each individually crafted. He had stepped forward, not back, when the height race demanded changes in the design. He even showed the mechanical engineer how to take the plumb lines for the elevators shafts. "If the elevator cabs travel less than straight," he instructed, "they will be more noisy than pistons in cylinders that are out of round. I want them perfect." Now they ran at a thousand feet per minute, two hundred and fifty feet faster than the building code allowed. Most important, he'd signed off on the addition of the steel-latticed vertex.

Although Chrysler had a personal stake in the building and took more than his share of credit for the building's design, this day was for

Van Alen. The vertex was not sixty feet tall, as had been rumored. The five sections of the vertex were instead 185 feet tall. These sections were now riveted together in the fire tower. Its 8-by-8-foot base strained the wooden planks on the sixty-fifth floor, where it stood. The needle's point reached through the dome's top to 935 feet in the sky. Only the derrick set to raise the vertex was higher. To hoist the vertex into position, the steelworkers had built an outrigger platform that projected over the four sides of the seventy-fourth floor. First they secured temporary extensions to the floor on each side and then lashed down planks so they had room to step around as they maneuvered the twenty-seven-ton vertex into place. On paper the vertex appeared a simple and clean addition to the skyscraper. Its lines were straight; its angles measured in exact degrees.

The men, however, had to erect the vertex 860 feet in the sky, raising it up through the fire tower and securing it to the dome's top while moving quickly about the narrow cantilevered platform that offered space for one misstep, but definitely not two. A gust of wind or the snap of a cable threatened to send the vertex pitching headlong into traffic below. This fifty-four-thousand-pound web of steel—some of whose braces were taller than the iron workers—was unlike anything any of these men had faced before, even the bolter-up, old John, who had seen much more than most. Balancing an elephant by his trunk on top of the building would have been an easier proposition. To add to the day's job, the derrick adjacent to the fire tower had only a twenty-ton capacity, but needed to lift the twenty-seven-ton vertex. Van Alen's engineers figured that by staging the derrick mast close to the fire tower opening, the boom could be in a vertical position as it raised the vertex. Derrick capacity was determined with the boom horizontal, its weakest position. With the boom and mast held upright against each other, the derrick would be able to handle the twenty-seven-ton pyramid of steel. At least that's what their calculations indicated.

The men were ready though. Fall lines from the guy derrick were lowered and attached to a connection on the vertex at its center of gravity to prevent the spire from tilting as it was being raised. With the derrick's boom set, the signal was given to the derrickman. The street car vendors, secretaries, and business executives had no idea of the danger that lurked above them. The papers hadn't been alerted. Only the construction photographers, Peyser & Patzig, who documented the building's progress every few weeks, had been informed to have their cameras loaded with film this day.

The vertex rose slowly from the dome, an American flag attached to its tip. Regardless of his faith in the design calculations or the confidence of the workers whose job it was to lift the vertex, Van Alen, "watching it from Fifth Avenue and Forty-second Street, had four sinking spells, continuous vertigo, and three attacks of mal-de-mer." The lines secured to the platform from the top of the derrick held. The hoisting connection to the vertex was centered and didn't slip. The derrick gangs and ironworkers shouted instructions to one another as the cables fed through the derrick's wheels and the vertex lifted higher and higher—five feet, then ten feet, then twenty, then fifty, then one hundred feet. The final section of the vertex, the first brought up the side of the building and set upon the timbers on the sixty-fifth floor, rose from the confines of the fire tower. At last, the entire length of the spire revealed itself like a "butterfly from its cocoon."

The foreman waved to the derrick crew's signalman, who then rung the bell to stop the lifting. The engineer shut off the power. The steelworkers manhandled the lower portion of the vertex to line up its rivet hole with that of one in the steel frame of the dome's top. The fall lines were dropped one inch, then two, until the holes met. The connectors rushed to place the temporary bolts. The faster they moved, the less chance a stray gale from yesterday's storm would endanger the operation. Once the connectors finished, an experienced plumber-up scaled the highest piece of stationary steel in the world to check that the vertex stood level. The plumb line fell true. Below him, the web of steel would have done little to stop his fall, but his skill and tight grip on the latticed vertex held him secure.

The riveting gang from Post & McCord moved in to finish the job. The rivets in the coke stove glowed a bright orange at eight hundred degrees. One bolt was removed, and a drift pin inserted in its place. With a pair of tongs, the capped end of a rivet was stuck into the hole. The bucker-up positioned his dolly bar against the rivet's mushroom end and then braced himself. The gunman swung the rivet hammer to the other end of the hole, squared his feet, and pulled the trigger. Sparks flew into the empty space below him. The shock of the pneumatic hammer shook his whole body. Twenty seconds later the concussion ended, and others hurried to seal the next connection. Ninety minutes from the first signal, the vertex was up and secured at 1,046 feet over the city.

No feat this spectacular had ever been dared, and the men celebrated—but quietly. Until the Manhattan Company Building crews finished their steel work, no announcements would be made. As Van Alen explained, "We'll lift the thing up and we won't tell 'em anything about it. And when it's up we'll just be higher, that's all." Walter Chrysler's skyscraper was higher than the Manhattan Company Building, and better yet, it was sixty feet taller than the Eiffel Tower, which had been the tallest man-made structure for over forty years. For now, however, Van Alen, Walter Chrysler, and the workers had to enjoy the achievement without recognition. There were no blinding flashes from photographers, no reporters on hand. No grand speeches, not even a press release. They were a team of climbers who could only appreciate the highest peak with those who had ascended with them.

That evening the papers ran photographs of a trolley that jumped its tracks and hurled into a subway excavation on Smith Street in Brooklyn, injuring eight passengers. The only race chronicled was the one run at the Empire City Racetrack where Kildare beat out Turf Writer and Okaybee in a photo finish. In fact, there was no mention in

the New York papers about the raising of the vertex. Perhaps everyone—reporters tracking the skyscraper race, people on the street, and
the 40 Wall Street team—simply mistook the slender spire for an un-
usually tall derrick. From a distance, they had a similar steel-latticed
design. For weeks, the only significant article featuring skyscrapers
was one about how one thousand years ago the Mayans built skyscrapers that rose two hundred feet high among the "cohune palms, giant
mahoganies and cedars of Central America." For a much more interesting story, the *New York World* reporter should have taken a longer
look at his skyline—as should have Severance. It was right there in
plain sight, if one knew what to look for.

When Chrysler wanted attention focused on the Chrysler Building,
he knew how to get it, yet the time was not right. Meanwhile, they
would move ahead with finishing the dome and covering the vertex
with Nirosta steel, giving it the force of an exclamation point.

Nobody knew that the next day the Roaring Twenties would be
ripped apart, nor that the skyscraper race had yet to be won. Tomorrow
would come, but today the Chrysler Building was king.

CHAPTER FIFTEEN

Crash

Prudent investors are now buying stocks in huge quantities and will profit handsomely when this hysteria is over . . . The pendulum has swung too far.

—*John Jakob Raskob*

I can only cry out that I have lost my splendid mirage. Come back, come back, O glittering and white!

—*F. Scott Fitzgerald*

Raskob removed his ticker-tape machine from the closet and placed it on his desk. He glared at the contraption, which was sitting quietly, at the moment, between the two crystal lamps that James Riordan had given to him for his birthday. It was 9:45 A.M., fifteen minutes before the stock exchange would open for trading on Thursday, October 24. Raskob knew the time exactly. Usually he needed to find a clock or ask for the time from a colleague. He hadn't worn a watch in years. This morning, his valet watched him slip one on his wrist and then ask for his chauffer to drive him to his office at 230 Park Avenue. Normally he walked. "I need to know the time—and I haven't the time to walk," he explained.

Due to yesterday's sharp market loss, many investors had suffered long, sleepless nights, worrying about what would surely be another day of heavy trading. In the moments before the opening bell, all of New York was on edge. Financier Michael Levine told his staff, "Nobody goes home until I say so." Pat Bologna, a shoeshine boy with years of wages in the market, said, "People just stood there, stopped talking, and looked toward the Stock Exchange. It was like the silence before the off of a big race."

When the market opened, the ticker-tape machine began to punch out market prices, indicating a surge of buying. The first twenty-five minutes of activity offered hope of a rally, but then a block of General Motors shares sold down. U.S. Steel, Westinghouse, and General Electric dropped as well. Switchboards across the city, and country, passed through the urgent message: "Sell at the market!" Within an hour, Raskob read the tale spilling from his ticker. The market was crashing.

At 11:15, sellers found no buyers for their shares, whatever the price. Fifteen minutes later, dread became fear; fear turned to panic; panic to mayhem. The ticker system failed to keep up with the trading and fed out quotations an hour behind the bids offered on the floor. In that space of time, some share prices fell ten or twenty points—others by that same amount in percentage terms. Crowds rushed down to Wall Street; they had to know what was happening, whether they were cleaned out. Police lined the streets to prevent a rush on the exchange. One investor paced back and forth on the street, shredding a sheet of paper into confetti. Some stared in disbelief. Others laughed at a joke they didn't get. Clerks hurried to manage the orders. Tempers flared at the exchange's selling posts. One broker mumbled unintelligibly and was led away. Another collapsed. Winston Churchill stood in the visitors' gallery above the floor watching the carnage unfold. "There they were, walking to and fro like a slow-motion picture of a disturbed ant heap, offering each other enormous blocks of securities at a third of their old prices and half their present value, and for many minutes together finding no one strong enough to pick up the sure fortunes they were compelled to offer."

Over eleven billion dollars in market value vanished by one o'clock. A collective moan echoed off the canyons of Wall Street. One speculator asked his broker the latest bid for National Casket. A steelworker eating his lunch on a beam hundreds of feet over Wall Street was thought to be a jumper. A producer ran down the aisle of the Shubert Theatre and shouted, "Boys, you can forget about the show. You can forget about everything. The bottom's just dropped out of the market!" In his office Raskob ate lunch alone, not wanting to be far from his ticker or distracted by another's misfortune. A market tailspin jeopardized his financing for the Empire State.

Under the din of construction from the Manhattan Company Building, the financial godfathers of New York gathered at 23 Wall Street, the office of J. P. Morgan and Company. They had come through in the Panic of 1907, and they had to come through now. After the meeting, they told the growing number of investors waiting outside to have faith. The break was "technical" and the market sound. At 1:30, the New York Stock Exchange's vice president, Richard Whitney, strode across the exchange floor to the post trading U.S. Steel. He bid 205 each for a block of ten thousand shares, a ten-point premium over the last bid. The order executed, he moved to the next post and the next. With the bankers' support, the market rallied in the last hours and by closing bell it had recovered eight billion in its lost value. The "minnows," as market player Jesse Livermore called small investors, suffered the brunt of the decline, having rushed to sell or had their margin accounts settled. Raskob placed several calls to those investing in his skyscraper. This kind of cataclysm could derail the smallest of projects, let alone one that cost double that of most other skyscrapers.

After his last phone call, Raskob calmed. At least for now his investors had weathered the worst.

Unfortunately, the worst hadn't yet occurred. The next day, John D. Rockefeller announced that "My son and I have for some days been purchasing sound common stocks." Merrill Lynch suggested that those "with available funds should take advantage of this break to buy good securities." For their efforts, the market rallied that Friday and in a short session on Saturday. But investors then had almost forty-eight hours in which to test their nerves before the market opened again. Should they sell or hold? Should they swoop in and grab some bargains or was this truly the beginning of the end? On Monday, October 28, the market fell again in a day of heavy trading. It was not cataclysmic, but in contrast to the previous Thursday's drop, there was no day-end recovery of prices. That evening many investors—big and small alike—decided they were finished. Many had bought their stocks on margin and needed to cut their losses.

In offices across the city Tuesday morning—Raskob's included—tickers fed out their first quotation: a 45,000 block of Anaconda Copper shares sold at 80, down 16 from the yesterday's closing. In the first half hour, brokers traded 3,259,800 shares, ten times what would normally be traded in that amount of time. Gigantic losses were posted on the board. Margin accounts were liquidated. Police blocked the entrance to the exchange, and hysteria reigned again on Wall Street. By the closing bell, 16,410,030 shares had been traded during the day, and the Dow Jones index was down forty percent from its position eight weeks before. The bubble had burst.

The knives came out to parse the blame. Some attacked Hoover and Mellon. Others harped at Charlie Mitchell for his optimism in the face of several breaks. Senate Republican leader Jim Robinson charged Raskob for encouraging "every one, even people with small means" to speculate. Raskob bit back that these claims were "false, vicious, wholly unwarranted and manifestly political . . . I do not gamble in the stock market." In fact, his biggest gamble was elsewhere.

As Wall Street and Washington slung mud slung back and forth, Raskob worked to keep the Empire State on track. They had yet to secure the major financing, and throughout the city buildings slated for construction were now put on hold or cancelled altogether. Charles Noyes quietly backed down from his one-hundred-fifty-story skyscraper, delaying it for at least eight years. W. B. Foshay, who financed the tallest tower in Minneapolis, filed for bankruptcy on November 2 and the thirty-two-story tower that bore his name was included in the receivership action. Spending $50 million on a speculative office building in this environment risked Raskob's fortune—and the fortunes of those he brought in. And as he would learn a few days later, it was a risk with consequences beyond money lost.

One of his closest friends, James Riordan, had grown despondent since Black Thursday: some said because of the losses so many of his colleagues suffered in the market collapse. Others feared that he may have been driven to desperation because of trouble at County Trust and several bad real-estate investments. On the morning of Friday, November 8, Riordan went missing. The bank's treasurer discovered that the .38-caliber revolver kept by the cashier for protection had been removed from his desk, and the treasurer notified Raskob, Al Smith, and several others, who feared Riordan might take his own life. They called his house on West Twelfth Street, but the maid didn't know where he was. A few hours later Riordan arrived at his home and let himself in without the maid hearing him. He went to his second floor bedroom, took off his coat and vest, sat down in a plush red chair, put the revolver to his right temple, and fired. The maid found him slumped in his chair at 3:50 P.M. and called for a priest. Raskob and Smith drove down to West Twelfth Street to meet the priest there. The Chief Medical Examiner, Dr. Norris, arrived soon after and they convinced him to withhold the news of the suicide for one day to prevent panic at County Trust. The police were not told.

Raskob assumed the bank's chairmanship, and over the weekend, he and several of Riordan's close friends made sure County Trust's finances were in order. They denied reports that $5 million in gold had been deposited into the bank to make it solvent. Eddie Dowling, "one of the inner circle," as he put it, admitted years later what most suspected at the time: "If he'd been discovered on Friday and the news had gotten out, it would have wrecked the bank. Anyway, they covered it all up. This was the power of these men. They got into vaults, they opened banks, they did things that nobody but people with their power could do . . . Nobody lost a cent. The bank was ten times stronger when it opened on Monday morning than it was before this thing happened."

The suicide shook Raskob deeply. He and Riordan had suffered many of the same obstacles and sacrifices on their career paths. Now Riordan, who had been one of the first to know about the Empire State and who was one of the few to understand its significance to Raskob, would never see it tower in the skyline. Much of the same power and influence Raskob wielded in order to prevent a run on County Trust, he used to ensure that the Empire State, and all it represented, wouldn't become another victim of the Wall Street crash.

––––––––

As Raskob and Smith served as pallbearers at James Riordan's funeral on November 12, the steelworkers on the Manhattan Company Building prepared to set the sixty-foot steel cap atop the pyramid crown. Not even the stock market crash stalled the momentum of the skyscraper race now. At 925 feet, New York would have a new winner— at least that was the race's progress as reported in the papers. Severance and Ohrstrom read nothing about the Chrysler Building's secret vertex or its height of 1,046 feet. The only photograph of the topped-out skyscraper ran in the *World's* gravure section above the caption: "The World's Tallest Building Raises the Stars and Stripes to the New York Heavens." But the caption continued that once the Manhattan Company Building completed their steel erection, they would take the height record from the Chrysler's 808-foot-tall tower. The *World* was only off by 238 feet. Other papers hardly mentioned the skyscraper at all. As awful as it was, the market crash helped Chrysler keep journalists focused elsewhere.

So those packed into Wall Street a few minutes before noon thought they were watching the final steel erection for the world's tallest structure. The site always gathered sightseers, who craned their necks to see the workers loop their legs up and around the pipe scaffolding hundreds of feet high to finish the exterior. As they watched a half-ton, ten-foot-wide block of granite ascend the side of the building to the thirty-fifth floor, there came a panicked cry. An engineer shouted to those below to look out. The thousand-pound block hurled downward—a hoist cable had broken. The bricklayers rushed to get out of the way, some diving through windows as the block roared past them. People on the street ran for cover.

The granite fell clear until the ninth-floor setback, where it crashed through several wooden planks (the concrete floors were not yet laid at this level). A thirty-five-year-old steamfitter, James Bellas, tried to scramble away. The block missed him, but it hit the planks at his feet. An upended piece of wood fractured his shoulder, and he was knocked to what was left of the floor. The granite block continued on its path, tearing through six more floors before connecting with a steel beam that split the granite in two. One half plummeted down the inside of the building, hitting other beams and eventually shattering into hundreds of shards on the ground floor. The other half shot out into the street. The stone missed the platform over the sidewalk, sparing the lives of several pedestrians. Instead the granite hit a steel beam in the bed of a truck. The granite crashed with such force that it twisted the beam and hurled it into the street, almost hitting a car driving past. The granite careened off the beam and exploded in the street, sending fragments shooting out like shrapnel. One piece broke through the rear window of a Rolls-Royce idling at 37 Wall Street, hitting Miss Pratt, a young woman waiting in the automobile while her chauffeur ran "the luckiest errand he ever went on in his life." A splinter of granite sliced through the leg of an eighteen-year-old office clerk heading across Wall Street.

As the cloud of dust settled over the site, Captain Edward Quinn and thirty of his policemen hurried to rope off the block as a crowd pressed forward for a look at the macabre scene. Dr. Salken, a physician for Starrett Brothers, ran to help the injured. Miss Pratt refused his aid and was driven away from the scene. An ambulance took Bellas and the young clerk to the hospital. One patrolman said, "it was miraculous that no others were injured." A chunk of granite the size of a soccer ball missed one woman by inches. A fragment landed near an evangelist praying on his knees in front of the old Subtreasury Building. Another tore off the brim of a man's hat on the sidewalk. The foreman ordered the street cleared and ordered his men on the seventieth floor to return to the day's task: finishing the steelwork.

One hour later, the sixty-foot steel cap was lifted into place above the pyramid crown and secured nine hundred feet above the sidewalk. Workers embraced one another on the seventieth floor. Photographers clicked pictures of the steelworkers waving from their perch. A flag was attached to the topmost steel, replacing the roof-tree in the ritual used for centuries to top out a building. Ohrstrom sent his congratulations, remarking on the unparalleled speed with which the tower had been erected. Reporters from the *Herald Tribune, World, New York Times*, and the *Sun* left the scene to file their copy about the half-ton block of granite crashing into the street, but also to herald the completion of the steelwork on the "tallest structure in the city" and the "world's tallest tower." The newspapers proclaimed it a great day for the city. Praise was showered upon the architects and builders.

Four days later the truth was revealed, from the most unlikely of sources: the Dow Service's *Daily Building Report*. The trade report usually devoted its pages to such titillation as the price differentials for a ton of cast-iron soil pipe between suppliers in Newark, New Jersey, and White Plains, New York. On November 16, Allen Beals surprised his readers and the world when he wrote:

> This is the story of how two architects, formerly partners, vied with each other to erect two of the world's tallest man-made habitable structures, and how one of them, by an ingenious engineering device, finally succeeded in passing the hitherto thousand-foot pinnacle of the Eiffel Tower in Paris . . . While the structural steel men were fabricating in the shops the final-framework for the lantern story on the Bank of Manhattan Building . . . there was being secretly fabricated 845 feet above 42nd Street at Lexington Avenue a spindle-like lattice ornament that only a few knew what it was to be used for . . .
>
> It grew in size two, three, four, until finally it reached a dozen stories tall before it dawned upon the workmen on the job that it was some kind of a pinnacle, but how was it going to be set, on so narrow and so precarious a footing as the structural steel beams and columns and girders more than 845 feet above the street, until the day came when a huge American flag, attached to its point, floated out 100 feet beyond the derrick boom that raised it, and the 185 foot vertex was fitted into place as the Stars and Stripes straighten out at the highest level the Flag ever flew from a fixed point in New York City—the top of the world's highest man-made structure.

Over the next week, newspapers splashed the story onto their front pages. Van Alen's defeat of Severance made great copy, even though this defeat had really played itself out weeks ago. Chrysler had fooled the same journalists who now headlined: "Architects' Race Jostles the Moon" and "Chrysler Tower Wins Sky Race: Architect, Spurred by Rival's Bank of Manhattan, Tops It and Eiffel, Too." The story prompted magazine articles and was the target of editorials, one reading "America is vindicated, and our national passion for the biggest, the tallest, the most stupendous, may gratify itself in the thought that at last we are supreme." Photographs of the late October emergence of the vertex finally found their way into editors' hands. Even cartoonists took a turn at the extraordinary set of events, one depicting the Chrysler Building as so tall that its elevators serviced such floors as Venus, Mars, Saturn, and Heaven—in that order.

The surprise finish between the architects captured the popular imagination. It was a welcome return of the decade's spirit of extravagance in a time when there wasn't much to be excited about, except the billions of dollars lost on Wall Street every week. In the American tradition of making nouns into verbs, "skyscraping" was introduced "to indicate what is undoubtedly the big major sport of our architects, engineers and their backers of today. It is, in many respects like a game of poker. The chips in this game cost about a million apiece which makes a certain amount of bluffing possible."

Severance had laid down his cards only to find Van Alen with an ace up his sleeve. Van Alen had outplayed him, and everyone knew it. Severance suffered the publicity in silence, not granting any interviews. However, he was not idle, nor did he sit for the widely accepted idea that he had lost out to the architect-artist. Now that the steelwork on the Manhattan Company Building was finished, height alterations would be more difficult and expensive, and more obviously an act of pride rather than good business. Yet even with the steel cap riveted into place, complicating matters greatly, Severance and the builders investigated ways to carry the skyscraper higher.

They now had two choices to pursue in the race: devise some structural addition of their own or spin their skyscraper as the tallest because it claimed "the tallest usable floor," as Severance, the architect-businessman, argued in private. They pursued both.

———

One afternoon, while journalists at newspapers and magazines across the country churned out ever more copy about the skyscraper race, earning the Chrysler Building a bonanza of free publicity, Van Alen and Chrysler entered a mine-cage elevator at the construction site. The gate shut, a bell rang, and the elevator lifted upwards with a jolt. The journey up was like an old wooden roller coaster—the ride was not for the faint of heart. As the elevator climbed upwards, the floor beneath their feet shook and they had to hold the sides tightly so as not be thrown against each other. They rattled past workmen finishing floors and installing electric wires. As the elevator gathered momentum, wind whistled through the floorboards and each floor became nothing more than a blur. When they reached the top floors, the ride slowed and was bookended with another jolt. They stepped out of the elevator into a different world than the one they had left behind.

A spiderweb of tubular scaffolding covered the arched dome and vertex. Workmen in overalls and caps moved about, no doubt stealing a glance at the visiting suits before continuing with the pinging and banging of Nirosta steel sheets. The noise they made sounded as if they were pounding together aluminum trashcan lids. Only the sharp rat-tat-tat of the pneumatic hammer could be heard above their ruckus. Chrysler and Van Alen climbed upwards through the aerie construction site, careful with each step. At the seventy-fourth floor, they reached the vertex's base. It was surrounded by a tangle of steel; the dome rose four more levels around the vertex until approximately 950 feet above the street, where the finial leapt clear. Chrysler and Van Alen climbed a set of ladders to the seventy-seventh floor. The wind howled through the three open triangular windows on each side of the dome. At this height above sea level, the temperature down on Forty-second Street was meaningless. Up here, workers weathered temperatures that dipped as low as ten to twenty degrees below zero. The constant wind drowned out the men's voices and numbed their hands.

According to the papers, the Chrysler Building ended at the seventy-seventh floor, but in the middle of this "last" floor another ladder led to the seventy-eighth floor, 906 feet above the street. This shrunken space wouldn't be available for rent, nor would the seven floors above it—each smaller than the one before. By the eighty-fourth and final floor, two men could barely stand together at one time. Above this, one could ascend a series of increasingly more narrow ladders through several trapdoors inside the vertex until it tapered to its point. There the darkness was complete.

The other way to get to the long, slender pyramid spire was to climb the scaffolding on the outside of the building. Chrysler and Van Alen took this route, one less claustrophobic but a lot scarier. They scaled the slim series of ladders and platforms, the wind blowing against them and even rocking the building slightly. Glancing down would reveal a thousand feet of empty space.

Several minutes later, they reached the top platform, a few planks of wood surrounding the vertex in a square. It wouldn't take much to pitch headlong over the side; to stand up straight was an act of valor, simple foolishness, or both. Van Alen and Chrysler stood up straight, placed their hands on the vertex—the tallest point man had raised above the Earth—and posed for the camera. (A photographer had clambered after them to record this moment.) The steel, which weighed as much as twenty thousand automobiles, rocked slightly underneath their feet. All they could hear was the muffled hum from the streets far below and the faint creaking of the building.

Few characterized better the feeling of reaching this height on the Chrysler Building than writer David Michaelis. "Deep-sea divers in deep-sea depth are said to experience something called the rapture of the deep. A diver's euphoria proves so overwhelming that he fails to return to the surface even when his air runs outs. From the 84th floor of the Chrysler Building, the city below appears as dreamy, distant, and unnecessary as the mercury-colored surface of the sea must look to an enraptured diver."

Van Alen must have experienced a well of emotion standing atop his skyscraper, especially after such a long struggle to see it built. The vertex had outstretched the Eiffel Tower and beat Severance, but in his heart he cared more for its purpose as a "natural and logical development of the tower," than its role in the height competition. As he instructed, the workers below him were fastening the forty-eight tons of Nirosta steel—shaped in a metalworking shop on the sixty-seventh floor—to the dome and vertex frame using screws, bolts, rivets, and nails made of the same alloy. The silver luster dominated the building's crown from the sixty-first floor to the vertex tip. "With all the surfaces of this spire turned toward the sky, it will reflect nothing but the sky, and because it will have no outline—all being in perfect reflection—it is expected to be almost invisible. Thus the tower will appear to join the sky and melt into any cloud that floats by." This "artistic effect," Van Alen knew, provided the perfect terminating point for the Chrysler Building. The eight eagles' heads for the sixty-first floor—now being shaped in the same metal as the vertex—spoke further to the truth he sought in designing for the modern world. No more "rusticated stone work, belt courses and heavy stone cornices," he said. The gargoyles that would stare out at the city were "very bold in outline, form and scale, and of proportions suitable for their great altitude."

Hand pressed to the pinnacle of his skyscraper, Van Alen had set aside convention in favor of eagle gargoyles and steel pyramid spires. Some called his designs capricious, the result of too much emotion and too few spare economic lines, yet in his own fearless way, Van Alen had answered the question posed years ago by Louis Sullivan, the first genius of modern skyscrapers: "How shall we proclaim from the dizzy height of this strange, weird, modern housetop the peaceful evangel of sentiment, of beauty, the cult of a higher life?" There was still much to do—design the vaulted ceiling of the observation floor, the passageways to the subway, the revolving doors, recessed lighting, shop fronts—each detail, even down to the pattern brickwork on the sidewalk, refined his answer: an architect should proclaim nothing less than the spirit of the age in which he lived.

Standing next to Van Alen, Chrysler shared the same view of the city stretching below them, but one colored by his own thoughts. The long lines of flat brownstone roofs of a nineteenth-century Manhattan had lost out to the towers of office, hotel, and apartment buildings, his now the tallest of them all. Cars, many of them built by his company, passed on the streets instead of horse-drawn wagons. Bridges (and unseen tunnels) conquered the Hudson and East Rivers that once were crossed only by ferries. Somewhere an airplane tracked through the sky, its passengers the rare few who could see, from an even higher altitude, the green spread of Central Park, the proud stance of the Statue of Liberty in the harbor, and the slope of the Palisades. Those who came to his building after its completion would pay a meager fifty cents to enjoy this same majestic sight, or at least the one from the seventy-first story. It was on this observation floor that Chrysler decided to display the tools he had fashioned at seventeen in the same wooden box he had carried around the railroad yards, evidence of what man could achieve with the strength of his own two hands. The mural planned for the Y-shaped lobby ceiling—the largest painting in the world, per his instructions—would first impress this on visitors, showing among its other images the "single figure, the naked torso of a man," which symbolized the individual's ability to harness the elements in the mechanical age.

For Chrysler, his skyscraper best represented this ability. He celebrated the building's engineering triumphs: the self-leveling, high-speed elevators; the latest fire protection; an underfloor electrical system; moveable steel office partitions; pressurized steam connections; a centralized vacuum system; mechanical lungs that breathed fresh air to every floor; and individual thermostats for each office. The skyscraper would be a self-enclosed city for over fifteen thousand people—stores, barbershop, hospital, gymnasium, restaurant, and transportation included. He planned to have an apartment and office in its penthouse floors as well as a three-story "Cloud Club" where the city's powerful could congregate in one of the private dining rooms or at the oyster bar. It would also serve as the world's highest speakeasy.

Few could understand the glory he experienced in standing atop this monument to his life, but the brochure published for the skyscraper offered a hint:

Heavenward spring the spires of man's aspiration. Through the ages, from the eternal pyramids brooding over Egypt's timeless sands, the soul has sought expression in a restless, ceaseless striving to reach the heights . . . And now, one more bold has attained a new eminence . . . into the glorious sky of eternal blue and billowy cloud springs the shining finial, fashioned of gleaming metal and flaunting its triumph like the upraised lance of a knight of old.

The photographer finished the shot, and Chrysler and Van Alen began the climb back down to the street. Chrysler and Van Alen didn't know it, but they would only have a few months to enjoy being the world's tallest. The men behind the Empire State were putting together plans to put up a lance of their own.

CHAPTER SIXTEEN

Pharaoh Against Pharaoh

If the race itself is a competition in advertising,
so . . . have been all the competitions in tall buildings from the time when Pharaoh vied with
Pharaoh, matching tomb against tomb, to the pious
rivalry of the cathedral builders, each seeking to
raise a pointed arch or spire nearer to god.

—*H. I. Brock*

[After hearing of another record-breaking sky-
scraper], the redoubtable Shreve, the gentle Lamb,
and the retired Harmon, met in their own private
office and swore to a suicide pact. They fished out
the old office revolver . . . and started to draw lots
for the first shot.

—*The Architect, 1929*

Van Alen and Severance had maneuvered and countermaneuvered
for nearly a year now, and although Severance still had some fight left
in him, the spotlight had turned to a much more spectacular battle. It
was now John Raskob pitched against not only Walter Chrysler, but also
a world fast disintegrating upon itself with the stock market's collapse.

On Monday, November 18, two days after the story broke about the Chrysler Building surpassing the Eiffel Tower, the Empire State, Inc., announced the purchase of the land adjacent to the Waldorf-Astoria Hotel, adding seven thousand five hundred square feet to the sky-scraper's site. Reporters wanted to know why they needed the additional land, suspecting the larger site anticipated a taller tower. No definitive height had been announced yet; a skyscraper of eighty stories and "at least 1,000 feet" were the firmest figures mentioned.

"We bought that property simply because we thought that it was cheap," Al Smith explained to reporters eager for the race to go on. They tracked down Shreve as well, who added: "The determination of the height of the building will be based on the sound development of useable space. As we proceed with the plans the owners will be in a better position to determine what the height of the building is to be. Any announcements as to dimensions and set-up must come from Governor Smith."

This announcement had to wait a day. The politician in Smith knew how to play the press for the greatest effect. The furor over the Chrysler Building's secret vertex had drawn attention away from the Empire State. The two skyscrapers were rivals, not only in vertical feet but also in their attraction to tenants. Millions had read about the race between the Chrysler and Manhattan Company towers, and Raskob meant to steal the story back—the decision as much economic as an act of pride.

Demanding that the Empire State stretch higher, Raskob wanted to add several stories to the tower, whether more elevator banks were needed or not. Utility cones be damned. The architects had told him those renting these offices, if tenants could be found, would have to switch cars to reach their offices. The board fielded these concerns in the days after learning of Chrysler's vertex. No doubt Raskob insisted that the significance of this monument far outweighed the architec-tural complications or cost of going higher. While Shreve specified what these complications and costs were, Lamb may have sketched out some design ideas on a scrap of paper, crumpling it before Raskob made him stick a needle or some other structure atop the Empire State. Du Pont and Kaufman likely thought about how their investment had made a great deal more sense when the economy was not in ruins. As for the Starrett brothers, they had already been beaten once in the height race and the addition of several stories would only affect their schedules by a week. Smith had much experience in mediation and must have brought his persuasive powers to bear, but ultimately it was a decision for Raskob to make. Despite the additional cost and unsuitability of these floors for commercial office space, he led the board to increase the Empire State's height to eighty-five stories. For as much as they heralded the skyscraper as the finest of collaborations among owner, architect, builder, real-estate agent, and engineer, when push came to shove, Raskob had the money, and the money talked.

On November 19, Smith sat at the head table for a luncheon of the Fifth Avenue Association. Members and journalists crowded the Hotel McAlpin to listen to his speech, which was also being broadcast by radio station WEAF. Few luncheons hosted by Lewis Flaunlacher, the association's chairman, warranted this kind of attention. He introduced Smith, saying he welcomed the Governor's switch "from the brown derby of Oliver Street and the gray fedora of the West Side to the silk hat of Fifth Avenue."

Smith began with his opinions on such topics as whether New Jersey should obtain a railroad price differential over other sections covered by the Port of New York (no) and if Fifty-ninth Street should serve as the northern limit for general business and office developments (yes). This was fine and well, but most wanted to hear what he had in mind for the Empire State. Smith didn't disappoint. "This building will be a monument to the dignity, power, growth and wealth of the imperial city of the Empire State," he predicted. As if unaware his comment would lead tomorrow's headlines, he casually mentioned that they now planned for the skyscraper to rise eighty-five stories, five more than originally announced. At first, he didn't even detail the height. He let the audience draw the conclusion that this would bring his skyscraper higher than any other in the city. Only later did he offer the specific figure—1,100 feet—though final plans had yet to be completed by the architects.

Several hours later, Richmond Shreve spoke at the Building Managers and Owners Association dinner at the Hotel Commodore, just across the street from the Chrysler Building. Entitled "The Economic Design of the Modern Office Building," his talk covered the factors that went into planning a skyscraper of the Empire State's proportions: "Since the building must pay, the designer must do his best to make this possible . . . After all the elements to make up the cost of the skyscraper are gathered together, we must locate the point at which the balance begins to swing back, where the additional floor space becomes too expensive and the rate of return on capital investment begins to diminish as the building goes higher. We must then set up a financial analysis, because it is the final test, of our capital investment, our financing, our income, and our fixed charges and our operating cost, which will finally determine if the building we have designed is to be built." He excluded from the speech anything about how the advertising value of greater height affected the equation, though it was a factor he later admitted.

The tandem speeches by Smith and Shreve shaped the message that the five stories added to the Empire State met the demands of maximizing profits. They argued it was an indisputable calculation of economic height, a decision as sound as the bedrock underneath their skyscraper. Beating out the Chrysler Building had nothing to do with it. Frank Rogers, who listened to Shreve's speech and knew the architect well, probably had a different read on the day. The timing of the change was too conspicuous to overlook. The title of the world's tallest remained in play.

The next day, people read only of the Empire State in their morning newspapers. "Smith to Break Height Record in 1,100-foot Tower" ran one headline. The eighty-five-story tower "settled, at least for the present, all question of height supremacy," said the *Evening Post*. All the newspapers mentioned that once built, the Empire State would out-top every skyscraper in the city.

"Make believe that you are 8 feet up and relax, take it easy," the steelworkers instructed photographer Margaret Bourke-White. "The problems are exactly the same." Seventy-one stories high in the Chrysler Building, she leaned over the elevator shaft's edge to take a picture. The workers, responsible for making sure she didn't hurt herself while on the site, wanted to lash a rope around her waist. She refused. She had to be free to compose her shots, so they held her waist and legs. Laying on her stomach, she had the better half of her upper body over the edge. Still she didn't quite get the right shot. She told the workers to release her. They feared this young woman with the thin face and short bob of black hair had a lesson in gravity awaiting her. It looked like the camera weighed more than she did. Finally they let her alone. There was no denying the demands of her photography. As for the danger, she always felt safe with her 5 ×7 Corona View camera in hand. She got the shot.

In the second week of December 1929, she came "to steeple jack for Mr. Chrysler," as she wrote her editor Parker Lloyd Smith at the new magazine *Fortune*. Only twenty-three years old, she had already made headlines with her photographs. She once braved the steel mills of Cleveland, nearly drowning in a pile of iron dust, to practice her craft. Months before the skyscraper race began in earnest, she met Chrysler on a job to photograph his mile-long automobile plant in

Detroit. The two shared an appreciation of the mechanical age. "Industry is huge and vital," she once wrote. "It is important because it is close to the heart of the people. Art must be sincere and active to have value. Art that springs from industry should have real flesh and blood, because industry itself is the vital force of this great age." The words might have come from Chrysler himself.

He commissioned Bourke-White to dramatize his skyscraper in photographs for newspapers and magazines. Some in New York questioned the vertex as a stunt and unworthy of the height crown. "In this battle of the skyscrapers . . . I was brought in as a sort of war correspondent on the Chrysler side," she wrote. "The scene of battle was that relatively narrow band of atmosphere ranging from 800 to 1,200 feet above the sidewalks of New York. . . . The principal target was prestige. A skyscraper was a tall and strong feather in the cap of that ultra-rare individual who could afford to build one. . . . Chrysler was aware of the stupendous advertising value generated when the world's highest building bears the name of your product. And this was where I came in."

It was bad enough for Chrysler that people questioned whether his skyscraper deserved the title of tallest (on account of the vertex offering no rentable space). Now the "Napoleon," John Raskob, looked like he was moving ahead with the Empire State despite the Wall Street crash. An incredible, but not altogether surprising show of resilience on his part. Given the uncertainty in the business community, rentals could prove difficult to find, particularly if tenants would rather wait to sign leases with Raskob's world's-tallest skyscraper. Chrysler couldn't support an empty skyscraper forever. Going on the offensive, he hired Bourke-White and the renowned publicity flak Ivy Lee to promote his building.

Ivy Lee had cut his teeth in political campaigns, and now represented the Rockefellers, Bethlehem Steel, and the Pennsylvania

Railroad. He was one of the first public relations spinmasters and had recently helped Chrysler shape his message for investors after a decline in his company's stock.

In early December, Chrysler began the campaign. First he announced that his renting agents had signed the Texas Company to lease seventeen floors. Furthermore, to handle the leasing of the nine hundred thousand square feet of office space, the agents had hired a "special staff of brokers, canvassers, layout men, stenographers and resident agents, equivalent in number to a full-fledged real-estate office." They had spread across the city in an orchestrated assault. Each time they leased a block of space, Lee would dash off an additional release to build the impression of success on success.

While Lee fed journalists copy and intensified the height war on the public front, Bourke-White scaled stairs and ladders into the tower dome, hauling her camera and wooden tripod with her. At a thousand feet above the sidewalk, amidst gales of wind and temperatures reaching subzero, she followed her orders to show the vertex as integral to Van Alen's overall design. One day the wind buffeted with such force that the tower seemed to sway eight feet. "With three men holding the tripod so the camera wouldn't fly into the street and endanger pedestrians . . . my camera cloth whipping and stinging my eyes as I focused . . . I tried to get the feel of the tower's sway in my body so I could make exposures during that fleeting instant when the tower was at the quietest part of its sway."

The vertex scraped the sky as Van Alen had planned, and Bourke-White photographed it for all the world to see.

───────

Raskob had been quick to add five stories to the Empire State, but the architects told him these floors put the skyscraper at 1,050 feet, not the

1,100 feet that Smith announced to the press. This provided a slim
margin over the Chrysler Building; too slim. Chrysler had shown himself willing to take extraordinary measures to win the height race.
Raskob knew of his drive to win, had witnessed it first hand in the years
they spent together at General Motors. His architect, Van Alen, was obviously full of clever ideas. He might have another secret plan to breach
the four-foot difference between the two skyscrapers. Hamilton Weber
said that his boss "was worried that Walter Chrysler would pull a trick,
like hiding a rod in the spire and then sticking it up at the last minute."
A cartoon published that year poked fun at this possibility, showing a
lank architect (not unlike Van Alen) explaining to his client with a
drawing (not unlike the Chrysler Building) that "You see, this spike
runs down the entire length of the building and if anyone builds a taller
building we can jack up the spike and still be tallest."

Raskob wanted to prevent this joke from becoming a reality. His
architects could add even more floors to the tower, but this plan lacked
boldness and begged the question: how many were enough? Shreve,
Lamb, & Harmon had made clear their prejudice against a hundred-
story building. The five floors above the eightieth story already presented a challenge to rent. Raskob didn't require another lecture in
service utility cones and the valuable space that elevator banks took
from rentable areas. If he wanted the building to be taller, it had to
generate that much more money.

While studying the latest plaster model made for him by the architects, Raskob hit upon the solution: "What this building needs is a
hat!" What in fact he had in mind was a mooring mast for airships.
Passengers could embark and disembark from zeppelins anchored to
this mast affixed to the Empire State's crown. Unlike Chrysler's vertex,
the "hat" would have a practical use. It would rise two hundred feet
over the eighty-fifth floor, put to rest any chance of Van Alen outma-
neuvering them again, and capitalize on the country's aviation obses-

sion. He would bring to life the future that Moses King had predicted thirty years before in *Views of New York*: airships launching from tall buildings and threading their way through the city's canyons.

If there was one thing that challenged the public's interest in skyscrapers and Wall Street, it was the romance with flight—or "airmindedness." Lindbergh's transatlantic flight to Paris made him a hero worthy of ticker-tape parades and keys to cities. Americans spoke of aviation as a "winged gospel" and those who mastered these flying machines as "apostles" and "prophets." Hollywood produced numerous films featuring daredevils and fighter pilots braving the skies. Henry Ford came out with a single-seat flying flivver, the supposed Model T of airplanes, causing one writer to script: "I dreamed I was an angel . . . And with the angels soared . . . But I was simply touring . . . The heavens in a Ford." Young boys and girls pestered their parents to help them build model airplanes. And zeppelins, traveling at seventy-five miles per hour, promised a bright future of available transportation for the masses. In Akron, Ohio, the Goodyear Zeppelin Company was building a 785-foot dirigible, the largest in the world, to be ready by August 1931. The Empire State could serve as its New York terminal.

As a way to win the skyscraper race and cause a publicity stir, the plan had legs. Finding a workable design, absorbing the seven hundred fifty thousand dollars of additional costs to build the mast, and radically changing the skyscraper's flat-topped crown, was an altogether different story. Raskob ordered his reluctant architects to make it happen. The board approved the proposal, authorizing sixty thousand dollars in alterations to the structural steel specifications to carry the mast. The effect of cost considerations on profitability was not calculated. The architects had little say on whether the plan made sense or not, despite the fact that Lamb didn't typically suffer the demands of clients, regardless how trivial. When designing the Reynolds Tobacco Building, he refused to smoke Camels instead of his usual Lucky Strikes, even after the company's executives complained to Shreve. He considered Van Alen's vertex worthy of "the Little Nemo school of architecture." Now Raskob asked him to perform a stunt design for the top of what was his most important commission. Shreve kept his disdain to himself, but his staff of draftsmen conveyed the firm's sentiment in an illustration drawn for him that showed a gargoyle sitting atop a column, hands covering its eyes, with the bubble quote: "Hear No Dirigible—See No Dirigible—Who Said Anything About a Dirigible!" Reservations aside, they had a job to do. The plan made sense to Raskob, so they began their sketches.

Two days after Chrysler's boast of "supremacy," Raskob had Smith announce the broad strokes of the plan in New York:

> The directors of Empire State, Inc., have come to the conclusion that in a comparatively short time Zeppelin airships will establish trans-Atlantic, trans-Pacific, transcontinental and, possibly, South American routes from New York. One of the chief problems is mooring facilities and landing spaces. At present our own Zeppelins and those of foreign countries that visit the Port of New York on a friendly trip are compelled to anchor at Lakehurst, New Jersey, about seventy-five miles from the center of the city.
>
> Building with an eye to the future, we have determined to build a mooring tower 200 feet high on top of the new Empire State Building. The roof of the building itself will be 1,100 feet from the sidewalk. That will mean that the Zeppelin would be anchored more than 1,300 feet in the air, with elevator facilities through the tower to land passengers downstairs seven minutes after the ship is anchored.

The next day Smith traveled to Washington, D.C., to meet with the Secretary of the Navy to discuss the plans. The day appeared more like a victory tour: an entourage of guards, cheering crowds, and a phalanx of reporters. "Hello, Al!" His fans yelled, pushing forward to shake his hand. He was scheduled to return to New York late that evening, but many wanted him to stay, urging him to rejoin the fight in the political arena.

"I am interested in constructing buildings and landing airships now and not politics," he said before meeting with the Secretary and a pair of admirals. They promised to provide any technical assistance Smith needed in designing the mooring mast, ignoring the fact that the Empire State's architects and engineers had already discussed their plans in secret with the Navy experts and had even sketched them out. Smith's trip served its main purpose: capturing headlines. It gave him the opportunity to declare to reporters that the mooring mast, though an expensive addition to the skyscraper's costs, would be "of inestimable advantage in national defense and as a means of developing commercial use of lighter-than-air craft."

The idea was so fantastic that "if it was bein' put up by just a regular politician and not Al Smith," noted a comic, "wouldn't any of us believe it. We would demand a recount." Given the swirling winds over New York, experts questioned the feasibility of mooring a zeppelin at this height. They also wondered what was to happen when the airship needed to stay at even keel and jettisoned several hundred gallons of water ballast down onto the streets. But Raskob had a height crown to claim. Whether the experts found a way to make the mooring mast work or not, its steel would top the Empire State over two hundred feet higher than Chrysler's vertex. Now they just had to build it.

Lest anyone forget the Chrysler Building after the long weekend and incredulous discussion of mooring masts and dirigibles, Lee sent a press release to newspapers Monday morning, recounting for editors that Chrysler's tower ranked "definitely as the tallest which has ever been erected," and that "the Eiffel Tower must bow before this latest addition to the skyline of New York." Furthermore, "If the building were located in Delaware, Florida, Louisiana, Mississippi or Rhode

Island, it would be theoretically possible to extend the lines of vision from the top of the Chrysler Building to all parts of the state without interruption." Unfortunately, his words were only a whisper in the hurricane roar of attention now swirling around the Empire State.

There was scarce word from those behind the Manhattan Company Building. Severance was spending many hours with his first grandchild, awed that "she's the most beautiful girl in the world—she's even got fingernails." He was also busy shoring up his business in the wake of the market collapse. Ohrstrom needed to travel to England to reassure several of his major investors and inform them as to how he intended to recover their losses. And the Starretts had the Empire State's construction to focus on. For them, as their partner Andrew Eken later said, "the battle for the possession of the world's highest structure goes on apace . . . Billions of dollars have been spent, millions of tons of steel and stone have been reared from Manhattan's rocky base in the struggle to come nearest to a literal interpretation of 'skyscraper.' "

However, the 40 Wall Street team's absence from the headlines didn't signal their surrender. The flagpole, scheduled to have been riveted into place a week after securing the pyramid cap, had missed its deadline and remained unraised. The builders promised it would be set before May; that was all they said. In secret they continued to discuss plans to go higher. They claimed the "mysterious scaffolding" was simply left above the pyramid to finish the lead and copper roof. It was foolish to ask any of them what they thought of the Chrysler Building beating their tower in the height race: blueprints were retrieved and laid out for the misinformed to discover the truth.

"Chrysler's only sixty-eight stories," explained one of Starretts' men after being confronted with the suggestion. "We're seventy. They put that flagpole, or whatever they call it, on the top, and it goes up higher, but you can't put offices in a flagpole, can you? We've got more construction. Clear up to the top penthouse, right under the pole, we've got space for things you have to put in a building like this." Then they invariably spoke of the speed of construction: the demolition crews razed the old building and cleared the site in three weeks—setting one record; the foundations were set into place during this work— an unheard of achievement; and, in a mere ninety-three days, the steelworkers erected the seventy stories of steel—the greatest record of them all. Speed measured as important as design or height. "This sky-scraper was built in less than a quarter of the usual schedule," said Matsui. Some confronted with this argument might have remembered that the Singer Building people had talked about speed as well, ex-plaining how the Cologne Cathedral required 641 years to build and "the great pyramid of Cheops, on which 100,000 men were employed for 30 years, which would be equivalent to 3,000,000 men working every day for one year—as against 1,200 men employed for one year and eight months on the Singer Building." Of course, the Metropolitan Life Tower stole the Singer's short-lived height record, speed or not. After that, the Singer Building's architect, Ernest Flagg, proposed a thousand-foot-tall skyscraper. Even he wasn't convinced that "fastest" was as important as "tallest."

CHAPTER SEVENTEEN

Aladdin's Genii and Paper Fights

Ah, but a man's reach should exceed his grasp.
Or what's a heaven for?

—Robert Browning

"I feel like my own boss up here," a steelworker told Margaret Bourke-White. "Nobody can reach me to give me orders." Throughout the winter months, she snapped photographs of the Chrysler Building, sometimes shimmying out onto an eagle's head, nothing but empty space far below her feet. She told her parents that the heights didn't bother her and that she understood the freedom the steelworkers enjoyed. Although she admitted that one evening, after a day on an open scaffold braving subzero temperatures and fierce winds, "I descended fifty steps of unfinished stairway under my own footpower. After summoning a cab, I found I couldn't make the step from the curb into the taxi. I fell and cut my shins." Her explanation? "It took more out of me than I was aware."

Perhaps that insignificant episode was a sign, or a warning unheeded, of what was to come in the days ahead for a city that had ascended great heights, but was worn out from the effort. The wild times, the late nights and early mornings, the music, the sex, the dance, the booze—every binge eventually ends with an empty bottle and the drift into an uneasy sleep. *Variety*'s column "Box Scores of the Havoc" described how Broadway, "famed for its mirth and jollity, became the locale of misery." Broadway producers stared dejected at the vacant seats their actors faced. Clubs closed. At the Hotel Pennsylvania, singer George Olsen looked out at the evening's crowd, passed out the music for "Happy Days Are Here Again" to his band, and said, "Sing it for the corpses." At the end of 1929—in just one of many such sad stories— Henry Grew Crosby, a thirty-two-year-old Boston blueblood, and Mrs. Josephine Roth Bigelow, a twenty-two-year-old married to a Harvard student, were found at the Hotel des Artistes, each with a gunshot wound to their head. In *Exile's Return*, Malcolm Cowley tried to get at what drove the two to their suicide pact, and in the attempt, evoked the country's mood: "Everywhere was the atmosphere of a long debauch that had to end; the orchestra played too fast, the stakes were too high at gambling tables, the players were so empty, so tired, secretly hoping to vanish together into sleep and . . . maybe wake on a very distant morning and hear nothing whatsoever, no shouting or crooning, [to] find all things changed."

Attendance spiked at the long-shunned Trinity Church. The Wall Street traders and lawyers who crowded the pews often found themselves singing the verses from "Lead, Kindly Light." On New Year's Eve, the 369th Infantry Band played on the exchange floor, but there was no good news to celebrate. Neglecting calls from Hoover and his cabinet that the worst was over, companies laid off thousands of workers and general despair began to settle over the economy. Their tax cut and loosening of credit showed how helpless they had become. Confidence in the American financial system had eroded to the point of nonexistence, causing several bank and industrial mergers to fall through. Automobile manufacturers, like Walter Chrysler, continued to speak of prosperous days ahead, but it was wishful thinking. Eventually they would have to cut production and close plants.

In this environment, only so much building and hundreds of thousands of square feet of new space could flood the market before, as one editorial noted, "the newest New York became a sixty-story city unoccupied above the twentieth floor." Plans for super-skyscrapers fell by the wayside as the economic slump deepened. John Larkin, who had first spurred imaginations with his one-hundred-ten-story tower in 1926, sold the land on Forty-second Street where the skyscraper was supposed to rise, saying "we were about five years ahead of time so far as the neighborhood was concerned and we couldn't afford to wait any longer." The directors of the Metropolitan Life Insurance Company went ahead with their hundred-story tower, erecting the base for this monster skyscraper, but eventually ended it there. The City Bank Farmers Trust Building, which was slated in October 1929 to be seventy-five stories, was trimmed back to sixty-five stories, then fifty-four stories.

Amidst these deflated ambitions, Raskob went ahead with his plans for the Empire State. He intended to see his skyscraper erected, even though each drop in the Dow Industrial index increased the risk of financial disaster. Putting three million square feet of office space into an already oversupplied rental market was not the kind of move that had won him acclaim as "Wall Street's greatest mind." Even after several friends sat him down to tell him that it would be perfectly understandable if he backed out of the project, Raskob told them that he meant to keep his promise of building the world's tallest skyscraper. It was about beating Chrysler, because Raskob didn't like the idea of another man out-topping his vision, but more importantly, the former stenographer wanted the world to see that all was not lost. With the Empire State Building, America would always have a symbol that represented the ability of any man, no matter his background, to achieve great things.

As for Bourke-White, her steeplejacking on the Chrysler Building ended just as the Empire State started, leading her to question whether her photographs would make a difference in a race whose late entrant appeared bent on winning. "I don't know whether the photographs proved anything," she said, "except that a photographer has to work in all kinds of weather."

———

Those who spoke of the Empire State—from Raskob, to Smith, to the architects and builders, to the men hired in its construction—spoke with a messianic tone. Each had a job to do to see this "vaulting ambition" stand in the skyline, and they intended to see it through until the end.

Raskob secured the money, a task made difficult by the market devastation, yet proving how much faith people had in him, not to mention his ability to twist a few arms when needed. It was one of the most remarkable, yet largely unrecognized, achievements in the building's rise. The syndicate originally put together to buy the land from Floyd Brown provided $10 million in initial funds: Raskob and Pierre du Pont contributed the first half ($2.5 million each) and the other members, namely Louis Kaufman, the other half. In December 1929 the Metropolitan Life Insurance Company granted Empire State, Inc., a loan for $27.5 million. They immediately paid $8 million into the building corporation, and subsequent installments were scheduled at certain stages in the construction. The remaining $13.5 million in capital came from the sale of bonds. Raskob and du Pont each purchased one quarter of these bonds and Chatham-Phenix the other half. Except for an additional $1 million in bonds, the financing arrangement matched to the dollar the amounts Raskob outlined to Kaufman several months before.

The Starretts harnessed their every skill in its construction, taking what they learned from the Manhattan Company Building and applying even more advanced methods. They were no less enthusiastic than Raskob about completing what Paul described as his career's climactic project. "I was to build the world's tallest—not only the tallest one but one which expresses most completely and honestly the skyscraper idea, whose beginnings I had seen fifty years earlier . . . The Empire State Building is truly an epitome of all that has preceded . . . all the spirit, the imaginative and technical daring, and even some of the frenzy, that animated the decade of which it was the culmination." By February 3, 1930, they completed the wrecking of the Waldorf-Astoria Hotel down to the sidewalk. They honored sentimental requests for souvenirs: the Iowan who wanted a piece of the Fifth Avenue iron railing; the couple who asked to have the key for the room they enjoyed on their honeymoon; and the calls for stained glass windows, flagpoles, and brass lighting fixtures. The sentiment ended there.

With seventeen oxyacetylene torches and five derricks, the workers brought down the 12,097 tons of structural steel of the hotel and Astor Court buildings. The demolition crew chipped away at the sidewalls and floors with Ingersoll-Rand pneumatic rotary jackhammers and concrete breakers. Five-ton Mack trucks were driven within the buildings and carried away 16,508 loads of debris. One story was demolished at a time and markers (like a circle of sticks placed on the floor or some trim nailed to a door) alerted workers where they risked having the ceiling crash onto them. Water was sprayed throughout the site to keep dust clouds from overwhelming neighboring tenants and pedestrians. At the peak of demolition, 719 men worked on the site. Two shifts working six days a week for fifty days completed the operation of drilling, blasting, and carting away the roots of a New York landmark reduced to figures in a "load of material" column: 6,246 loads of debris, 56 loads of firewood, and 298 loads of structural steel and miscellaneous scrap iron.

Simultaneous with this activity, the Starretts began the pier holes excavation and the pouring of concrete to support the steel columns. Over twenty-six thousand cubic yards of earth and stone were scooped out from the site for the basement floors. The City Inspector tested the depth to where the pier holes hit and surpassed hard rock—roughly thirty to forty feet below the sub-basement floor. Six weeks later, on March 29, 1930, the 210 piers had been excavated and concrete poured into their holes. On April 1, the first grillages were placed on top of these piers; on April 7, a crane lifted the first steel column. Post & McCord were going to outdo their Manhattan Company Building speed record. In total, the Empire State required 57,480 tons of structural steel, as compared with 17,000 tons for the Manhattan Company Building and 21,000 tons for the Chrysler Building. In relative scale, the Starretts were erecting two Manhattan Company Buildings and one Chrysler Building in the span of six months on a site 197 feet long and 425 feet wide. It was an awesome task.

Shreve, Lamb & Harmon planned out the entire skyscraper before the first story was raised. They knew the number of beams and columns, their lengths, and the amount of bolts and rivets needed to put them together. Usually the firm invested little emotion in its architectural commissions, big or small. Once charged with designing the mausoleum for Adolph Ochs of the *New York Times*, the unfinished drawing on a draftsman's board was labeled "In this Box Lies Adolph Ochs." They got the job, they finished the job, they were paid for the job, and they moved to the next one. But the Empire State was no ordinary assignment; this time, the firm was swept up in the mission. Shreve, Lamb, and Harmon knew the skyscraper would be their most amazing achievement, and Shreve wrote of harnessing "the powers of Aladdin's genii" to manage this "miracle of a modern skyscraper."

In reality, Shreve worked with more mundane tools. He developed what he called his "bug diagrams," a graphical system of events that needed to occur simultaneously (like a truck driver arriving at the docks to carry the steel brought by a ferry crossing the Hudson River, while the engineer on the site had the structural plans in hand and the derrick crew in the right position once the trucks returned) in order to avoid losing one hour, let alone one day, from the schedule. The system predated by decades "critical path" techniques that now require more technology than penciled drawings on a large board—but Shreve's method was no less efficient. Andrew Eken said of the firm's superhuman focus on the Empire State, "They knew when we would need the electrical layout or the plumbing blueprints, for example, and we didn't even have to ask. We'd just send a messenger to their office, and the right number of the right prints would be packed and ready for us."

A month before the steel work began, the *New York Sun* reported on the plans filed for the Empire State at the Manhattan Bureau of Buildings. There was nothing secret about their delivery, nor any reason for there to be. Although the plans listed the skyscraper's height at 1,044 feet (and 11½ inches), Lamb explained to reporters that the mooring mast would bring the skyscraper to its full height of 1,250 feet. The mast was both feasible from an engineering standpoint, he said, and more important, it was decided upon by the board. The architect reserved most of his comments for the skyscraper's design. He spoke of its clean, modern lines and the vertical rise of the tower. He described the silver panels running parallel to the windows and how they would reflect brilliantly in the sunlight. He told the press that despite the extra expense, his firm had chosen large slabs of Indiana buff limestone instead of small bricks for the façade. "Stone of this size will be used all the way to the top of the building, in keeping with its massiveness." He had considered every piece of the building, down to the last detail. It was a passion that his partners shared.

For all the grand speeches, plaster models towering beside Al Smith, press interviews, and releases of architectural plans, none did better justice to the enormity of the Empire State and the challenges ahead than the sight of four massive central columns set on their concrete piers. They would soon carry a load of 10 million pounds, requiring the reinforced plates riveted to their sides. Those peering into the site from Fifth Avenue on April 11 witnessed the placing of column #115, which weighed 72,795 pounds. The derrick gang set it next to column #105, the heaviest of the bunch at 102,830 pounds and stretching nearly twenty-seven feet high. The workers in the excavated pit looked like ants in a forest of steel, but with the sum total of their commitment and labor, and that of architects, owners, and builders, they were creating something bigger than themselves, something that the *New York Sun* suggested would "produce a blaze of light in the clouds" higher than any other structure in the skyline.

————

Walter Chrysler made as much noise as he could in the time he held the title of world's tallest skyscraper. Throughout the first half of 1930, in anticipation of the Chrysler Building's opening, he placed ads in scores of newspapers, promoting his skyscraper as the highest structure in the world. It was as if through repetition he hoped to negate the existence of the Empire State. One ad, entitled "On Everyone's Tongue," displayed a photograph of the building over the expression "Tallest in the World" translated into thirteen languages. Another promoted the high tower floors as "so far above the earth as to be literally in the clouds—so near the sky the sun shines there an hour longer every day . . . You will find here the inspiration and isolation of an eagle's nest on a towering crag—an atmosphere of such peace, of such quiet and seclusion that you seem miles removed from the bustling city below."

His press flak Ivy Lee released a drawing of the Chrysler tower next to distortedly scaled-down images of the Eiffel Tower, Manhattan Company Building, and Woolworth Building (again the Empire State was absent). Time and again Chrysler laced his speeches with references to the height crown. At a simple craftsmanship award ceremony, he found several ways to reaffirm his victory, saying "It is the first time that any structure in the world has reached such a height" and "You men are responsible for this building. You built it as a monument to yourselves and to me—the highest structure of its kind in the whole world." He also mentioned that "erecting the tallest building in the world" won out as the most thrilling event in his life. In press statements, the skyscraper's 1,046 feet took center stage. It reached higher than the natural elevation of five states. It caused the Eiffel Tower to supplicate in its presence. It provided the longest vertical run for its elevators in the world.

Despite the Empire State's imminent rise, the 40 Wall Street team couldn't help but strike back. They insisted the Manhattan Company Building was taller; the automobile giant was simply misguided. In March 1930, Yasuo Matsui published a long article reprinted in several newspapers that offered an explanation (graphical depictions and scorn included) about why this was so:

Generally speaking, one thinks of Cleopatra's Needle as an obelisk in Central Park, but William Van Alen's skyline project is truly a sharp steel needle. We have been told that this has been done by a patented method and secret plan . . . The legitimate height of skyscrapers should be considered of the building only, in accordance with the Building Code, and shouldn't include the flagpole or the radio needle, so the Eiffel Tower still holds the crown for the highest structure, its observatory being 905 feet, 11 inches above grade.

The Bank of The Manhattan Company's tower on Wall Street ranks second, its observatory being 836 feet, 5 inches above the Wall Street grade. A good third is the Chrysler Building, its observatory being 783 feet, 1½ inches above Lexington avenue grade, or 53 feet below that of the Bank of the Manhattan Building . . . the growth of skyscrapers is only by public demand and economic necessity. Therefore purely ornamental towers, such as the Metropolitan and the Woolworth of today, have no particular significance from a commercial standpoint.

Unfortunately for Severance and the owners of the Manhattan Company Building, they were part of a small minority who saw it this way. For most, tallest was tallest. Having made this argument, however, they boxed themselves out of raising a spire of their own. It was sense-less to go higher when they were already highest. On March 12, they ended speculation that they planned to out-top the Chrysler Building. "No, the rumor is baseless," said Andrew Eken's secretary to an *Evening Post* reporter. "True, we did discuss putting up an additional spire to top the Chrysler Building, but that's all off. The original plans still hold. She's as high as she'll go." The scaffolding over the pyramid crown didn't hide a flagpole; it was there to place the silver ball atop the skyscraper, as earlier planned. In advertisements, they were forced to claim their skyscraper "as the tallest, with one exception."

Severance continued to shun the press or any attention whatso-ever, now ranking his fondness for the Manhattan Company Building somewhere below that of his Pekinese. He refused to participate in an American architectural exhibit of skyscrapers held in Sweden and Budapest that year. Van Alen participated, of course, sending a large plaster model of his design labeled "Tallest Building in the World—Exceeding 1,000 feet in height and having 78 stories." There was no room in the spotlight for second place.

In late May, the Chrysler Building and the Manhattan Company Building officially opened. Their openings—only a day apart from each other—gave the press and public another chance to focus on the height controversy. The Manhattan Company Building managed to woo Mayor Jimmy Walker to speak at its opening. The Mayor was sched-uled to attend the Chrysler ceremony the next day, but neglected to show. Perhaps this was a final jab that Ohrstrom or Severance—or one of the Starrett brothers—had arranged. Regardless, neither event made much of a splash. The spotlight on these two buildings had grown dimmer each day as the steel rose on Thirty-fourth Street and Fifth Avenue. Guests down at 40 Wall Street enjoyed some tedious speeches about the history of the bank, the event feeling more like an annual board meeting than a celebration. One bank executive commented that "there wasn't going to be any celebration; we're all going to work like hell to pay for all this."

Indeed, they spared no expense on their new quarters. Over the Wall Street entrance was a ten-foot-long bronze statue of Oceanus, the Greek god of the waters, by the noted sculptor Elie Nadelman. Through the sliding bronze doors was a space as luxurious as a French palace. Ornamental bronze fixtures hung from the ceiling. A wide marble staircase with balustrades of black and gold led into the two-story main banking room whose floor and tall columns were also of rich marble. Along the walls Ezra Winter had painted six murals, each depicting a historical Wall Street scene. The executive offices had marble-framed doorways, wood-paneled rooms, and working fireplaces. On the fourth floor, the bank's boardroom was a reproduction—down to the furniture, carpets, and mantelpieces—of the Signers' Room in Philadelphia's Independence Hall. The private executive luncheon clubs on the upper floors, including the one on the fifty-fourth floor that was used for the opening ceremony, were designed in early Colonial Farmhouse style, fitted with wood beam ceilings and French wallpaper. If the interiors were not enough to impress, guests could climb a wrought-iron staircase from the sixty-ninth floor to the small glass-enclosed, tubular chamber on the seventieth floor, the city's highest observation point at 836 feet, fifty-three feet higher than Chrysler's. But as one reporter noted, other than a worker who had penciled the message, "What hath Starrett Brothers wrought!" on the windowsill, most seemed indifferent to the tower's height achievement or the building's lavish quarters.

Chrysler tried to make his opening more newsworthy, gathering five hundred guests into the building's fan-shaped lobby, a master-piece of Art Deco design in its own right. A silver line in the Siena travertine floor led people from its entrance to the elevators. Nickel chrome steel in geometric shapes decorated storefront grills and stair-case railings. Neon tubes surrounded by stainless steel reflectors pro-vided the lobby a soft amber glow that seemed to emanate from the Rouge Flamme marble walls. Bringing everything together was the Edward Trumbull mural overhead, an awe-inspiring set of images: a Herculean figure mastering the elements; fifty construction workers laboring at their tasks; symbols of fire, water, and lightning giving way to electricity, heat, steam; ocean liners, trains, airplanes, and dirigi-bles defeating "time and space by energy"; and through the center of it all a portrait of the Chrysler Building rising into a blue sky.

Dressed in a checkered business suit and colorful necktie, Chrysler posed for photographers, officially accepted the mural from Trumbull (making sure to mention it was the largest one in the world), and received a bronze tablet from the 42nd Street Association in honor of his civic contribution to the skyline. He then ushered his guests into the elevators for a tour of his skyscraper. Each elevator cab was unique, including each set of doors. The steel was overlaid with a veneer of rare woods—Japanese ash, oriental walnut, satinwood, American walnut, maple, Cuban plum-pudding wood, and English gray harewood—and handcrafted into various designs. The elevator cabs were only outdone by the observation floor, a chamber with a vaulted ceiling of deep blue, painted with stars, the moon, and other celestial motifs. Light streamed through the triangular windows and the fixtures overhead looked altogether like glass Saturns.

In contrast to the wholesale reproductions of past architectural styles executed by Severance for the Manhattan Company Building, Van Alen offered designs in the lobby and throughout the skyscraper that were unlike anything the guests had ever seen, yet few reports of the event mentioned the building's architectural details. Nor did journalists recount to any great degree what Chrysler spoke about at the luncheon afterward. Al Smith unexpectedly stopped by during the meal and offered some impromptu remarks about how he recalled the days when this land was famous for its bleating goats, and if "Mr. Chrysler and I could get together and form a little corporation, we could own the whole city." As always, he attracted a great deal of attention and a good bit of the newspaper-column space devoted to the ceremony. For the opening of the tallest building in the world, one surpassing the Woolworth Building and the Eiffel Tower after so many years and featuring some of the most original design work seen in the city, it was a decidedly uneventful event. "The king for a day," as the *New York World* called the Chrysler Building, was soon to be topped, and that was all that mattered.

As for Smith, his appearance was likely as much of a coincidence as the first release of Empire State ads at the time when tenants began moving into Chrysler's tower. The footsteps of the approaching giant were deafening.

CHAPTER EIGHTEEN

The Chase into the Sky

Never before in the history of building had there been, and probably never again will there be an architectural design so magnificently adapted to speed in construction.

—*Paul Starrett*

The Chrysler and Manhattan Company buildings had pushed as high as they would go. The construction gangs had packed their equipment and left. Suits now crowded the hallways and elevators. Instead of bells and whistles, phones rang. Instead of talk about steel deliveries and hoisting machines, people spoke of sales projections and client meetings. The race was over for Chrysler and Ohrstrom, Van Alen and Severance. The remaining question was whether or not the Empire State would complete its rise. As the months unfolded, as the media campaign staged by Raskob and Smith was only outdone by the roar of construction and impending celebration for the Empire State's opening, the answer became all too clear.

From the skyscraper's first announcement, Raskob and Smith launched a media blitz that left every other skyscraper in the city fighting for attention. The two men followed dictates from the political arena: always stay on message and in the public eye. With Smith, the press guaranteed the latter, and their message was simple: the Empire State was the largest and tallest skyscraper in the world. There was no comparison. On April 29, 1930, they started the advertising campaign, buying space for ads re-creating the 1799 listing posted by John Thompson for the sale of twenty acres "situated in the heart of New York Island." The next day, a rendering of the Empire State rising over the Waldorf-Astoria and Thompson's farm appeared in place of the 1799 listing. The ad was their opening salvo, invoking the epic proportions of the skyscraper and its place in the city's history.

To compete with Margaret Bourke-White's dramatic shots of the Chrysler Building, Raskob and the board commissioned the famed photographer Lewis Hine to record the feats of the "poet builders" and "sky boys" constructing the Empire State. The portraits were remarkable for their aerie backdrops, but more so for capturing the ease with which the steelworkers scaled cables, rode the derrick ball, and sprinted across beams. By mid-construction, Hine's photographs must have seemed ubiquitous to Chrysler, showing up in hundreds of newspapers and magazines and even in Manhattan store display windows. Making it more difficult for Chrysler to escape the assault, Josef Israels II, the Empire State's publicist, had manufacturers involved in the building's construction—Corbin Locks, Otis Elevators, and Campbell Metal Windows—pay for promotional pamphlets and full-page advertisements boasting of their role in this "magnificent Colossus in the making."

Not yet satisfied, the major players involved in the Empire State's construction also wrote articles heralding the skyscraper's enormity and what went into creating it, many of which were syndicated nationwide in 1930. Even the mechanical engineer and renting agent had the opportunity to expound on their role and the challenges involved in building this tallest of tall skyscrapers. The Happy Warrior led the charge, writing articles of his own about how the Empire State would realign the power center of New York. Raskob had chosen his spokesman well, as newspapers printed nearly every sentence Smith penned, and every word he uttered in public, whether about the building's nickel façade, observation gallery, or the terrace reserved exclusively for women. A photograph of the Governor standing next to a plaster model of the skyscraper was published so many times that it was easier to count the number of newspapers that didn't carry it than did. Most titled the photograph: "Al Smith Shows His Skyscraper—World's Tallest!" When he revealed on July 21 that the new plans filed for the Empire State officially extended its height to 1,248 feet (for the equivalent of one hundred and two stories) and that they had officially adopted plans for landing dirigibles, he captured headlines again: "Tallest Building to Have Tower Quarter Mile Up" and "Rivalry in Skyscrapers Still Advancing in New York." It was a merciless barrage.

Chrysler tried to counter in the only way he could, by sending out a series of statements right after Smith's announcement: on July 24, "The prestige of having the tallest structure in the world has sunk so deeply into the Parisian mind that recent press dispatches from Paris indicate that the French are considering adding sufficient height to the Eiffel Tower to make it surpass the 1,046 feet of the Chrysler Building"; on July 26, "The world's tallest structure which tops Manhattan's skyline with its 1,046 feet . . . is really five buildings one on top of the other"; on July 31, "During the daytime the sun turns the tip of the building into a blazing beacon, and at night it is distinguishable by the reflection of the light from the hundreds of buildings surround it." Smith only had to lead journalists over to the "steel giant" rising on Thirty-fourth Street to show Chrysler that his press releases couldn't outmuscle the efforts of thousands of men backed by fortunes won from his greatest competitor, General Motors. "Temporarily is the tallest in the world" was the description associated now with his skyscraper.

The Empire State rose four and one-half stories a week, a rate without equal in building history, especially given the size of each floor and the amount of steel and stone needed for each. Some related its construction to that of the Tower of Babel, but there was no confusion of tongues on a Starrett Brothers site. They organized the construction around four elements in the schedule (the "pacemakers"): structural steel erection, concrete floor construction, exterior metal trim placement, and limestone setting. They scheduled material deliveries and the direction of the men around these four pacemakers and checked their progress by them. They averaged ten thousand tons of steel erected per month, and by the end of July, eighty percent of the total structural steel to be used was already in place. The workers kept to the schedule of the other three pacemakers as well. Neither the crowds choking on the Fifth Avenue sidewalk, nor the mounted police keeping them at bay, knew of these pacemakers or their precision. Nonetheless, by simply watching this leviathan rise at such a rate, particularly amidst the creep of the Depression, many understood they were witnessing one of man's greatest achievements.

August 14 marked the busiest day in the skyscraper's construction. Starrett Brothers oversaw the labor of 3,439 men on the kind of mild day that workers pray for during the summer months. In the morning the steel arrived at Thirty-third Street. Eighty hours before it was being rolled in a Pittsburgh mill. To reach the site on time, the steel had been rushed by freight train to a New Jersey supply yard, brought across the Hudson, and taken by truck through Manhattan's streets. After the derrickmen lifted the steel from the truck beds to the sixtieth floor, the bolter-ups rode the beams on the last leg of their journey before jockeying them into position. The steel was still warm to the touch. Meanwhile, eighteen riveting gangs climbed about the narrow spans of steel on the fifty-sixth floor, securing beams to their column connections. Rivets flew through the air and plinked against the catcher's can before the pneumatic gun roared. Steelworkers cut half-ton girders with torches, sending sparks cascading down the sides of the building before using these same torches to light their cigarettes. It was a typical day on an atypical job.

On the fifty-fifth floor, mechanics set brackets for the elevators and plumbers laid fire lines. Laborers poured the cinder concrete arches for the fifty-third floor and stripped the wooden forms from the arches that had set. Within calling distance, men from C. E. Halback & Company set the ten-inch wide exterior metal trim on the north side of the building, while the W. H. Jackson Company handled this task on the south side. Men from each of these companies were also placing spandrels between the windows. Stone setters on the thirty-ninth floor set the exterior limestone walls and bricklayers followed to back these up. Half a dozen floors below them, a foreman directed a team of five men as they caulked the space between the stone and steel and the window frames. "Mopping up" gangs moved throughout, removing the dirt and debris to prevent mishaps.

Legions of workers installed the guts and nerves of the building on the lower floors, everything from wiring the elevators, placing the under-floor ducts, and installing radiators. Others raised scaffolding, fireproofed wind braces, repaired concrete buckets, laid out terracotta partitions, repainted the street bridge, answered job telephones on the twentieth, thirtieth, and fortieth floors, and stenciled "E. S." on the windows. It was a scene of constant movement—a great vertical assembly line of floor added upon floor. Civil and mechanical engineers visiting the site—some of whom came from as far as China, Russia, South Africa, New Zealand, and South America—were stunned at how fast and efficiently the building rose.

The weekly payroll for all these construction workers, including those hired by the subcontractors, averaged $250,000. The Starretts eked out every dollar's worth of labor from them by employing 104 men to supervise the construction. Throughout the day they moved in and out of the office shanties above the Fifth Avenue sidewalk bridge to check on the men and ensure the prompt delivery of supplies. To expedite the movement of materials, railway tracks were laid on each floor and flat cars carried tons of brick, terra-cotta, and other material to their needed positions. It was the first time this kind of railway system had ever been used. So the men never had to venture too far from their day's task, the Starretts installed a restaurant on the third floor and spaced lunch stands throughout the building to distribute sandwiches, hot coffee, near beer, and cigarettes. Temporary toilets were constructed every six stories above the twenty-third floor.

When Richmond Shreve was not charting ways to shave off minutes or expenses in his small office, he walked down to Thirty-fourth Street to check on the building's progress. Shreve was a generous man, one who had a standing agreement with Schrafft's restaurant to feed any man who entered bearing his business card, which he often gave out to those asking for money on the street. However, he didn't tolerate idleness or waste in the Empire State's construction. One time, finding a water faucet running, he called the plumber over, ordered him to shut off the faucet, then fired him on the spot. The skyscraper was designed with the same merciless attention to detail. Lamb explained that the "Windows, spandrels, steel mullions and limestone, all fabricated in various parts of the country, were designed so that they could be duplicated in tremendous quantity with almost perfect accuracy and brought to the building and put together almost like an automobile." They limited the size of the limestone placed on the exterior in order that the material hoists operating inside the building could bring the stone to its needed floor. When a marble supplier balked at the schedule the builders required for delivery, the architects chose another type and the Starretts bought an entire German quarry to meet their needs.

The pace on the Empire State rarely slackened. Five hundred trucks a day delivered material to the site. In an eight-hour day, that meant one truck a minute. Journalist C. G. Poore wrote of the extraordinary "chase up into the sky" that he witnessed in midsummer: "Following one of the trucks, an observer finds himself in a forest of concrete covered piers. Here there is an infinity of operations. Truckloads of brick are being unloaded with a roar as the truck chassis tips up and the load goes thundering down through the floor into a basement hopper. Truckloads of tile are unloaded more gingerly, by hand. Sheet-iron, metal parts, bales of wire and coils of cable, sand and cinders and lumber and pipe arrive. Each is unloaded in a special corner of the block-wide floor, presently to go shooting up in elevators to the floor where each is needed."

The Starretts calculated every brick used and yard of wire mesh cut. They had to track costs, but these figures served a higher purpose: grist for statements like "If all the materials which came to the corner of Fifth Avenue and Thirty-fourth Street for the construction of Empire State had come in one shipment, a train fifty-seven miles in length would have been needed. When the locomotive of such a train would have entered New York, the caboose on the rear end would have come to a halt in Bridgeport, Connecticut. Ten million bricks were used in building Empire State. A single workman, had he continued at it every day, would have had to work for 25 years before he could have finished mortaring these bricks." Lengths of wire were expressed in miles; marble by the hundreds of thousands of square feet; and plaster by how far a three-foot-wide sidewalk could be surfaced with the amount of the material used on the Empire State (according to the Starrett brothers, a sidewalk stretching from Manhattan to the Capitol Building in Washington, D.C.). Not only was the skyscraper tall, but it was also gargantuan in proportion, bigger than any other building in New York, and it went up like a rocket ship.

———

By the first week of August 1930, Chrysler and Van Alen had only a short time left to enjoy their victory in the height race. The observation deck opened on August 3 and ticket sales were brisk. The tower stood distinctly in the skyline, its seven-tiered dome reflecting the sun. Of the many elements of the Chrysler Building, the tower was the most revealing element of the collaboration between architect and client. Van Alen had used steel in an original design and shown what was possible outside of classical decorative details. Chrysler had selected the particular type of steel, knowing Nirosta's metallurgical qualities and how, as the *New York Sun* reported, "it will automatically keep glittering, so long as nature provides rain and snow."

But for Van Alen this ideal collaboration—as had happened with Severance six years before—was about to end badly. With the skyscraper complete, Van Alen called on Chrysler to receive the fee he thought he deserved. He wanted to be paid the six percent of the building's $14 million cost that the American Institute of Architects suggested as the standard fee for services. Chrysler balked; he had no intention of paying Van Alen $840,000, particularly since the two had never signed an agreement specifying that amount. In fact they had never signed any agreement, and Chrysler argued that since he had been paying him $8,000 a month on top of the buyout of his $100,000 contract with Reynolds, he owed Van Alen nothing more.

Lawyers entered the fray, and a flurry of meetings and phone conversations ensued, attempting to settle the matter privately. Neither side would give. There is no way to know how much of this bitterness was due to Chrysler's impending loss of the height crown, but there was no doubt he hated being beaten and was unwilling to part with another dollar on an affair that had already cost him many millions.

With negotiations stalled, Van Alen decided to file a mechanic's lien, which meant that he was claiming an interest in the building and property until he was paid the balance due him. Theoretically, if Van Alen won a judgment in court that the lien was valid, he could have the skyscraper put up for auction. Once the lien was filed, the dispute between Chrysler and Van Alen hit the newspapers. Each side made public statements to defend their position in what was becoming an embarrassing affair, particularly for Van Alen, whose case was presented in the *American Architect* as "a lesson to other architects who are inclined to depend on their artistic rather than on their business ability."

The lawsuit promised to be expensive. Depositions would have to be taken, and Chrysler had a team of lawyers who would want evidence of an employment agreement that was never made, not to mention details of every drawing Van Alen completed, who he had presented it to, why it had been created, and when it had been approved. Expert witnesses would have to be called, complaints answered, and calls for dismissal refuted. Throughout, the acrimony between Chrysler and Van Alen was bound to deepen and the bad press widen. Yet Van Alen pursued the suit, as he had no other recourse to be paid adequately.

The project that had once been all about Van Alen seeing his vision of the skyscraper stand above every other was reduced to a battle over money. Neither he nor Chrysler could have expected their relationship to end this way. Then again, the Empire State had changed everything.

CHAPTER NINETEEN

Excelsior

Mightiest peak of New York's mighty skyline, tallest of all tall buildings stands Empire State . . . It stands, a marvel for the sight of men, a challenge to their awe . . . It is done.

—Empire State: A History

On September 9, Al Smith wielded a silver trowel to cement the 4,500-pound cornerstone of the Empire State. As usual, photographers surrounded him, and journalists scribbled down every word he said. It was an underwhelming task given his speech on the history of New York was forty-nine words long: "Eighty years ago, a very short time when one stops to think, this land was part of a farm. More recently it was the site of one of the great hotels of the world; and soon it will be the location of the tallest structure ever built by man."

Half the crowd of five thousand that Smith addressed was workers. He told them that a copper box had been placed inside the granite cornerstone to commemorate the day's importance and to inform future generations about the skyscraper and the decade in which it was built. Contained within the box were coins and bills in every denomination from one hundred dollars down to one cent; a history of the Empire State, Inc.; photographs of the architects, builders, and officers of the company; and an edition of the *New York Times*. During Smith's speech, the workers goodheartedly jeered him for the way he held the trowel. One asked if the Eighteenth Amendment was included in the copper box.

Smith assured him, "So that there will be no mistake or misunderstanding about it, I declare, and firmly, that I have a right to use this trowel as a member of the union. My dues are all paid and I have my card in my office at 200 Madison Avenue."

Throughout the ceremony Raskob stood next to Smith. Above him the steelwork was a few days away from being secured at the height where his office would be located. Perhaps Raskob said something, but if so, the press didn't think it was worth reporting. What the press did find interesting, and had earlier reported, was that within "the black skeleton of a new mammoth of stone and steel, one-fifth higher than anything ever built . . . the honor of occupying the highest office in the world will fall to Democratic National Chairman John J. Raskob, who is a director of the Empire State, Inc. He has leased the entire eighty-fifth floor of the building, beyond which there will be no rentable office space." Raskob didn't need to court the press or have his name emblazoned on the skyscraper's side to know he was the one responsible for its rise. Having the highest private office in the world, decorated in a rich Georgian style, was apparently reward enough. Looking down on Chrysler's office would be a part of this reward.

Ten days later, the steelworkers set the last steel for the eighty-fifth floor at 1,048 feet in the air, overcoming Chrysler's victory after a short ten months—and by a margin of two feet. The men on the Empire State unfurled the American flag over the tens of thousands of tons of steel. The *New York Times* described it as a "flag of triumph." "You should have heard those workmen cheer," noted another journalist there to see the workers wave their hats at the crowds below. As always, Smith was on hand to mark the occasion, announcing the construction was almost two months ahead of schedule and that the building's grand opening was slated for May 1, 1931.

Photographs of the flag raising and the workers at the building's crown splashed across broadsheets in newspapers from Bayonne, New Jersey, to Huntsville, Alabama, to San Francisco to Honolulu to London and Paris and Johannesburg. The headlines read "A New Monarch" and "New Tower Dwarfs Once Mighty Spires." A comparison of the tallest structures in the world showed the Empire State towering above the Eiffel Tower and diminutive illustrations of the Chrysler, Woolworth, and Metropolitan Tower crowns. Steelworkers like Neil Doherty and Carl Russell were heralded as having "nerves of steel" and many of their photographs were framed with the Chrysler Building in the distance, looking altogether much shorter. The six men who died during the construction—laborers Giuseppi Tedeschi and L. DeDominicki, steelworker Reuben Brown and carpenters Sigus Andreasen, Frank Sullivan, and A. Carlson—were regarded as "unsung heroes of peace," their names recorded by the builders with the same respect as those who fought in the Great War. When the largest dirigible in the world, the *Los Angeles*, flew beside the Empire State in October, papers ran the photograph beside the banner "A King and a Queen Meet." No description of the building was understated.

On November 18, the last beams for the mooring mast arrived at the site. The mast was supposed to have been erected in October, but the structural engineers delayed the schedule. They had to decide what bracing and wind-load resistance was needed for the airship dock and for the gangplank that would transport passengers into the ship, a quarter-mile high. The weather also proved difficult. Some days the wind blew so hard that the men could barely stand, and other days rain and fog reduced visibility to the point that the top of the steel disappeared from sight. Nonetheless, in the fourteen days since they had begun, they had set the forty-seven-foot, four-story base; completed the one-hundred-five-foot, five-story main shaft; and riveted into place all but the last beams of the fifty-three-foot-high, thirty-two-foot-diameter conical top. In total, the mast was built of six hundred tons of steel, enough to resist a one-hundred-thousand-pound horizontal pull.

Through winds and a constant drizzle, the derrick swung the steel toward the bolter-up who straddled a column and used a hoist cable to hold his balance. The engineer pulled his levers to bring the beam into the exact position in the web of steel, and temporary bolts were stuck in to secure the connection. In three days, Smith would arrive for a ceremony, shoot the last rivet (made of gold) on the one-hundred-and-second story, and watch as the men unfurled a flag; but today, without fanfare or recognition, the steelworkers set the tallest steel in the world. The public celebrations were not to be theirs. They went home with their grade pay as reward.

———

Al Smith stood next to his two grandchildren, Mary and Arthur, in front of a red-white-and-blue silk ribbon stretched across the Fifth Avenue entrance of the "House that Al Built," as some called the Empire State. Stone eagles were perched atop the two columns to either side of the thirty-foot-high portal. Ready to get the show moving, the children kicked their feet against the sidewalk, then danced back and forth in front of their grandfather. Fighting for his attention as well was a large crowd who pressed forward, eager to get a smile or simply a glance from the Happy Warrior. Al Smith was dressed for the occasion, wearing a morning coat, bowtie, striped pants, and his ever-present black derby, and flashbulbs popped from the line of photographers around him. Policemen supported by state militia and some private detectives watched over the crowd, ensuring that only the invitees could enter, plus a few journalists.

A ticket to the May 1, 1931, opening of the Empire State was the most difficult invitation to get in town. The event made the openings of the Chrysler Building and Manhattan Company Building look insignificant at best. The board had sent out two hundred engraved invitations. Two days later, everyone had accepted, some of whom pleaded to allow their wives or close friends to attend. This was *the* event in the city. Raskob sent a note to Walter Chrysler, offering a personal tour of the skyscraper, but Chrysler refused the olive branch, not willing to make himself available to reporters' questions about what he thought of the Empire State or its mooring mast. Instead, he sent a diplomatic telegram to Smith that read "My congratulations and best wishes on your achievement and the greatest possible success for the Empire State Building." He reserved further comments, at least publicly, but the defeat must have been debilitating, particularly at the hands of GM's Raskob, who had outfoxed, outspent, and outdistanced him. It would be several years before the two would even attempt to interact with each other. Although the rumors that he removed his handmade tools from the Chrysler Building's observation floor because it was no longer tallest turned out to be false, it was telling that in his autobiography he devoted only two pages to his involvement in the skyscraper. He would relegate one of his most remarkable legacies to little more than a footnote—"It belongs to the kids," he later said. "I haven't got a nickel in it." As for Van Alen, his name didn't even appear in the book. His efforts were anonymously referred to as having been performed by "the architect."

At 11:15 on the cool, slightly overcast Friday morning, Smith leaned down to Arthur and Mary and said, "All right kids, go to it." With scissors awkward in their hands, with thousands bottlenecked in the streets around them, with the city and nation eager to unveil this great monument, his grandchildren had trouble bringing the scissors' edge to ribbon. They slashed but didn't cut it. Smith moved to their side and snapped the ribbon apart with his hands. After the police pushed wide the doors, the two children tiptoed through the entrance. Halfway across the dark corridor, having marshaled courage with every step, they finally rushed forward into the expansive lobby, their eyes wide as half dollars.

In Washington, D.C., the President of the United States, Herbert Hoover, excused himself from a Cabinet meeting, much as Wilson had eighteen years before for the opening of the Woolworth Building. He waited at his desk until the clock struck 11:30 and then pressed a golden telegraph key wired to the Empire State, and the lights brightened throughout the skyscraper. The illumination revealed the large mural opposite the Fifth Avenue entrance. On the dark marble wall the Empire State was outlined in strips of stainless steel set over a map of the northeast United States and bordering Canada. Rays of light shot from the mooring mast, as if it was the sun, and spread across the map. On the ceiling the architects had designed an array of stars and circles with gold and platinum leaf. Compared to the Chrysler Building, the Empire State's lobby was an exercise in restraint, but it was no less powerful to the guests.

"Come on everybody!" Al Smith waved his derby. "Follow me and we'll go around to the elevators that will take us up to the eighty-sixth floor, the observatory deck, and when we get there I'll show you the hills of Westchester, the Narrows, and Newark, anything you like. Come on, let's go!"

On the eighty-sixth story tables and chairs were spread across the observation floor for a celebratory lunch. Only the mooring mast towered above them, its skeleton structure clothed in stainless steel and flanked by narrow wings at its base (in a sense, the modern version of flying buttresses). "I'd like you to remember you are eating higher up in the air than any human being has ever eaten," Smith said, waving a sandwich. "There may have been loftier meals on mountain tops or in airplanes but not in buildings. This is the world's record." The guests admired the vista more than the food. Many had never traveled by airplane and the view inspired awe.

"There's Central Park, no bigger than a football gridiron," said one. Arthur Brisbane, the owner of the first Park Avenue apartment tower commented that from this height his building "looked like a chicken coop." An elderly lady feared the "rarefied air." To the north were the low canyons of the Great White Way and then Central Park, its pathways and stretches of water seen in a way that its designer Frederick Law Olmsted never could have imagined. To the northeast, the Chrysler Building and the other Forty-second Street skyscrapers looked Lilliputian compared to the girth of the Empire State under their feet. Directly east, Brooklyn's shoreline of smokestacks and grain elevators appeared like toy models of industry. To the south, the guests peered down at the Statue of Liberty, the Woolworth Building, and the 40 Wall Street tower. Tugs moved across the bay and around Staten Island, looking no greater than water spiders. To the northwest was the new Hudson River bridge (later named the George Washington Bridge), an engineering marvel in its own right, but from this altitude its steel cables looked no wider than strings.

At noon, with sirens wailing from his motorcade, Franklin Delano Roosevelt, Smith's successor as Governor of New York, arrived by black limousine at the Thirty-fourth Street entrance. He made it in time for the end of lunch and a rendition of "The Star-Spangled Banner" played by a full orchestra. Once the last note struck, Smith stood to read a telegram from Hoover, congratulating him on the completion of the skyscraper and assuring that it would "long remain one of the outstanding glories of a great city."

Absent from the opening was the man who had ensured the Empire State's rise: John Jakob Raskob. Happy to enjoy the pride of his accomplishment in solitude, Raskob was aboard the steamer *Augusta* heading to Italy. Smith briefly mentioned that he had sent a telegram

offering his gratitude to the workmen and all involved in the construction. Smith never said what the telegram's exact words were. Perhaps
Raskob made mention of his son William or their friend James
Riordan, or of what he and Smith could have done if they had won the
1928 election. It must have been too personal to reveal to the guests
and media, so instead Smith launched into a speech about how the
Empire State "stands today as the greatest monument to ingenuity, to
skill, to brain power, to muscle power, the tallest thing in the world
today produced by the hand of man." He thanked the newspapers,
magazines, radio, and moving pictures for helping spread the univer-
sal interest in the skyscraper. He thanked the Starrett brothers and
Andrew Eken. He thanked the architects, sadly informing his guests
that Lamb, too, had set sail for Europe but had also sent a telegram that
read: "One day out and I can still see the building." To avoid the cere-
monial backslapping, Lamb had booked a ticket on the *Ile de France* to
leave that morning. While Smith regaled his guests with the Empire
State's greatness, the architect stood on the ship's deck with his wife
and poured two martinis from a cocktail shaker. Three miles from the
coast and free from the Prohibition laws, they raised their glasses and
Lamb said, "Isn't this marvelous? Here we are and we don't have to go
to the party and listen to all those speeches."

Throughout the afternoon many speeches were made. Smith
stirred his guests with the vision of the Empire State standing in the
skyline for many generations to come. Roosevelt talked of the tremendous service the owners, architects, and builders had rendered and of
losing his "sense of proportion" after seeing New York from such a
vantage point. He concluded by echoing a sentiment that Raskob held:
"This building is needed not only by the city, it is needed by the whole
nation." Mayor Walker joked that Smith had the skyscraper built so
that "there might be a place higher, further removed than any other in
the world, where some public official might like to come and hide."
Once the laughter quieted down, "Jimmy"—as Smith introduced him—

spoke of transcendence and vision and the determination to build such a structure as the Empire State. Shreve followed, giving credit to Lamb for his stunning design and then offering a list of facts and figures about the building. Most notably, he discussed how the skyscraper weighed 600 million pounds, but the pressure on any square inch of the foundation was "as light as that sometimes exerted upon a French heel" on the sidewalk because of the load distribution about the forest of columns. Paul Starrett stood to tell how the Empire State rose over a land once populated with tepees and the cabins of early settlers, of how great progress and great change had brought about this triumph.

Smith concluded the ceremony by sending a return telegram to Hoover "from the highest telegraph station in the world." Later that day, he hosted a "sky party" with comedians, entertainers, and the broadcast of an original score for a march entitled "The Empire State." In the many grand speeches, the mooring mast was not mentioned, likely because attempts to negotiate an airship amidst Manhattan's crosswinds proved too difficult. The mooring mast had made for great news though—Josef Israels commenting that it was his most successful publicity stunt ever—and it provided 200 feet in "World's Tallest" insurance (or 215½ feet if one included the staff on which the wind-recording instruments were placed). Nor did they mention that the building was only twenty-three percent rented, half the number they would have wanted at that point. Raskob had defied the odds by following through to completion on the Empire State, but now he faced a struggle to make his skyscraper pay.

What the Empire State lacked in tenants, it made up for in the number of sightseers who rushed to take the elevators to the eighty-sixth- and one-hundred-and-second-story observation posts. In its first month, the building welcomed eighty-four thousand visitors, who each paid one dollar to stand atop what some considered the eighth wonder of the world. Newspaper editors ran headlines like "Highest Structure in the World Is Opened" and "Empire State Building Tops

Chrysler Building by Over 200 Feet." A newspaper in Bohl, Idaho, asked, "What more can man do?" A writer in Kansas City, Missouri, remarked, "Not the Tower of Babel, the Pyramids of Egypt, or the Leaning Tower of Pisa can compare." Photographs showed the upper reaches of the tower lost in the clouds. Smith informed the press that a chamber at the mooring mast's top could be fitted with 200-ampere lights and parabolic reflectors to create the tallest lighthouse ever erected. "Nowhere in the world," he said, "will there be a mariner's beacon at all comparable to the Empire State Building's far-reaching pencils of gold."

Of all the editorials published after the building's completion, the *Lewistown-Democrat News* of Montana made the most insightful comment of all: "One wonders where the daring of American architecture and engineering will end. This latest realization of what, a few years ago, would have been held as a most fantastic dream, would seem to mark the limit of height; but so it was thought when each of its preceding skyscrapers was finishing." Several days later reports spread that for the 1933 World's Fair in Chicago, a 1,600-foot skyscraper—more than 350 feet taller than Empire State—was being planned.

Spirit—Not Steel and Stone

From the ruins, lonely and inexplicable as the sphinx, rose the Empire State Building and, just as it had been a tradition of mine to climb to the Plaza Roof to take leave of the beautiful city, extending as far as eyes could reach, so now I went to the roof of the last and most magnificent of towers. Then I understood—everything was explained: I had discovered the crowning error of the city, its Pandora's Box. Full of vaunting pride the New Yorker had climbed here and seen with dismay what he had never suspected, that the city was not the endless succession of canyons that he had supposed, but that *it had limits* . . . And with the awful realization that New York was a city after all and not a universe, the whole shining edifice that he had reared in his imagination came crashing to the ground. That was the rash gift of Alfred E. Smith to the citizens of New York.

—*F. Scott Fitzgerald, "My Lost City"*

Three months before the Empire State's opening, the Society of Beaux-Arts Architects threw their annual ball at the Hotel Astor, which Van Alen had worked on nearly three decades before as a draftsman. It was one of the city's great social events, and three thousand guests crowded the ballroom for a "Fête Moderne," the first ball in the event's history not to have a theme from a historical French period. At midnight, trumpets blared, and dancers lined the stage to present "Modernistic Impressions of the Blues." This was followed by costume contests, including one called the "The Skyline of New York." One by one, architects dressed in elaborate representations of their buildings walked onto the stage to the cheers and jeers of the guests: William F. Lamb as the Empire State, Raymond Hood as the Daily News Building, Ely Jacques Kahn as the Squibb Building, Leonard Schultze as the new Waldorf-Astoria Hotel, and William Van Alen as the Chrysler Building. Of the forty-four costumes, Van Alen's impressed the most. It was made of silver cloth, black patent leather and flexible wood. The cape was designed like one of the first floor elevator doors. His shoulders were bedecked with eagle ornaments, and his headpiece was a near exact reproduction of the skyscraper's dome (arches and vertex included). He stood center stage as photographers took his picture among his colleagues.

It was typical of Van Alen to spend so much time on the costume, but the thin set of his smile that evening barely disguised the troubles he faced. The Chrysler Building had been eclipsed by the Empire State. His plan for a twenty-six-story hotel at Fifty-sixth Street and Lexington Avenue was hopeless, due to the economy. His lawsuit against Chrysler continued and looked like it might drag out for months, maybe years. And Van Alen's name was synonymous with how not to conduct business with a client.

On top of all that, his Chrysler building design received one bad review after another. Critics thought the addition of the vertex, which

Van Alen considered a masterstroke, to be architecturally irrelevant, and it cast a pall on their perception of the skyscraper. The *New Yorker* began the attack weeks after the building's opening, saying, "it is distinctly a stunt design, evolved to make the man in the street look up. To our mind, however, it has no significance as serious design; and even if it is merely advertising architecture, we regret that Mr. Van Alen didn't arrange a more subtle and gracious combination for his Pelion-on-Ossa parabolic curves . . . We cannot help feeling, too, that all this exposed sheet metal is a part of temporary construction to be covered up later with masonry." The *Architectural Forum* offered some kinder comments, but largely dismissed the building's more innovative designs as nothing more than advertising for the automobile magnate. In the first of a series of architectural reviews in the *Nation*, the soon-to-be-renowned critic Douglas Haskell accused Van Alen of not living up to his potential with the Chrysler Building, saying, "it embodies no compelling, organic idea." Haskell blamed the lack of solid architectural criticism for Van Alen's failure to build upon his ambitious designs of the Bainbridge Building and Childs Restaurant. Curiously, it was Severance's suit against the *New Yorker* in 1926 that had stunted much of the decade's criticism. Meanwhile, Van Alen's former partner's Manhattan Company Building received the Downtown League's gold medal for design, despite its conservative French Gothic style. At least to his colleagues and the industry, Van Alen had failed to express a new vision in skyscraper design. Like so many others, he headed into the new decade with an uncertain future. The costume balls lost their exuberance, and clients with extravagant dreams were no longer knocking at his door.

————

The gaudy spree of the Roaring Twenties had come to an end, and its finest chronicler, F. Scott Fitzgerald, suffered its consequences with all the rest. His wife, Zelda, was cloistered away in a mental hospital, and the writer drank heavily so as not to face his departed golden youth. The Great Crash of 1929 precipitated the economy's collapse, and by 1931 the economy was dealing with a host of troubles: industrial overexpansion, a dearth of business confidence and consumer demand, a foreign trade imbalance, and neglect in a banking structure that one historian said had "provided everything for their customers but a roulette wheel." A depression held the country in its terrible fist.

Over a million men in New York paced through the streets, wearing the leather off their shoes trying to find work. Where they found it, wages had been slashed. This scene played itself out in cities across the country. Automobile plants ran at one-fifth of capacity, steel plants at one-tenth. Banks closed by the hundreds, then thousands. Corporate earnings stalled. By July 1932, the Dow Jones Industrial Average fell from its September 1929 high of 452 to a lowly 58. Crippled by drought and low crop prices, the American farmer, who hadn't exactly enjoyed the twenties boom, now witnessed his darkest days yet. Breadlines and soup kitchens filled with the middle class. Riots ensued in Newark, New York City, Washington, D.C., Detroit, and Cleveland. Heroes of the previous decade—Jimmy Walker, Charlie Mitchell, Henry Ford, Babe Ruth, Al Capone, and H. L. Mencken—found themselves cast aside. Herbert Hoover, the "Great Engineer," was tarred and feathered in the press for not pulling the country back from disaster's brink. Even technology, once championed far and wide, fell into disrepute; labor-saving machines were replaced by hoes, shovels, and picks. Joseph Stalin rejoiced at capitalism's demise, and membership lists in the Communist Party of America grew longer.

In these tough times, there was no place for a culture of excess. Shoppers cancelled orders for jewels and sable coats, while travelers called off European voyages. Men tried to hawk cars at ten percent of the price they had paid during the market heyday and found no buyers. Only pawnshops hummed with business. Fashion designers lengthened hemlines, seemingly with every drop in the market, and endurance contests, prizefights, and aerial adventures drew little of the fascination they once had. People now had mouths to feed, not their curiosity or overtaxed libido. The grim faces on the street revealed the loss of hope that happier days were around the corner. *Business Week* prophetically remarked: "It is becoming clear that it will take longer than expected for all the king's horses and all the king's men to put Humpty-Dumpty together again."

Not surprisingly, the construction and real-estate market followed suit, despite optimistic statements that the industry wouldn't be stalled. Within a year of the crash, construction fell fifty percent. Builders began searching for projects, mostly government supported, to keep their businesses afloat. Thanks to the millions of square feet of office space added to the market during the boom time, vacancy rates skyrocketed. The Chrysler Building opened in the best shape, having rented space to several large industrial companies before the rental glut. The Manhattan Company Building was hit early and hard, particularly because many of its tenants were securities firms. Several tenants went bankrupt, others reduced the amount of square feet needed, and some demanded cheaper rents. Friends joked to Ohrstrom that he owned his skyscraper "only for one day." Forty Wall Street barely covered its operating costs, let alone the $1 million a year in interest payments on bonds sold to finance what one critic called "a promise, a hope, a gambler's optimism, an opium-eater's dream."

Although the builders of the Empire State managed to reduce its construction cost from an estimated $43 million to an actual $24.7 million due to cheap labor and a ready supply of materials in the downturn, it suffered the weak real-estate market most famously, earning the moniker "Empty State Building." It was nearly three-quarters empty and earning a square foot rate five dollars less than some downtown skyscrapers. While traveling around the world after the building's completion, Richmond Shreve ruefully wrote in his diary, "From the stories [I read], the owners might as well lay the building end-for-end, for all the good that rentable area is doing them." The eighty-sixth and one-hundred-and-second observation floors may have taken away all the visitors from the Woolworth and Chrysler buildings, as Al Smith boasted to du Pont and Raskob, but they had rented no offices from the forty-fifth to the seventy-ninth floors and shut down the elevators servicing them. At night they kept the lights lit on these floors so the mooring mast didn't look like it was supported on air.

In 1932 the *New Republic*'s Elmer Davis wrote a indictment of New York's skyscrapers in an article entitled "Too Stately Mansions," reflecting what many perceived as the wasteful exercise of ego that had driven these buildings so tall: "So there they stand, those magnificent monuments to the faith of the nineteen twenties—a perpetual inspiration to the beholder, provided he never invested any money in them. What is to become of them? The setback skyscrapers of Babylon have crumbled into hills of mud, but steel and concrete do not melt so easily. Of the faith that built the cathedrals of Ile-de-France, enough has survived to keep those buildings in repair; but the faith that built the Empire State and Chrysler buildings may presently be as dead as Bel and Marduk." With couples hosting rent parties to pay the landlord and street corners crowded with men selling apples, these skyscrapers were evidence of what had brought them to such a state of affairs.

Those behind the world's-tallest race never had to push around apple carts, but few passed through the Great Depression unscathed, including the winners. For publicity purposes, Al Smith was forced to escort countless politicians, dignitaries, and the rich and famous to the top of the Empire State, a task that became irksome over the years. His efforts to shore up the building's finances by recruiting tenants and reducing the tax assessments proved inadequate, and the skyscraper slipped further into debt. Meanwhile, thousands of constituents wrote him every year, sometimes addressing the envelopes only "Al, New York," but there was little he could do to help them find a job, let alone turn around the state of the country. That was a job for Franklin Delano Roosevelt, who had first succeeded Smith in the governor's mansion and then won the presidency that Smith had wanted for himself. Worse still, many of the social reforms that Smith first promoted as governor became part of the New Deal, yet he now rejected these policies, thinking that Roosevelt had gone too far with government intervention. Fed up by 1936, Smith jumped parties to support the Republican presidential candidate. He felt powerless and ineffective at his job as the president of the Empire State. Slowly he withdrew from the public eye and died in the fall of 1944, a far cry from the political warrior he once had been.

The Starrett brothers had labored for decades shaping city skylines across the country, and their greatest success was the Empire State, but the pressure and deadlines involved in the construction of two of the world's three tallest skyscrapers, not to mention the management of millions of dollars in other projects, wore them both to exhaustion. At fifty-five years old, William Starrett passed away in 1932, "a victim of overwork and long nervous strain," his brother wrote. Paul Starrett lived to see his company weather the Depression, finding work building large-scale housing projects in several New York boroughs, but his partner Andrew Eken eventually ran the business. Paul admitted: "After forty years of intense activity, the strain of erecting the Empire State Building in eleven months was too much for me, and I suffered a rather severe nervous breakdown." The two brothers had poured every energy into the skyscraper race, and once completed, they had nothing left to give.

The harmonious relationship between Shreve, Lamb & Harmon and Starrett Brothers & Eken continued after 1931, and the architectural firm worked with the builders on housing projects in the

Bronx and Brooklyn. Richmond Shreve considered his work in clearing slums and providing low-cost housing as his finest achievement,
but he knew it was the Empire State for which he and his partners
would be remembered. In 1931 their design won gold medals from the
Architectural League, American Institute of Architects, and the Fifth
Avenue Association—a clean sweep. The *New Yorker* said its design was
endowed "with such clean beauty, such purity of line, such subtle uses
of material, that we believe it will be studied by many generations of
architects." Editorial pages praised the skyscraper as "a union of
beauty and strength" and the *New Republic* called the building "New
York's handsomest skyscraper." Short of some negative remarks about
the mooring mast, Lamb's design was considered genius and won him
a place in *Vanity Fair*'s ten "Poets in Steel," an honor not granted to either Severance or Van Alen. The firm Shreve, Lamb & Harmon expanded in 1943 to include several partners, but the three founders
remained active. Before his death, Richmond Shreve suffered a stroke
that left him partly paralyzed and bound to a wheelchair. His son wrote
that "it was the first time in his life that he had encountered a problem
he couldn't lick. He never stopped trying; he never accepted failure; he
just wore himself out." This description might have applied to his two
partners as well, both who persisted in taking on commissions and involving themselves in architectural associations until their final days.

After the completion of the Empire State, there was nobody more
supportive of Shreve, Lamb & Harmon than John Raskob, who several
times wrote recommendation letters for the architects. It was not the
architects' fault, nor the builders', that his financial commitment to
the skyscraper had only just begun. The economy was in far worse
shape than he could have imagined. Fortunately for him, he had di-
vested a good percentage of his stock market holdings before the crash.
He would need the money. For nearly two decades, the Empire State
operated in the red. It was a struggle to keep the bankers from fore-
closing. Raskob managed to convince Metropolitan Life to reduce the

interest rate on their loans by half, then further still, yet the skyscraper was not earning enough to meet their diminished mortgage payments. Several times Raskob had to pump millions of his own money to keep the building afloat. When the skyscraper finally began turning a profit in 1948, du Pont wrote to congratulate the Empire State's new president, General Hugh Drum, and concluded his note: "John [Raskob] should be set up on a pedestal for his patience in working out this splendid investment against serious odds. The pedestal of his monument is the Empire State Building itself."

By 1950 with tenants "jammed to the rafters," as *Time* magazine described, it was netting close to $5 million a year. Raskob's gamble at Thirty-fourth Street and Fifth Avenue had taken a long time to pay out, but his monument was now one of the world's most profitable buildings. He died in October of that year and donated much of his estate to the Raskob Foundation for Catholic Activities, which promotes through its charitable works the same philosophy that made the Empire State possible in the first place: "Go ahead and do things, the bigger the better, if your fundamentals are sound. Avoid procrastination. Do not quibble for an hour over things which might be decided in minutes. However, if the issue at stake is large, stay as long as the next man, but go ahead and do things." Raskob lived his words to the end.

———

Like him, George Ohrstrom and Walter Chrysler went into the Depression facing a tough road ahead, but both managed to sustain themselves through the desperate times, although one had to give up ownership of his skyscraper.

In the crash, the boy wonder of Wall Street forfeited most of the water companies he had assembled during the market bubble, leaving him in a precarious financial position, but his voyage to Europe in the wake of Black Tuesday was a success, helping him to maintain the support of his investors. Once again he began acquiring small industrial businesses within a larger holding company. The market implosion taught him not to leverage his companies against one another. They had to stand on their own, or he was not interested in a relationship. Slowly he began putting together another fortune. Fortunately he had more success in these dealings than he did racing horses or financing skyscrapers. By 1939, there was no saving his investment in the Manhattan Company Building, given the lack of tenants, and though he maintained offices on its top floors for many years, he and the Starretts lost the building. The mortgage bonds sold for eleven cents on the dollar and the sale offer was "less than we paid for the 43 high-speed elevators," Ohrstrom said. The young banker, however, was on his way to amassing another empire of companies. At his death in 1955, he was one of the richest men in America and the tower at 40 Wall Street was only one of his many achievements—not bad for a kid whose mother had to take in sewing to help pay his way through school.

Chrysler maintained control of his skyscraper, but the last decade of his life was not without challenges, particularly since the automobile industry was so hard hit by the Depression. The market value of his company stock was decimated and for six quarters straight he operated at a loss of $1 million per month. To his credit, Chrysler didn't retreat from his plans to battle Ford and General Motors. Instead of cutting back on research and development, he pumped more money into both, introducing a new Plymouth model at the end of 1932. Despite the economic downturn, he managed to boost his car sales significantly. In the following years, he came out with one new design after another, branched out into businesses like marine engines and air-conditioning (from research done for the Chrysler Building), and built several new plants across the country. While others retrenched, he used the hard times to surge ahead, leading the company from his office on the fifty-sixth floor of his skyscraper. At street level, a two-story showcase of his cars lured pedestrians to stop at the windows and gaze at his newest models. It was a far cry from the days when he had to negotiate for a spot to display his first Chrysler car at the Hotel Commodore during an automobile show.

In 1935 he resigned as president of the Chrysler Corporation and passed away five years later at his Long Island mansion, ostensibly of a stroke, but more from heartbreak over his wife's death. More than fifteen hundred people attended his funeral in New York, and newspapers and magazines throughout the world praised his great works. Many published editorials about the significance of his death, the best from a small trade report called *Automobile Topics*: "He truly left the world a better place than he found it."

———

Neither of these two owners could have known what they started in hiring former partners Craig Severance and William Van Alen to design their "world's tallest" skyscrapers. Even after the race, the two architects didn't speak, and Severance argued to the last that the Manhattan Company Building was taller than his rival's because of its higher rentable offices.

Like Shreve, Lamb & Harmon, Severance designed a few projects for the Starrett Brothers after the crash and won commissions from the government, including a series of dirigible hangars and administration buildings for the U.S. Naval Air Station in Lakehurst, New Jersey—but the days of big commissions were over. Fortunately, the house he owned outright in Point Pleasant, New Jersey, was a large one, as his brothers, sisters, and daughter's young family all moved in with him there. He supported them through the Depression, frequently making trips down to Washington, D.C., to pitch for more work. Then in August 1941, he grew suddenly ill. His daughter, Faith, remembered him coming down from his bedroom for the last time, putting his hat on in front of the small mirror in the hallway and then heading outside to his car. He told her that "this is only hard on you, dear" and drove off to check himself into the hospital. Three days later he was dead. A condolence letter from a former suitor of hers captured what his death meant to those closest to him: "Dear Faith, [your father] stood somehow for the grand manner of life, for that way of things that the crash of 1929 knocked into a cocked hat and that Hitler finished off ten years later. So it is much more than the passing of an individual; it is an end of an epic."

William Van Alen didn't send a letter to Severance's family after his death. Simply too much had passed between them. Of the many people involved in the skyscraper race, nobody suffered more after its end than Van Alen. According to Chesley Bonestell, once a close friend, the architect died "unloved and unmourned." He ended up settling his lawsuit against Chrysler in April 1931, winning most of the fees he had demanded after Cass Gilbert testified that six percent was indeed the industry standard. Nonetheless, he had to bear the distinction of a widely publicized lawsuit, worsened by the rumor that Van Alen had taken kickbacks from several subcontractors. The accusations were never proven, nor even raised in any of the lawsuit's depositions, but as with most such rumors, the mention of them was enough to ruin his reputation. The rumors, coupled with an industry-wide lack of commissions and a spate of bad reviews, ended his career. Nobody hired him again for a major building, and a great talent was never given another chance to shine.

In the mid-1930s, he attempted to advance a new type of prefabricated house: constructed of steel panels, the small home cost a mere four thousand dollars and could be erected by six men in two days. His design didn't find any takers and only a couple exhibition displays were ever built. Desperate for someone to accept his work, he offered to design homes for relatives or friends. In the end, he taught sculpture at the Beaux-Arts Institute of Design and spent more and more time handling his real-estate investments.

It would be many decades before his design found favor in the architectural establishment, and this acknowledgment was likely pushed by popular sentiment. One could hear the critics saying to themselves: how could so many people love this meritless skyscraper? At the time the skyscraper race ended, there was a new trend in design quickly gaining force in the United States, a trend that originated in Europe with the likes of Le Corbusier, Walter Gropius, and Mies van der Rohe. They celebrated function over form and were devoted to designing a "machine for living." Ornamentation and extravagance had no place in the clean, precise world they imagined. The lean Depression years helped foster this "International Style," and for many, the Chrysler Building was a lightning rod for what had gone wrong in American architecture. Lewis Mumford wrote in a 1931 article entitled "Notes on Modern Architecture": "The ornamental treatment of the [Chrysler Building] facade is a series of restless mistakes [which] could easily have been corrected by a plain, factual statement of the materials . . . Such buildings show one the real dangers of a plutocracy; it gives the masters of our civilization an unusual opportunity to exhibit their barbarous egos, with no sense of restraint or shame. Among the many blessings of depression, one must count the diminution of such opportunities."

Sadly for Van Alen, this kind of thinking guaranteed that he would be held in little regard throughout his remaining years. He died in 1954, leaving half of his estate to the Beaux-Arts Institute of Design, which later took his name and continues to educate the architects of tomorrow.

———

Since their openings, the three skyscrapers that competed in the race have endured many worse crimes than a critic's sharp pen. On May 20, 1946, an army transport plane flying through a thick fog crashed into the fifty-eighth floor of the Manhattan Company Building, killing five people and tearing a 20-by-10-foot hole in the masonry. The building fell into disrepair, was foreclosed on twice, bought by the husband-and-wife dictators Ferdinand and Imelda Marcos, and eventually taken over by a developer whose renovations included a great deal of burnished bronze and marble surfaces and who emblazoned the letters "T-R-U-M-P" across the front of the building.

Decades after the raising of the Chrysler Building's vertex, a renovation crew inspected the vertex and discovered a considerable number of perforations in the nickel sheath; lightning had punctured the vertex's skin dozens of times. By the 1950s, the Chrysler family lost management control, and as writer David Michaelis chronicled, "a procession of Murdstones, grim as a cortege, marched in and took control. The building suffered flogging after flogging, for each stepfather was more selfish and cruel and pitiless than the last, and each turned a cold shoulder as the building slid further and further into tatters, misery, wrack and ruin." The tower leaked. Holes were drilled into the lobby ceiling for lighting, and wheelbarrows of junk were pushed into the spire. At its most depressed in the early 1970s, the building's occupancy rate was a mere seventeen percent, providing no money for upkeep. Eventually the economy improved, workers patched up some of the damage, and in 1981 Van Alen's original lighting design for the tower's triangular windows was discovered and installed, giving the building the distinctive appearance it now enjoys in the city's skyline at night.

On Saturday morning, July 28, 1945 (ten months before the Manhattan Company Building crash), a B-25 bomber pilot lost his bearings while flying near the city and suddenly found himself dodging several midtown skyscrapers. Tragically, he couldn't outmaneuver the massive Empire State, and his ten-ton plane slammed into the seventy-eighth and seventy-ninth floors. Its fuel tanks exploded.

Smoke billowed from the shattered windows, and pedestrians scrambled away from the skyscraper, fearing its collapse. A cascade of glass, brick, and debris fell from the top stories. Rushing to the scene, firemen attempted to save those injured and prevent the fire from consuming the building. Fourteen died, but the skyscraper survived.

The Empire State has had its share of owners, some more neglectful than others. Much to William Lamb's regret, a 222-foot television antenna was affixed atop the mooring mast and his eighty-sixth-story observation floor became infamous for its suicide jumpers.

Today many of the wounds inflicted on these structures have been healed, and each building is now protected by landmark status. But nothing could save them from losing their rank as the tallest in the world. Although the Manhattan Company Building was pushed out of third place as early as 1932 by another downtown skyscraper, the 952-foot Cities Services Building, it would be some forty years before the Empire State and Chrysler buildings had to give up their positions as number one and two. When the height of the World Trade Towers was announced at 1,350 feet, the Empire State's owners sued to stop their erection, and after the suit was thrown out, they hired Shreve, Lamb, & Harmon (which continued, despite the deaths of the three founders) to design an addition so as to retain the height crown. Several plans were published, including one that had the mooring mast removed and thirty-three stories added to its crown, carrying the skyscraper to 1,494 feet. Ultimately, the owners scuttled these plans, and the World Trade Center claimed the height crown in December 1970 (with the north tower's topping-out ceremony), only to be surpassed four years later by Chicago's Sears Tower, which rose to a height of 1,454 feet. Two decades after its completion, the crown was passed once again, this time to Malaysia's Petronas Towers at 1,483 feet tall.

Plans for higher skyscrapers continue to make headlines, and perhaps one day Frank Lloyd Wright's idea of a mile-high tower may be built. As Daniel Burnham, one of the first architects to design a sky-scraper, said, "Remember that our sons and grandsons are going to do things that would stagger us."

—————

Stolen height titles, ruined careers, vicious reviews, miserly neglect, lost fortunes, and terrible accidents—these may seem to be the legacy of the skyscraper race, but they aren't. Fitzgerald was too soaked in re-gret to understand that the Empire State was far from the "crowning error" of the city. Lewis Mumford was too enthralled by functionalism to see that the Chrysler Building reflected not plutocracy, but democ-racy. George Ohrstrom was too sullen after investing so much in the Manhattan Company Building to understand its value far outweighed that of its forty-three high-speed elevators.

If they had taken a step back, had looked at who designed and drove these buildings to such great height, perhaps they would have come to a different conclusion. Yes, the builders were fat-cat industri-alists and financiers who hired the top names in architecture. But these men, all of them, came from humble backgrounds. The journey-man mechanic raised in a house where snow accumulated on the floor at night; the sons of a Presbyterian minister and Quaker taskmaster; a former fishmonger and subpoena server with a gift for gab; a $7.50 per week stenographer supporting his family; an immigrant's son who put himself through college; a kid born into a family that squandered its wealth before he turned eighteen; a Nova Scotian who came to the United States as a child and ran his own paper route; and an office boy—draftsman who dropped out of school yet labored long into the night to master his craft. In the decade when America finally came into its own, thanks to the efforts of thousands of others who also lifted themselves up from nothing, these men, and the skyscrapers they con-structed, reflected the spirit of a country in the making.

All the exuberance, daring, romance, moxie, innovation, and pride that infused the decade is seen in these pinnacles. No misfortune or turn of events could take that away. Even if these skyscrapers were "torn down, as others have been before them," Chrysler said at the time of the race, "the spirit of men working together that they represent will build new ones." It was this spirit—not steel and stone—that carried these skyscrapers higher.

Acknowledgments

When I started this book two years ago, I was a member of that dangerous club: the armchair architects. I had my opinions about new designs
on the cityscape, but scarce understanding of the complex web of decisions, compromises, and bold stands by architect to owner (or by
owner to architect) that go into every building. Plus, I was "unburdened" by decades of studying architectural history. I liked—or dis-
liked—a new museum, house, or skyscraper simply out of a gut
reaction. Suffering from such naked ignorance when beginning this
book, I enjoyed a pair of advantages. One, investigating the history of
the New York City skyline was a voyage of discovery. Two, I had no pride
to lose in asking any question, reading any book, or searching any
archive to add another detail to the broad canvas that was this story.
Fortunately I had quite a few companions for the voyage, many who
helped guide me, entertaining hundreds of questions along the way. I
would like to credit them here.

First to the librarians—my eternal gratitude. Notably, I would like
to thank Janet Parks and her assistant, Lou Di Gennaro, of the Avery
Architectural and Fine Arts Library at Columbia University. They tol-
erated innumerable "Do you have . . . ?" and "Do you know where I
can find . . . ?" questions and always had either an answer straight-
away or insight into where I needed to look. It did not hurt that they

had at their disposal one of the world's finest architectural libraries. I am also grateful to Shelley Diamond (JPMorgan Chase Archives), Nancy Shader (Princeton University Library), Marjorie McNinch (Hagley Library), Judy Throm (Architectural League of New York), Maricia Battle (Prints and Photographs Division, Library of Congress), Janet Wells Greene (Tamiment Library, New York University), Diane Cooter (Syracuse University), and Carol Salomon (Cooper Union Library). Thank you also to the keepers of the records at Yale University, Cornell University, Columbia University, and the University of Pennsylvania; Archives of American Art; New York County Clerk's office, New York Building Department, and the New-York Historical Society. And finally, a great expression of gratitude to the dedicated staff at The New York Public Library at Fifth Avenue and Forty-second Street. Fortunately Carrère & Hastings had the vision a century ago to provide you a building worthy of your efforts.

One of the sad circumstances of researching this story was that its participants had long since passed away and left little record of their thoughts at the time of the race to the sky. Of course, their actions spoke volumes, but where these failed to provide answers, their family and friends stepped in to help—not to mention adding some wonderful anecdotes and insights that have never before been published. I am grateful to Faith Severance Hackl Stewart, George C. S. Hackl, Faith Hackl Ward, Benjamin Raskob, Patsy Bremer, Mary Louise "Boo" Duffy, Maggie Ohrstrom Bryant, Richmond B. Shreve, Thomas Shreve, Herbert and Elizabeth Cowden, Frank Rhodes, Thomas Sutton, and William Edwin Squire Jr. Thank you also to Donald Friedman, Wil Roussos, and Carlo Bartoli, who illuminated for me some of the finer points of engineering and the laws of physics. Ray Gastil of the Van Alen Institute was kind enough to open his records about the organization's namesake, and Ron Miller provided some fascinating details about Van Alen through his research on Chesley Bonestell.

My efforts were aided by Mark Jupiter and Tyler Schmetterer, who first brought this story to my attention. Without their excitement and passion, not to mention their hard work in researching the events behind the race, this book would have been like so many of the hundred-and-fifty-story, mile-high skyscraper announcements of the late 1920s: a great idea, but now what do we do? Thank you as well to my good friends Tim Elliott and Neil Pakrashi for their legal research guidance. Most notably, Neil made the heroic discovery of the documents related to the lawsuit between William Van Alen and the W. P. Chrysler Building Corporation amongst the antiquated and mazelike filing system of the New York State courts. This lawsuit proved of great value in tracking the architect's work on the skyscraper and his relationship with Walter Chrysler. In my photographic research, I must credit the aid of David Stravitz, Christopher Gray, and Erika Gottfried.

Most writers, especially this one, need good readers, and I had the benefit of several talented professionals. Thanks to Daniel Abramson, Janet Parks, and Donald Friedman for making sure I did not mistake a column for a beam and preventing other architecture and engineering gaffes. Any mistakes that may have crept into the book are most certainly my own. Joe Veltre and Todd Keithley proved critical in helping smooth out my early drafts; they must also be acknowledged for not relinquishing our friendship subsequently.

I owe a great debt to my literary agent, Scott Waxman, who shaped the early idea for this book and was time and again an essential partner in its publication. He was a good friend in the process. I am especially thankful as well to Bill Thomas and Jason Kaufman at Doubleday. Bill's enthusiasm was instrumental to my pursuit of this project and Jason brought his keen editorial eye to the manuscript and steered me through the publication with great energy. Every author should be as lucky to find such champions for their first book. Your passion and guidance—and that of Team Doubleday as a whole—never ceased to astound. The drinks are on me.

This book is dedicated to my parents. They suffered every moment with me before the book sold, read (and saved on their home computer) every draft, enjoyed every step with me on the way to publication, and most important, supported me with unflagging faith in the thirty years it took to get to this point. I know it could not have been easy. And finally I want to thank Diane. She was my companion, motivator, shrink, editor, researcher, ballast, masseuse, helpful but firm critic, patient listener (even at midnight when I insisted on reading to her a line I wrote earlier in the day), and everything in between and beyond. I wish I could do justice in explaining how much of this book belongs to her.

My high school English teacher once told me that the best acknowledgment is simply said. So to one and all, thank you.

Notes

To spare the reader countless footnotes interrupting the story, I decided to use endnotes. Hopefully, these allow readers interested in greater details about particular facets of *Higher* to sate their curiosity. Reconstructing the events behind the skyscraper race of the 1920s proved an exercise in detective work. Sadly, few architectural practices of the time saved their records for posterity. The discovery of legal records related to William Van Alen was one boon. The notebook detailing the construction of the Empire State Building brought to light by Carol Willis (*Building the Empire State*) was another. I found invaluable information in the archives of John J. Raskob, The Bank of The Manhattan Company, Empire State, Inc., and Yasuo Matsui. Then there was the kindness and patience of my interview subjects, who gave great color to the principals in this story. And finally, I negotiated lengthy, but critical stays in the New York Public Library and Avery Architectural Library. At the former I scanned through the microfilmed pages of the *New York World*, *New York Sun*, *New York American*, *New York Evening Telegram*, *Evening Post*, and *New York Herald Tribune*—an effort that makes one appreciate the indexed *New York Times*. That said, I discovered scores of articles that helped put flesh on the bones of this story—for example, the one by William Van Alen ("Architect Finds New Designs in Frame of Steel," *New York Herald Tribune*), which offers a rare explanation of his thought process behind the Chrysler Building design. At the Avery Library I paged through decades' worth of journals like *Pencil Points, Architectural Forum, The Architect, The American Architect, Architecture,* and *Engineering News Record,* getting a clear-eyed picture of the life of an architect in the 1920s. It was a marvelous time.

PROLOGUE

1   *"What floor, please":* F. Scott Fitzgerald, "May Day," *Smart Set* (July 1920).

2   *Severance's role:* Faith Severance Hackl Stewart, personal interview.

3   *"Well, how do you like":* Francis Swales, "Draftsmanship and Architecture, V, as exemplified by the work of William Van Alen," *Pencil Points* (August 1929).

3   *"All my French is coming":* Faith Severance Hackl Stewart, personal interview.

4   *"In William Van Alen's work":* Leon Solon, "The Passing of the Skyscraper Formula for Design," *The Architectural Record* (February 1924).

4   *"the greatest energy":* Ibid.

4   *"We're going to ask McKim":* Allan Keller, "For Rockefeller Center Or a Small Home," *New York World Telegram* (February 16, 1938).

5   *They skirmished over money:* Faith Severance Hackl Stewart, personal interview. [Note: Unfortunately, the full details of the lawsuit have been lost in the New York courts. Several attempts to locate the files proved fruitless.]

5   *To understand this chase:* Francisco Mujica, *History of the Skyscraper* (Da Capo Press, 1977).

6   *bird's-eye:* George H. Douglas, *Skyscrapers: A Social History of the Very Tall Building in America* (McFarland & Company, 1996), p. 7.

6   *"Architects said nothing":* Harvey Wiley Corbett, "The Limits of our Skyscraping," *New York Times Magazine* (November 17, 1929).

7   *"extreme height":* "City's Tallest Structure from Base to Top," *New York Times* (January 1, 1905).

7   *"With the trees of Madison Square":* Sarah Bradford Landau and Carl Condit, *Rise of the New York Skyscraper, 1865–1913* (Yale University Press, 1996), p. 304.

7   *A year later, the slender Singer:* Anthony Robins, "The Continuing Saga of the Tallest Building in the World," *Architectural Record* (January 1987).

8   *The loan denial cost:* Douglas, *Skyscrapers,* pp. 50–60.

8   *Thirty years and millions of nickels:* Ibid., pp. 50–60.

9   *He and Gilbert then settled:* Landau and Condit, *Rise of the New York Skyscraper,* pp. 381–91.

9   *"How high do you want"*: Ibid., pp. 381–91.

9   *"There would be an enormous"*: Louis Horowitz and Boyden Sparkes, *The Towers of New York: The Memoirs of a Master Builder* (Simon & Schuster, 1937), p. 2.

10   *Dubbed the "Cathedral of Commerce"*: Robert A. M. Stern, *Pride of Place: Building the American Dream* (Houghton Mifflin, 1986), p. 251.

10   *"80,000 lights instantly"*: Edwin Cochran, *The Cathedral of Commerce* (Broadway Park Place Company, 1916).

11   *"The lamps are going"*: Barbara Tuchman, *The Guns of August* (Macmillan, 1962), p. 117.

11   *"The rain drives on"*: Modris Eksteins, *Rites of Spring: The Great War and the Birth of the Modern Age* (Houghton Mifflin, 1989), pp. 146–47.

11   *Worse than all of it*: Ibid., pp. 146–65.

12   *President Wilson hesitated*: Paul Johnson, *A History of the American People* (Weidenfeld & Nicolson, 1997), pp. 645–48.

12   *Her efforts decided*: James Truslow Adams, *The Epic of America* (Little, Brown, & Company, 1931), p. 386.

12   *Instead they danced and drank*: Eksteins, *Rites of Spring*, pp. 259–69.

12   *"A fresh picture"*: F. Scott Fitzgerald, "Early Success" in *The Crack-Up: with Other Uncollected Pieces, Note-Books and Unpublished Letters*, ed. Edmund Wilson (New Directions, 1956), p. 87.

13   *"think of any temptation"*: Ann Douglas, *Terrible Honesty: Mongrel Manhattan in the 1920s* (Farrar, Straus, and Giroux, 1995), p. 193.

13   *"It is a European city"*: Ric Burns and James Sanders, *New York: An Illustrated History* (Knopf, 1999), p. 317.

CHAPTER I

17   *"The heart of all"*: Thomas Van Leeuwen, *The Skyward Trend of Thought: Five Essays on the Metaphysics of the American Skyscraper* (AHA Books, 1986).

17   *The lobster shift returned*: William H. Whyte, *The WPA Guide to New York City: A Comprehensive Guide to the Five Boroughs of the Metropolis—Manhattan, Brooklyn, the Bronx, Queens, and Richmond* (The New Press, 1992), pp. 49–53.

19   *"The bravest thing"*: Gene Fowler, *Skyline: A Reporter's Reminiscence of the 1920s* (Viking Press, 1961), p. 50.

19   *It was not just another day*: Supreme Court of the State of New York, "William Van Alen versus Cooper Union for the Advancement of Science and Art, Reylex Corporation, W.P. Chrysler Building Corporation and National Surety Company," 1930–31 (New York, NY). [Note: Many of the details about this first meeting with Chrysler as well as precise information

about the dates and types of drawings/revisions that Van Alen executed for Chrysler are found in the files related to this lawsuit.]

20   *Regardless, Reynolds assured Van Alen:* Ibid.

22   *"stores and other improvements":* Ibid.

22   *"In designing a skyscraper":* William Van Alen, "Architect Finds New Designs in Frame of Steel," *New York Herald Tribune* (September 7, 1930).

22   *"a fire-proof office building":* Supreme Court of the State of New York, "William Van Alen versus Cooper Union for the Advancement of Science and Art, Reylex Corporation, W.P. Chrysler Building Corporation and National Surety Company."

23   *"leading the New York modernists":* Allene Talmey, "Raymond Hood—Man Against Sky," *New Yorker* (April 11, 1931).

24   *The last charge:* "W. H. Reynolds, Builder, Dead at 63," *New York Times* (October 14, 1931).

24   *Over the next fifteen years:* Cooper Union, "Minutes of Trustees Meetings," 1915–1930, Cooper Union Library (New York, NY).

25   *"In a rich baritone voice":* Kenneth Murchison, "Mr. Murchison of New York Says—," *The Architect* (April 1928).

25   *"successful addition to the skyscraper":* "Approve New Skyscraper," *New York Times* (June 6, 1928).

26   *With nine hundred thousand square feet:* "Plan to Start 67-Story Reynolds Building Soon," *Record and Guide* (August 25, 1928).

26   *"without turning a spadeful":* Colonel W. A. Starrett, *Skyscrapers and the Men Who Build Them* (Charles Scribner's Sons, 1928), p. 110.

27   *Walter Chrysler was a bear:* "A Man of the Year—Walter Chrysler," *Time* (January 7, 1929).

27   *"Where did you get this":* Horowitz and Sparkes, *The Towers of New York*, p. 194.

28   *"Walter, you'll go broke":* Vincent Curcio, *Chrysler: The Life and Times of an Automotive Genius* (Oxford University Press, 2000), p. 394.

28   *"step in the campaign":* New York World (October 4, 1928).

28   *"I was well aware":* Curcio, *Chrysler*, pp. 406–7.

29   *"After a long harrowing day":* Nicholas Kelley Papers, Manuscripts and Archives Division, The New York Public Library, Astor, Lenox and Tilden Foundations.

29   *There were two main issues:* "Reminiscences of Nicholas Kelley" in the Columbia University Oral History Research Office Collection, Columbia University (New York, NY).

29   *"I think it's great":* Nicholas Kelley Papers.

30   *When out in social situations:* Herbert Cowden, telephone interview.

30   *"Actually, I had two":* Curcio, *Chrysler*, p. 639.

30 *Van Alen was to abandon:* Supreme Court of the State of New York, "William Van Alen versus Cooper Union for the Advancement of Science and Art, Reylex Corporation, W.P. Chrysler Building Corporation and National Surety Company."

30 *"I want a taller building":* Ibid. [Note: Paraphrased from recollections of William Van Alen]

CHAPTER 2

32 *"You shall no longer take things":* William Lescaze, *On Being an Architect* (G. P. Putnam's Sons, 1942), title page.

32 *Fifty years before:* Chrysler Tower Corporation, *The Chrysler Building* (Chrysler Tower Corporation, 1930), pp. 3–4.

33 *Despite a few tall buildings:* Sarah Bradford Landau and Carl Condit, *Rise of the New York Skyscraper, 1865–1913* (Yale University Press, 1996), p. 111.

33 *Jacob Van Alen ran:* Benjamin Taylor Van Alen, *Genealogical History of the Van Alen Family* (Chicago, 1902), p. 37.

34 *"His name, tripping":* Francis Swales, "Draftsmanship and Architecture, V, as exemplified by the work of William Van Alen," *Pencil Points* (August 1929).

35 *When one of the builders:* Henry Saylor, *The AIA's First Hundred Years* (Octagon, 1957), p. 2.

35 *"It was torn by dissensions":* Ibid., p. 13.

36 *"Yahoo or Hottentot creations":* John Burchard and Albert Bush-Brown, *The Architecture of America: A Social and Cultural History* (Little, Brown & Company, 1961), p. 262

36 *"the damage wrought to this country":* Louis H. Sullivan, *The Autobiography of an Idea* (Dover Publications, 1956).

37 *Practices of the day:* Anonymous, "The Story of an Architect." *Century Magazine* (1917).

38 *"herd by themselves":* Ibid.

38 *"it might not take":* Swales, "Draftsmanship and Architecture."

39 *After work and late into the night:* Francis Swales, "Master Draftsmen, VII, Emmanuel Louis Masqueray," *Pencil Points* (1917).

39 *First awarded in 1904:* Joseph Freedlander, "What Is the Paris Prize?" Van Alen Institute Archives (New York, NY), source unknown.

40 *As Van Alen departed:* Swales, "Draftsmanship and Architecture."

40 *"He must have both":* Vitruvius, *On Architecture*, edited and translated by Frank Granger (Harvard University Press, 1931), pp. 7–9.

41 *Students spent little time:* Letters to parents, *1908–1911*, Clarence S. Stein Papers at Division of Rare and Manuscript Collections, Cornell University Library (Ithaca, New York).

42 *"Everyone was shouting":* Letter to parents—March 10, 1908, Clarence S. Stein Papers at Division of Rare and Manuscript Collections, Cornell University Library (Ithaca, New York).

43 *"Unless you were":* Ely Jacques Kahn Papers, Avery Drawings and Archives, Avery Architectural and Fine Arts Library, Columbia University (New York, NY).

43 *"The training was providing him":* Swales, "Draftsmanship and Architecture."

45 *"Van Alen was the only American":* Kenneth Murchison, "The Chrysler Building as I See It," *The American Architect* (September 1930).

CHAPTER 3

46 *"All Great Ages":* William Lescaze, *On Being an Architect* (G. P. Putnam's Sons, 1942), p. 23.

46 *"to recognize that in steel-frame":* William Van Alen, "Architect Finds New Designs in Frame of Steel," *New York Herald Tribune* (September 7, 1930).

47 *"stark nakedness of silos":* Ralph Walker as quoted in Norbert Messler, *The Art Deco Skyscraper in New York* (Peter Lang, 1986), p. 45.

47 *"an architectural character":* William Van Alen, "Architect Finds New Designs in Frame of Steel."

47 *"It must be tall, every inch":* Rosemarie Haag Bletter and Cervin Robinson, *Skyscraper Style: Art Deco New York* (Oxford University Press, 1975), p. 36.

47 *"frozen fountain":* Claude Bragdon, "The Frozen Fountain," *Pencil Points* (October 1931)

48 *On the initial design of the Reynolds Building:* Francis Swales, "Draftsmanship and Architecture, V, as exemplified by the work of William Van Alen," *Pencil Points* (August 1929). [Note: based on study of sketches included in the article.]

49 *"top piece which looked":* Kenneth Murchison, "The Chrysler Building as I See It," *The American Architect* (September 1930).

49 *From these early sketches:* Supreme Court of the State of New York, "William Van Alen versus Cooper Union for the Advancement of Science and Art, Reylex Corporation, W.P. Chrysler Building Corporation and National Surety Company", 1930–31 (New York, NY).

50 *"giving life and interest":* William Van Alen, "Architect Finds New Designs in Frame of Steel."

51 *"a great jeweled sphere":* "Final Sketch of the Reynolds Building," *The American Architect* (August 20, 1928).

52 *"neck of a demijohn":* "They Do Say," *The Architect* (May 1929)

52 *When the architect presented:* Walter P. Chrysler in collaboration with Boyden

Sparkes, *Life of an American Workman* (Dodd, Mead & Company, 1950), p. 198.

53   *"several van loads":* Supreme Court of the State of New York, "William Van Alen versus Cooper Union for the Advancement of Science and Art, Reylex Corporation, W.P. Chrysler Building Corporation and National Surety Company."

53   *Throughout this process:* Andre J. Fouilhoux, "Drawings, Specifications and Inspection," *Engineering News Record* (February 19, 1931).

53   *Born in Springfield, Massachusetts:* "Obituary—Fred Ley," *New York Times* (July 14, 1958).

54   *Wreckers utilized:* "Novel Methods are Tried," *New York Times* (June 30, 1929).

55   *Each rig cost $14,500:* "Skyscrapers: Builders and Their Tools," *Fortune* (1930).

55   *"move in every direction":* Ibid.

56   *"Chrysler Building—Being Erected":* John B. Reynolds, *The Chrysler Building* (Chrysler Tower Corporation, 1930).

57   *"At night the tower":* "Chrysler Plans are Announced," *New York Sun* (March 7, 1929).

58   *"Tower of Babel look":* *New York Times* as quoted in Robert A. M. Stern, Gregory Gilmartin, and John Montague Massengale, *New York 1930: Architecture and Urbanism Between Two World Wars* (Rizzoli, 1987), p. 601.

58   *Others announced plans:* "Mussolini to Build Highest Skyscraper," *New York Times* (September 30, 1924).

CHAPTER 4

59   *"I am perhaps a little quick":* Thomas Hine, *Burnham of Chicago: Architect and Planner* (Oxford University Press, 1979).

59   *In March 1929, Craig Severance:* Faith Severance Hackl Stewart, personal interview.

61   *"the only architect who owns":* "A Practical Point," *The Architect* (November 1929).

61   *"an unpleasant, tall funny man":* Faith Severance Hackl Stewart, personal interview.

61   *"I want. I get":* Ibid.

62   *Severance came from a well-established:* Nell Jane Barnett Sullivan and David Kendall Martin, *A History of the Town of Chazy, Clinton County, New York* (Little Press, 1970).

63   *"Stand there and hold":* Bell Sullivan, *Severance* (J. C. Hubbell Papers, County History, Clinton and Franklin County).

63 *"the intervention of an architectural police"*: Montgomery Schuyler, "Recent Buildings in New York," *Harper's New Monthly Magazine* (September 1883).

64 *"It wouldn't have mattered"*: Faith Severance Hackl Stewart, personal interview.

64 *"I'll plan anything a man"*: Paul R. Baker, *Stanny: The Gilded Life of Stanford White* (Free Press, 1989), p. 21.

64 *"I like your architecture"*: Francis Swales, "Obituary—Thomas Hastings," *Pencil Points* (1929).

64 *"There was always Carrère"*: Harold Van Buren Magonigle Papers, Manuscripts and Archives Division, The New York Public Library, Astor, Lenox and Tilden Foundations.

65 *One time while overseeing a man:* Faith Severance Hackl Stewart, personal interview.

66 *"John, you ought to delegate"*: Tom Shachtman, *Skyscraper Dreams: The Great Real Estate Dynasties of New York* (Little, Brown & Company, 1991), Chapter Two.

67 *"the idea of refinement"*: Matlack Price, "A Renaissance in Commercial Architecture," *Architectural Record* (May 1912).

67 *"I don't know any architects"*: Faith Severance Hackl Stewart, personal interview.

67 *Severance and Van Alen first met:* Christopher Gray, "An Architect Called the Ziegfeld of His Profession," *New York Times* (March 22, 1998).

68 *Soon more commissions for office buildings:* John Taylor Boyd, "The Newer Fifth Avenue Retail Shop Fronts," *The Architectural Record* (June 1921).

68 *"Our office is entirely organized"*: Letter from H. Craig Severance to James Ewing, President of Morewood Realty Holding Company, November 19, 1921. (Supreme Court of the State of New York.)

68 *When Van Alen began missing deadlines:* Faith Severance Hackl Stewart, personal interview.

69 *"Every proportion appears to be unfortunate"*: T-Square, "Skyline," *New Yorker* (October 16, 1926).

69 *"We wish to clear our conscience"*: T-Square, "Skyline," *New Yorker* (February 11, 1928).

69 *It was much more than an isolated:* Robert A. M. Stern, Gregory Gilmartin, and John Montague Massengale, *New York 1930: Architecture and Urbanism Between Two World Wars* (Rizzoli, 1987), p. 204; p. 548.

70 *"machine that makes"*: Carol Willis, *Form Follows Finance: Skyscrapers and Skylines in New York and Chicago* (Princeton Architectural Press, 1995), p. 19.

70 *"History will record"*: "Mechanics Hear Chrysler," *New York Times* (January 21, 1930).

70   *"Make no little plans"*: Daniel Burnham as quoted in Ralph Walker Papers at Department of Special Collections, Syracuse University Library (Syracuse, New York).

CHAPTER 5

72   *"The raison d'être of the skyscraper"*: Claude Bragdon, "The Frozen Fountain," *Pencil Points* (October 1931).

73   *"Boy Wonder"*: Thomas Sutton, personal interview.

73   *"could be tucked away on one floor"*: *Michigan State Journal* (George Ohrstrom Archives), undated.

73   *The call of World War I*: Maggie Ohrstrom Bryant, telephone interview.

73   *"rocked sharply, lifted"*: online article (http://members.livingalblum.net/robert110/pages/pageeight.html.

74   *"I haven't reached the top"*: B. C. Forbes, "Romance Behind World's Tallest Skyscraper," *Boston American* (April 17, 1929).

75   *"only person who bothered"*: Thomas Sutton, personal interview.

75   *"There was no bullshit"*: Ibid.

76   *In September 1928 Ohrstrom formed*: "Skyscrapers: Pyramid in Steel and Stock," *Fortune* (1930).

76   *"the reverse of those of Foch"*: Ibid.

77   *First Ohrstrom took Lot I*: Ibid.

78   *"there is no intention on our part"*: Letter from George Ohrstrom to P. A. Rowley, Vice Chairman, January 11, 1929 (JPMorgan Chase Archives (New York, NY).

79   *"in earning power than in brick"*: "Skyscrapers: Pyramid in Steel and Stock," *Fortune* (1930).

79   *As Ohrstrom prepared the financing*: Yasuo Matsui, *Skyscraper: Multiple Business Dwellings* (JPMorgan Chase Archives, 1930).

80   *the new Golconda*: John Brooks, *Once in Golconda: A True Drama of Wall Street 1920–1938* (W. W. Norton & Company, 1969), pp. 1–13.

80   *"the man who builds a factory"*: William Klingaman, *1929: The Year of the Great Crash* (Harper & Row, 1989), p. 9.

80   *Retail chains consolidated*: Frederick Lewis Allen, *Only Yesterday: An Informal History of the Nineteen-Twenties* (Harper & Row, 1931), pp. 160–80; E. S. Turner, *The Shocking History of Advertising* (E. P. Dutton & Company, 1953).

81   *"picked up twelve men"*: Allen, *Only Yesterday*, p. 180.

81   *"No money down"*: James Playsted Woods, *The Story of Advertising* (Ronald Press Company, 1958), pp. 360–79.

81 *"It was a great game":* Klingaman, *1929*, p. 12.

82 *"Look down there":* Ibid, p. 56.

82 *"Four More Years of Prosperity":* Allen, *Only Yesterday*, p. 304.

82 *Amidst this boom:* Stanley Peter Andersen, *American Ikon: Response to the Skyscraper, 1875–1934* (University of Michigan, Ph.D. dissertation, 1960), p. 142.

82 *"Never . . . it would be difficult":* John Taurenac, *The Empire State Building: The Making of a Landmark* (Scribner's, 1995), pp. 67–68.

83 *Skyscrapers were a self-fulfilling prophecy:* Carol Willis, *Form Follows Finance: Skyscrapers and Skylines in New York and Chicago* (Princeton Architectural Press, 1995).

83 *To make way for the hundreds:* Robert A. M. Stern, Gregory Gilmartin, and John Montague Massengale, *New York 1930: Architecture and Urbanism Between Two World Wars* (Rizzoli, 1987), pp. 19–23.

83 *After rumors early in 1928:* Taurenac, *The Empire State Building*, p. 120.

83 *"it is a difficult matter to shake":* Klingaman, *1929*, p. 57.

84 *Although they denied participation:* Brooks, *Once in Golconda*, pp. 65–85.

84 *"If the attitudes of Americans":* Ibid., p. 84.

85 *By March 12, 1929, Severance was given:* David Bareuther, "Japanese Designs Great Towers," *New York Sun* (January 11, 1930).

85 *It was not like Severance:* Faith Severance Hackl Stewart, personal interview.

86 *"You can build anything in New York":* "A Practical Point," *The Architect* (November 1929).

86 *At fifty-three years old, Matsui:* David Bareuther, "Japanese Designs Great Towers."

86 *"What is your hobby?":* Ibid.

86 *The tower featured a pyramidal crown:* Yasuo Matsui, *Skyscraper*.

87 *"the theme of the symphony":* "Skyscrapers: The Paper Spires," *Fortune* (1930).

87 *Once the tower plan was fixed:* Daniel Abramson, *Skyscraper Rivals: The AIG Building and The Architecture of Wall Street* (Princeton Architectural Press, 2001), p. 55.

87 *Later that year economist W. C. Clark:* "75-Story Skyscrapers Found Economical," *New York Times* (September 22, 1929).

88 *Radio Corp shares rose:* Klingaman, *1929*, p. 151.

88 *"the first time we led":* Yasuo Matsui, *Skyscraper*.

89 *There were many factors still to overcome:* Board minutes of The Bank of The Manhattan Company, March 1929 (JPMorgan Chase Archives, New York, NY).

CHAPTER 6

91   *"When Americans find themselves"*: Ric Burns and James Sanders, *New York: An Illustrated History* (Knopf, 1999), p. 232.

91   *"This reversal of building methods"*: Colonel W. A. Starrett, *Skyscrapers and the Men Who Build Them* (Charles Scribner's Sons, 1928), p. 35.

91   *Coined for the winning horse:* Sarah Bradford Landau and Carl Condit, *Rise of the New York Skyscraper, 1865–1913* (Yale University Press, 1996), pp. ix–x.

92   *In 1867 New York:* Frederick Simpich, "This Giant That Is New York," *National Geographic Magazine*, (1930); Bassett Jones, "The Modern Building Is a Machine," *The American Architect* (January 30, 1924).

93   *"Before us is spread the most"*: Landau and Condit, *Rise of the New York Skyscraper*, p. 71.

93   *"one might believe that the chief end"*: Winston Weisman, "New York and the Problem of the First Skyscraper," *Journal of the Society of Architectural Historians* (Volume XII, 1).

94   *"the loss of property was greater"*: George H. Douglas, *Skyscrapers: A Social History of the Very Tall Building in America* (McFarland & Company, 1996), pp. 8–10.

95   *"All lost except wife"*: Ibid., pp. 8–10.

95   *In the ensuing years, they ushered:* Landau and Condit, *Rise of the New York Skyscrapers*, pp. 19–39.

96   *"He reached a snag early one"*: Douglas, *Skyscrapers*, p. 24.

98   *"a steel bridge structure on end"*: David Bareuther, "Structure on End," *New York Sun* (January 12, 1929).

99   *"if the building goes down"*: Ibid.

99   *"I secured a plumb-line"*: Landau and Condit, *Rise of the New York Skyscraper*, p. 163.

100   *"like a human being in its organization"*: Norbert Messler, *The Art Deco Skyscraper in New York* (Peter Lang, 1986), p. 45.

CHAPTER 7

101   *"Mr. Chrysler is a big man"*: W. Parker Chase, *New York, The Wonder City* (Wonder City Publishing Company, 1932), p. 94.

101   *"To me this building"*: "Chrysler Gives Credit to Men," *New York Telegram* (January 24, 1930).

102   *"mind so real, so complete"*: Vincent Curcio, *Chrysler: The Life and Times of an Automotive Genius* (Oxford University Press, 2000), p. 64.

103   *"Banker at 34"*: *New York Herald Tribune* (April 10, 1929).

103   *"64-Story Bank Building"*: *New York Herald Tribune* (April 7, 1929).

103   *"Wall Street Building to Top All"*: *New York Times* (April 10, 1929).

103 *"in its tracks the rumor"*: "Lights of New York—Downtown Record" (George Ohrstrom Archives), no date/source reference.

103 *"a beacon for airplanes and ships"*: "Planning 63-Story Wall Street Building," *Boston Herald* (April 14, 1929).

103 *"the newest skyscraper will cost more"*: "Hot Off the Griddle" (George Ohrstrom Archives), no date/source reference.

104 *"This young man calls himself"*: B. C. Forbes, "Romance Behind World's Tallest Skyscraper," *Boston American* (April 17, 1929).

104 *"Twentieth century pyramid builders"*: "George Ohrstrom, 34, Now a Bank President" (George Ohrstrom Archives), no date/source reference.

104 *"monument"*: "Chrysler Gives Credit to Men," *New York Telegram* (January 24, 1930).

105 *"prodigious, fabulous, a torpedo-headed dynamo"*: "A Man of the Year—Walter Chrysler," *Time* (January 7, 1929).

105 *Such was the story of his life*: Vincent Curcio, *Chrysler: The Life and Times of an Automotive Genius* (Oxford University Press, 2000). [This section draws heavily on this fine autobiography of Walter Chrysler.]

105 *"You had to be a tough kid"*: Walter P. Chrysler in collaboration with Boyden Sparkes, *Life of an American Workman* (Dodd, Mead & Company, 1950), p. 12.

106 *"I wasn't willing to stick around"*: Ibid., p. 69.

107 *"You can take her away"*: Curcio, *Chrysler*, p. 81.

107 *"It was painted ivory white"*: Chrysler and Sparkes, *Life of an American Workman*, p. 99.

108 *"What a job I could do here"*: Ibid., pp. 126–27.

109 *"staring at the wall as if in a daze"*: Curcio, *Chrysler*, p. 253.

110 *"If that's the way you feel about"*: Ibid., p. 279.

111 *Van Alen was buried in revisions*: Supreme Court of the State of New York, "William Van Alen versus Cooper Union for the Advancement of Science and Art, Reylex Corporation, W.P. Chrysler Building Corporation and National Surety Company," 1930–31 (New York, NY).

111 *More details had been published*: "Wall Street Tower to Rise 850 feet," *New York Sun* (April 13, 1929).

112 *This was a character who*: George C. S. Hackl, personal interview.

112 *"Make this building higher than the Eiffel Tower"*: Chrysler and Sparkes, *Life of an American Workman*, p. 198.

112 *"Van, you've just got to get up"*: Kenneth Murchison, "The Chrysler Building as I See It," *The American Architect* (September 1930).

113 *"Running up a building's like playing"*: William Bridges, "In the Eyes of a Steel Worker," *New York Sun* (January 29, 1930).

114 *The main power on the building site*: "3½ Tons of Girders Plunge," *New York*

Times (April 21, 1929); "4 Killed, 11 Hurt as Girders Fall," *New York Sun* (April 20, 1929); *New York World* (April 21, 1929).

115 *Steel work was dangerous business:* F. D. McHugh, "Manhattan's Mightiest 'Minaret,'" *Scientific American* (April 1930).

CHAPTER 8

116 *"Let's speed—speed—speed":* Colonel W. A. Starrett, *Skyscrapers and the Men Who Build Them* (Charles Scribner's Sons, 1928).

116 *"The idea is my own":* Meryle Secrest, *Frank Lloyd Wright* (Knopf, 1992), p. 7.

116 *When settlers crossed the Atlantic:* Edwin G. Burrows and Mike Wallace, *Gotham: A History of New York City to 1898* (Oxford University Press, 1999), pp. 3–26.

117 *It was a long way:* "Stock Exchange on Pillory Site," *New York Sun* (May 24, 1930).

117 *"the proposed building may later":* "Great New Structure to Rise on Old Site," *Manhattan Family* (May 1929).

118 *"a parade in which each marcher":* "Ability and Team-Work Are Features of the Crew Which Built Empire State," *World-Telegram* (February 18, 1938).

119 *On most jobs, the demolition crew:* Yasuo Matsui, *Skyscraper: Multiple Business Dwellings* (JPMorgan Chase Archives, 1930); W. T. McIntosh, "Unusual Foundation Procedure for 71-Story Building," *Engineering News Record* (April 24, 1930). [Note: This section on the foundation work on the Manhattan Company Building is largely based on these two accounts.]

121 *"irreducible minimum":* Matsui, *Skyscraper*.

121 *The structural steel had long since begun:* "The Story of Steel," *Scientific American* (January–September 1924).

123 *"When it was decided that the topmost":* William Van Alen, "The Structure and Metal Work of the Chrysler Building," *The Architectural Forum* (October 1930).

124 *"I am not particularly interested":* District Court of New York, "Van Alen versus Aluminum Company of America," March 18, 1942 (New York, NY).

125 *It gave the appearance:* Claudia Roth Pierpont, "The Silver Spine," *New Yorker* (November 18, 2002).

125 *The question was how to be faithful:* Ibid.

125 *"To my mind, Van Alen was the best":* Ron Miller and Frederick C. Durante, *The Art of Chesley Bonestell* (Sterling Publications, 2001).

126 *"Your house is finished":* Secrest, *Frank Lloyd Wright*, p. 419.

127 *"far away from paper and pencil":* Robert Twombly, *Louis Sullivan: His Life and Work* (Viking, 1986).

127 *"liveliest spot on Earth"*: W. Parker Chase, *New York, The Wonder City* (Wonder City Publishing Company, 1932), p. 230.

127 *"As soon as the dusk falls"*: Ric Burns and James Sanders, *New York: An Illustrated History* (Knopf, 1999), p. 347.

129 *"If this is to be a skyscraper"*: "Automobiles in Architecture—Row of Motors Cars Placed in Design of Chrysler Tower," *New York Sun* (January 1930).

CHAPTER 9

130 *"Therefore when we build"*: John Ruskin, *The Seven Lamps of Architecture* (John Wiley, 1890).

130 *"nearest peace-time equivalent to war"*: Colonel W. A. Starrett, *Skyscrapers and the Men Who Build Them* (Charles Scribner's Sons, 1928), p. 63.

131 *400 masons and common laborers*: John B. Reynolds, *The Chrysler Building* (Chrysler Tower Corporation, 1930), p. 13.

132 *There were actually five Starrett brothers*: Paul Starrett, *Changing the Skyline* (Whittlesey House, 1938), pp. 3–14; John Taurenac, *The Empire State Building: The Making of a Landmark* (Scribner's, 1995), pp. 179–200.

132 *"You can hire any number of engineers"*: "Paul Starrett, Builder, 90, Dies," *New York Times* (July 6, 1957).

133 *"not to erect steel, brick, or concrete"*: Colonel W. A. Starrett, *Skyscrapers*, p. 87.

134 *If you stopped at the 40 Wall Street site*: Pietro Di Donato, *Christ in Concrete* (Signet Classic, 1939); "Skyscrapers: Builders and Their Tools," *Fortune* (1930).

135 *On the site, Mr. Adams*: "Building a 71-Story Skyscraper in 33 Weeks," *Engineering News Record* (May 15, 1930); Carol Willis, *Building the Empire State* (W. W. Norton, New York, 1998). [Note: Many details drawn from the activities of Starrett Brothers on the Empire State Building.]

136 *"is a fascinating game"*: Colonel W. A. Starrett, *Skyscrapers*, p. 63.

136 *Every morning before 8 A.M.*: O. F. Sieder, "Steel Design and Erection on a 900-Foot Tower Building," *Engineering News Record* (May 8, 1930).

137 *"We will make our deliveries on time"*: Raymond Jones, "Our New Main Office to Be World's Tallest Building," *Manhattan Family* (October 1930).

CHAPTER 10

139 *The summer should have been*: Faith Severance Hackl Stewart, personal interview.

140 *"modern interpretation of the ancient Greek"*: "Modern Architecture," *The Architect* (May 1930).

140 *"Distressingly pretentious"*: T-Square, "The Sky Line: One Silver Lining—Madison Mixture—And Contents Noted," *New Yorker* (June 1, 1929).

140 *"his most strikingly original and interesting"*: Francis Swales, "Draftsmanship and Architecture, V, as exemplified by the work of William Van Alen," *Pencil Points* (August 1929).

141 *"Never, so far as [Van Alen] knew"*: T-Square, "The Sky Line: Up and Up," *New Yorker* (August 17, 1929).

141 *George Ohrstrom was just as stalwart a competitor*: Maggie Ohrstrom Bryant, telephone interview; Thomas Sutton, personal interview.

142 *"last as long as the pyramids"*: 40 Wall Street, Inc., "Report as of June 30, 1956," JPMorgan Chase Archives (1956).

142 *"Why did you make it so high?"* Frederick Simpich, "This Giant That Is New York," *National Geographic Magazine* (1930).

143 *"Don't tell me how it can't"*: Maggie Ohrstrom Bryant, telephone interview.

143 *"lure of having the highest"*: Yasuo Matsui, *Skyscraper: Multiple Business Dwellings* (JPMorgan Chase Archives, 1930).

144 *In August of 1929, a rumor*: John Taurenac, *The Empire State Building: The Making of a Landmark* (Scribner's, 1995), pp. 120–21; "Syndicate Gets Waldorf Site," *New York Herald Tribune* (June 4, 1929).

145 *"Instead of having the feeling"*: "Waldorf Diners Clink Glasses," *New York Herald Tribune* (May 2, 1929).

146 *"There would be no limit"*: "Raskob Plans to Aid Workers by Investors," *New York Herald Tribune* (May 7, 1929).

146 *"Hello, Al"*: "Smith Plays Hurdy Gurdy in His Hotel Apartment," *New York Herald Tribune* (March 13, 1929).

146 *"Please do not trouble to acknowledge"*: Letter from John J. Raskob to Louis Kaufman, July 23, 1929, John Jakob Raskob Papers at the Hagley Museum and Library (Wilmington, Delaware).

147 *"enormous size of the building"*: Letter from Louis Kaufman to John J. Raskob, July 24, 1929, John Jakob Raskob Papers at the Hagley Museum and Library (Wilmington, Delaware).

148 *"Wickedest Ward in New York"*: Robert Slayton, *Empire Statesman: The Rise and Redemption of Al Smith* (Free Press, 2001), Chapter 2.

149 *"I'm to be an Irish landlord"*: "Smith to Head Firm Erecting 80-Story Tower," *New York Herald Tribune* (August 30, 1929).

149 *"Mr. Speaker, I have just heard"*: Slayton, *Empire Statesman*, Chapter 3.

150 *"There are no pikers in this organization"*: "Smith Denies He's through with Politics," *New York Telegram* (August 30, 1929).

150 *"But this building we're going to put up"*: "Smith to Head Firm Erecting 80-Story Tower," *New York Herald Tribune* (August 30, 1929); "Smith Denies He's through with Politics," *New York Telegram* (August 30, 1929); "80-Story Tower Will Rise Soon," *New York Sun* (August 30, 1929); "Smith to Build Highest Skyscraper," *New York Times* (August 30, 1929); "New

Waldorf-Astoria Building 80-Stories High," *Record & Guide* (September 7, 1929); "Al Smith, Builder, to Stay in Politics," *New York Evening Post* (August 30, 1929). [Note: This scene is brought together by weaving together these sources.]

152 *But on or about September 1:* "New Skyscraper Race Is Won by The Bank of The Manhattan Company," *New York Telegram* (October 18, 1929).

152 *"Made to learn the closely guarded":* Paul Starrett, *Changing the Skyline* (Whittlesey House, 1938), p. 283.

INTERLUDE

155 *"If a man saves fifteen dollars":* William Klingaman, *1929: The Year of the Great Crash* (Harper & Row, 1989), pp. 211–12.

155 *Labor Day weekend offered:* New York Times (September 2–4, 1929); New York Evening Post (September 2–4, 1929).

156 *"Dow Jones could climb":* Gordon Thomas and Max Morgan-Witts, *The Day the Bubble Burst: A Social History of the Wall Street Crash of 1929* (Doubleday, 1979), p. 274.

156 *"Wall Street was pandemonium":* Ric Burns and James Sanders, *New York: An Illustrated History* (Knopf, 1999), p. 367.

156 *"You could talk about Prohibition":* John Brooks, *Once in Golconda: A True Drama of Wall Street 1920–1938* (W. W. Norton & Company, 1969), p. 82.

157 *Throughout the summer the bull market:* John Kenneth Galbraith, *The Great Crash: 1929* (Houghton Mifflin Company, 1988).

157 *"a new era of prosperity":* Vincent Curcio, *Chrysler: The Life and Times of an Automotive Genius* (Oxford University Press, 2000), p. 462.

158 *"a young banker had put every dollar":* Klingaman, *1929*, p. 219.

158 *"as little an intrest or shear":* Ibid., p. 220.

159 *"The summer holiday is now":* New York Evening Post (September 3, 1929).

CHAPTER 11

163 *"What figure the poet":* Robert A. M. Stern, Gregory Gilmartin, and John Montague Massengale, *New York 1930: Architecture and Urbanism Between Two World Wars* (Rizzoli, 1987), p. 505.

163 *"an absence of motion":* William Van Alen, "Architect Finds New Designs in Frame of Steel," *New York Herald Tribune* (September 7, 1930).

164 *Above these setbacks, the tower rose:* Eugene Clute, "The Chrysler Building, New York," *The Architectural Forum* (October 1930).

165 *"The tower should grow out of the lower":* William Van Alen, "Architect Finds New Designs in Frame of Steel."

166 *"This is not a building for investment"*: "Chrysler Awards Given," *New York Times* (September 11, 1929).

167 *"the better you do your work"*: "Chrysler Building Workers Honored," *New York Sun* (September 10, 1929).

167 *A race between skyscrapers suited*: Edwin Emery and Henry Ladd Smith, *The Press and America* (Prentice Hall, 1954), p. 514; pp. 624–29.

168 *Safe from the spotlight*: Ross King, *Brunelleschi's Dome: How a Renaissance Genius Reinvented Architecture* (Walker & Company, 2000), pp. 49–52; pp. 160–61.

168 *Under the guidance of Rogers*: William G. Wheeler, "Safeguarding Construction Crews in a Great Skyscraper," *Buildings and Building Management* (December 2, 1929).

168 *The steelworker's premium rate, $15.40 a day*: C. G. Poore, "The Riveter's Lofty Panorama," *New York Times Magazine* (January 5, 1930).

169 *"Prince of Wales of the Girders"*: Margaret Norris and Brenda Ueland, "Riding the Girders," *Saturday Evening Post* (April 11, 1931).

170 *"wore out the most clothes"*: Ibid.

170 *When the derrick brought up*: "Skyscrapers: Builders and Their Tools," *Fortune* (1930).

171 *"the most dangerous part of the work"*: C. G. Poore, "The Riveter's Lofty Drama."

171 *"find themselves on a narrow beam"*: Norris and Ueland, "Riding the Girders."

172 *"We have an old axiom"*: Harold McClain, "Above and Beyond the Ladders," *Empire State Building Commemorative Issue* (April 30, 1981).

172 *"When a steel man gets through"*: William Bridges, "In the Eyes of a Steel Worker," *New York Sun* (January 29, 1930).

172 *"You get to love it and can't quit it"*: Norris and Ueland, "Riding the Girders."

173 *Paul Starrett had long since traded in his scuffed-up*: Paul Starrett, *Changing the Skyline* (Whittlesey House, 1938), pp. 287–92. [Note: This scene, including quotations, is based on Paul Starrett's account.]

174 *Raskob was there, no doubt*: Benjamin G. Raskob, Patsy R. Bremer, and Mary Louise ("Boo") Duffy, personal interview.

174 *The mild-mannered Shreve*: R. B. Shreve, "RHS—The Life of Richmond Harold Shreve" (August 1, 1984); Thomas Shreve, email interview.

175 *"thought his idea in danger"*: "Richmond Harold Shreve—The Empire State Architect," *The Architect* (1947).

CHAPTER 12

178   *"Men are only as great":* Louis Hautecoeur, *Histoire de l'architecture classique en France* (A. and J. Picard and Cie, 1953), p. 148.

     On October 2, 1929: Gordon Thomas and Max Morgan-Witts, *The Day the Bubble Burst: A Social History of the Wall Street Crash of 1929* (Doubleday, 1979), pp. 314–18.

178   *At the table sat Billy Durant:* Dana Thomas, *The Plungers and the Peacocks: An Update of the Classic History of the Stock Market* (William Morrow & Company, 1967), pp. 175–77.

179   *top end of the scale:* Thomas and Morgan-Witts, *The Day the Bubble Burst,* p. 315.

179   *"that sooner or later a crash":* John Kenneth Galbraith, *The Great Crash: 1929* (Houghton Mifflin Company, 1988), p. 85.

180   *"Don't part with your illusions":* Ibid., p. 87.

180   *The market had continued a slow:* John Brooks, *Once in Golconda: A True Drama of Wall Street 1920–1938* (W. W. Norton & Company, 1969), pp. 110–11.

180   *The president of the New York Yankees:* William Klingaman, *1929: The Year of the Great Crash* (Harper & Row, 1989), pp. 241–44.

180   *"In a healthy market we prosper":* Thomas and Morgan-Witts, *The Day the Bubble Burst,* p. 317.

181   *His final move was to express:* Benjamin G. Raskob, Patsy R. Bremer, and Mary Louise ("Boo") Duffy, personal interview.

181   *"There are only about four hundred people":* Theodore James, Jr., *The Empire State Building* (Harper & Row, 1975), p. 23.

181   *Raskob came from squalor:* James Walsh, "Chronicle—John Jakob Raskob," *Irish Studies Quarterly* (September 1929).

182   *"the best education you can give a boy":* Ibid.

182   *Only days after his father passed away:* Benjamin G. Raskob, Patsy R. Bremer, and Mary Louise ("Boo") Duffy, personal interview.

182   *"fortunate accidents":* S. J. Wolf, "Raskob Takes Off His Coat for Smith," *New York Times Magazine* (September 30, 1928).

183   *The reserved, unassuming Raskob:* Matthew Josephson and Hannah Josephson, *Al Smith: Hero of the Cities* (Houghton Mifflin Company, 1969), p. 357.

183   *"What's a Raskob?":* "John Raskob of General Motors Made 80 Millionaires in 4 Years," *New York Sun* (March 12, 1928).

184   *"contains the following ingredients":* "National Affairs—Raskobism," *Time* (November 18, 1929).

184   *"there is a divinity which shapes":* Earl Sparling, *Mystery Men of Wall Street: The Powers Behind the Markets* (Blue Ribbon Books, 1930), p. 208.

185 *"something big and really worthwhile"*: Letter from John J. Raskob to Louis Kaufman, August 28, 1929, John Jakob Raskob Papers at the Hagley Museum and Library (Wilmington, Delaware).

185 *"a small town boy's idea"*: "Reminiscences of Eddie Dowling" in the Columbia University Oral History Research Office Collection, Columbia University (New York, NY).

185 *"Eddie, I could cry"*: Ibid.

186 *One account had Raskob*: Thomas and Morgan-Witts, *The Day the Bubble Burst*, p. 167.

187 *"what the poor are able to achieve in America"*: Benjamin G. Raskob, Patsy R. Bremer, and Mary Louise ("Boo") Duffy, personal interview.

187 *"Gentleman, this is part of what"*: Thomas and Morgan-Witts, *The Day the Bubble Burst*, p. 318.

188 *The location of the proposed Empire State*: John Tauranac, *The Empire State Building: The Making of a Landmark* (Scribner's, 1995), pp. 134–35.

188 *"Gentleman, stand back while I start"*: "Waldorf Razing Started by Smith," *New York Evening Post* (October 1, 1929).

CHAPTER 13

190 *"New York is the San Gimignano"*: Thomas Van Leeuwen, *The Skyward Trend of Thought: Five Essays on the Metaphysics of the American Skyscraper* (AHA Books, 1986).

190 *In early October, Severance drove down*: Faith Severance Hackl Stewart, personal interview.

190 *"vertical coffin"*: Chester Morrison, "Bold Post Climber Explores Bank of Manhattan Peak," *New York Evening Post* (December 26, 1929).

192 *She knew this kind of promise*: Faith Severance Hackl Stewart, personal interview.

192 *The pride Severance felt*: Ibid.

192 *"a few feet of stone that bears"*: online article (http://www.aboutfamouspeople. com/article1145.html).

193 *"King of Skyscrapers"*: "Bank Skyscraper to Rise 925 Feet," *New York Evening Post* (October 2, 1929).

194 *"Desire for height supremacy has no part"*: Gustav Zismer, "The 100-Story Building Looms," *New York Sun* (October 4, 1929).

194 *At least Lefcourt suggested*: "105-Story Tower Planned at Broadway," *New York Herald Tribune* (October 4, 1929).

194 *He didn't have to wait long*: "150-Story Super-Skyscraper," *New York Herald Tribune* (October 6, 1929).

194 *Skyscrapers had plenty of detractors*: Stanley Peter Andersen, *American Ikon:*

Response to the Skyscraper, 1875–1934 (University of Michigan, Ph.D. disser-
tation, 1960); Arnold L. Lehman, *The New York Skyscraper: A History of Its
Development, 1870–1939* (Yale University, Ph.D. dissertation, 1974); Isabelle
Jeanne Gournay, *France Discovers America, 1917–1939, French Writings on
American Architecture* (Yale University, 1989).

195 *"feared for the angels in flight":* "150-Story Skyscraper Will Revolutionize,"
New York Herald Tribune (October 13, 1929).

195 *"They seem to be springing up":* Kenneth Murchison, "Thousand Footers,"
The Architect (November 1929).

195 *In Los Angeles, plans were under consideration:* "Los Angeles to Have
Airport," *Evening Telegram* (November 16, 1929).

195 *"How long will it be before":* "An Architectural Dream," *New York Times*
(February 11, 1929).

196 *"the tallest building in the world":* "Chrysler Building Now Tallest Edifice,"
New York Times (October 16, 1929).

196 *"It was manifestly impossible to assemble":* William Van Alen, "The Structure
and Metal Work of the Chrysler Building," *The Architectural Forum* (October
1930).

197 *Each section was made up of stacks:* "Steel Erection Problems on a 1,000
Foot Building," *Engineering News Record* (January 28, 1930).

197 *Van Alen grabbed a menu:* "Note Cast from Ship Drifts to Scotland," *New York
Times* (January 30, 1932).

197 *Another example of Van Alen's engineering:* "Automobiles in Architecture—
Row of Motors Cars Placed in Design of Chrysler Tower," *New York Sun*
(January 1930).

198 *Squire, Van Alen's younger cousin:* William Edwin Squire Jr., personal interview.

198 *"great tower . . . improves steadily as it progresses":* T-Square, "Skyline," *New
Yorker* (October 12, 1929).

198 *"seems to me better than nearly":* Francis Swales, "Draftsmanship and
Architecture, V, as exemplified by the work of William Van Alen," *Pencil
Points* (August 1929).

CHAPTER 14

199 *"The architect examined his plans":* Kenneth Murchison, "The Chrysler
Building as I See It," *The American Architect* (September 1930).

199 *"When you get a guy down":* Christopher Gray, "A Race for the Skies, Lost by
a Spire," *New York Times* (November 15, 1992).

200 *"Even in building a dog house":* Paul Starrett, *Changing the Skyline*
(Whittlesey House, 1938), p. 178.

200 *"will rise to a height of"*: Raymond Jones, "Our New Main Office to Be World's Tallest Building," *Manhattan Family* (October 1930).

200 *The article featured photographs:* "New Skyscraper Race Is Won by The Bank of The Manhattan Company," *New York Telegram* (October 18, 1929).

201 *"Because of pyramiding in the upper floors"*: "Denies Altering Plans for Tallest Building," *New York Times* (October 20, 1929).

201 *"the very limit of allowable error"*: Colonel W. A. Starrett, *Skyscrapers and the Men Who Build Them* (Charles Scribner's Sons, 1928), p. 64.

202 *"definitely established"*: J. P. Lohman, "Speaking of Real Estate," *New York American* (October 22, 1929).

202 *As for the Chrysler Building:* Ibid.

203 *The unease that hung over Wall Street's brokers: New York Evening Post* (October 22, 1929).

203 *Governor Smith presented Starrett Brothers':* Memorandum of Information Desired from John J. Raskob as to Empire State Building, John Jakob Raskob Papers at the Hagley Museum and Library (Wilmington, Delaware).

203 *"the biggest and the highest building"*: Theodore James, Jr., *The Empire State Building* (Harper & Row, 1975).

203 *For "practical purposes"*: Letter from Hamilton Weber to Robert C. Brown October 21, 1929, John Jakob Raskob Papers at the Hagley Museum and Library (Wilmington, Delaware).

204 *"How high can you make it"*: Glenn Fowler, "Tall Lady Is Gainly and Gainful at 40," *New York Times* (May 9, 1971).

204 *"would have been fine"*: "RHS—The Life of Richmond Harold Shreve" (August 1, 1984); Thomas Shreve, email interview.

204 *"he was afraid that the day"*: "Ability and Team-Work Are Features of the Crew Which Built Empire State," *World-Telegram* (February 18, 1938).

205 *"heavy black pencil long hair"*: R. H. Shreve, "The Empire State Building Organization," *The Architectural Forum* (June 1930).

205 *"The program was short enough"*: William Lamb, "The Empire State Building—The General Design," *Architectural Forum* (January 1931).

205 *"Well, there's one thing"*: Theodore James, Jr., *The Empire State Building* (Harper & Row, 1975).

206 *Lamb put away his fifteenth scheme:* Lamb, "The Empire State Building."

206 *Just in case, they would leave:* Letter from Alfred Smith to Mr. Norton, Comptroller of Metropolitan Life Insurance Company, November 26, 1929, John Jakob Raskob Papers at the Hagley Museum and Library (Wilmington, Delaware).

207 *"It is fortunate that up to this time"*: Matlack Price, "A Renaissance in Commercial Architecture," *Architectural Record* (May 1912).

207 *On October 23, 1929:* The date of the erection of the finial spire has been an

item of conjecture for decades. Many believed it was raised in late November 1929 after The Manhattan Company Building had completed its steel work. The earliest newspaper photograph of the finial spire was printed in the November 3, 1929, gravure edition of the *New York World*. Studies of New York newspapers prior to October 23, 1929, do not reveal the spire. That narrows the window of when the spire was raised. In 2002, Princeton Architectural Press published *The Chrysler Building* by David Stravitz, which includes a construction photograph of the raised spire stamped with the date October 23, 1929. Given all of the evidence, this is the most likely date.

208 *Down on the street:* "Rainstorm and 52-Mile Gales Batter City," *New York Times* (October 23, 1929).

208 *"elongated packing boxes":* "Obituary—Thomas Hastings," *New York Times* (October 23, 1929).

208 *"fascinating visions of the fantastically":* Walter P. Chrysler in collaboration with Boyden Sparkes, *Life of an American Workman* (Dodd, Mead & Company, 1950), p. 123.

208 *"If the elevator cabs travel less":* Ibid., p. 129.

209 *The five sections of the vertex:* "Steel Erection Problems on a 1,000 Foot Building," *Engineering News Record* (January 28, 1930).

209 *The men, however, had to erect:* F. D. McHugh, "Manhattan's Mightiest 'Minaret,'" *Scientific American* (April 1930).

210 *Only the construction photographers:* David Stravitz, *The Chrysler Building* (Princeton Architectural Press, 2002).

210 *"watching it from Fifth Avenue":* Murchison, "The Chrysler Building."

210 *"butterfly from its cocoon":* Ibid.

211 *"We'll lift the thing up":* Ibid.

211 *The only race chronicled:* New York *Evening Post* (October 23, 1929).

212 *"cohune palms, giant mahoganies":* "Mayans Reared First Skyscraper," *New York World* (October 27, 1929).

CHAPTER 15

213 *"Prudent investors are now buying":* New York Times (October 30, 1929).

213 *"I can only cry out":* Ric Burns and James Sanders, *New York: An Illustrated History* (Knopf, 1999), p. 376.

214 *"I need to know the time":* Gordon Thomas and Max Morgan-Witts, *The Day the Bubble Burst: A Social History of the Wall Street Crash of 1929* (Doubleday, 1979), pp. 352–53.

214 *"People just stood there":* William Klingaman, *1929: The Year of the Great Crash* (Harper & Row, 1989), pp. 262–63.

214 *"There they were, walking"*: Ibid., p. 265.

215 *"Boys, you can forget"*: Arnold Shaw, *The Jazz Age: Popular Music in the 1920s* (Oxford University Press, 1987), p. 225.

215 *A market tailspin jeopardized:* Thomas and Morgan-Witts, *The Day the Bubble Burst*, pp. 370–71.

215 *At 1:30, the New York Stock Exchange's:* Klingaman, *1929*, p. 267.

216 *Unfortunately, the worst hadn't yet occurred:* John Brooks, *Once in Golconda: A True Drama of Wall Street 1920–1938* (W. W. Norton & Company, 1969), p. 118.

216 *In offices across the city Tuesday morning:* New York Times (October 29–30, 1929).

216 *"false, vicious, wholly unwarranted"*: Klingaman, *1929*, p. 263.

217 *W. B. Foshay, who financed the tallest:* "Foshay Bankrupt," *New York World* (November 2, 1929).

217 *One of his closest friends:* "James J. Riordan Ends His Life," *Evening Telegram* (November 9, 1929); "Riordan at 48 Credited with Midas Touch," *New York Herald Tribune* (November 10, 1929); "News Is Kept Secret," *New York Herald Tribune* (November 11, 1929).

218 *"If he'd been discovered"*: "Reminiscences of Eddie Dowling" in the Columbia University Oral History Research Office Collection, Columbia University (New York, NY).

218 *The only photograph of the topped-out:* "The World's Tallest Building," *New York World* (November 3, 1929).

219 *The granite fell clear:* "Half-ton Block Crashes from 70-Story Bank," *New York Herald Tribune* (November 13, 1929); "Two Hurt in Wall Street," *New York Times* (November 13, 1929); "Big Stone Falls in Wall Street," *New York Sun* (November 12, 1929); "Falling Stone Perils Wall Street Throng," *Evening Telegram* (November 12, 1929).

221 *"This is the story"*: Allen Beals, "Daily Building Reports," *Architects' Weekly Building Material Price Supplement* (November 16, 1929).

222 *"Architects' Race Jostles the Moon"*: New York Evening Post (November 18, 1929).

222 *"Chrysler Tower Wins Sky Race"*: New York Herald Tribune (November 18, 1929).

222 *"America is vindicated"*: "The Race Upward," *New York Herald Tribune* (November 23, 1929).

222 *Even cartoonists took a turn:* "Continued Stories," *New York World* (November 19, 1929).

223 *"the tallest usable floor"*: Faith Severance Hackl Stewart, personal interview.

223 *One afternoon, while journalists:* David Michaelis, "77 Stories—The Secret Life of a Skyscraper," *Manhattan, Inc.* (June 1986). [Note: this scene is

based on a photograph referred to in Michaelis's article where Van Alen
and Chrysler are photographed on top of the Chrysler Building. Many of
the details referred to in the experience of the climb and the comparison to
20,000 automobiles were also sourced from his fine article.]

225 *"natural and logical development of the tower"*: William Van Alen, "Architect
Finds New Designs in Frame of Steel," *New York Herald Tribune* (September 7,
1930).

225 *"With all the surfaces of this spire"*: "Automobiles in Architecture—Row of
Motors Cars Placed in Design of Chrysler Tower," *New York Sun* (January
1930).

225 *"rusticated stone work, belt courses"*: William Van Alen, "Architect Finds New
Designs in Frame of Steel."

225 *"very bold in outline form"*: William Van Alen, "The Structure and Metal
Work of the Chrysler Building," *The Architectural Forum* (October 1930).

226 *"How shall we proclaim"*: Robert Twombly, *Louis Sullivan: His Life and Work*
(Viking, 1986).

226 *"single figure the naked torso of a man"*: Chrysler Tower Corporation, *The
Chrysler Building* (Chrysler Tower Corporation, 1930), p. 15.

227 *For Chrysler, his skyscraper best*: Louis Ralston, "The Engineer's Problems in
Tall Buildings," *The Architectural Forum* (June 1930).

227 *"Heavenward spring the spires"*: Chrysler Tower Corporation, *The Chrysler
Building*, p. 3.

CHAPTER 16

228 *"If the race itself"*: H. I. Brock, "New York Completes Highest Office
Buildings in All the World," *New York Times Magazine* (February 9, 1930).

228 *"[After hearing of another record-breaking skyscraper]"*: Kenneth Murchison,
"150-Story Super Skyscraper," *The Architect* (November 1929).

229 *"We bought that property"*: "New Plans for Tallest Skyscraper," *New York Sun*
(November 18, 1929).

229 *"The determination of the height"*: Ibid.

230 *"from the brown derby of Oliver Street"*: "Smith to Break Height Record in
1,100-Ft Tower," *New York Herald Tribune* (November 20, 1929).

230 *"This building will be a monument"*: Ibid.

232 *"Smith to Break Height Record"*: *New York Herald Tribune* (November 20,
1929).

232 *"settled, at least for the present"*: "Skyscraper Leads Sea-Land Contest," *New
York Evening Post* (November 23, 1929).

232 *"Make believe that you are 8 feet up"*: Margaret Bourke-White, *A Portrait of
Myself* (Simon & Schuster, 1963), pp. 76–78.

232 *As for the danger:* Question and Answer Interview in Margaret Bourke-White Papers at Department of Special Collections, Syracuse University Library (Syracuse, New York).

232 *"to steeple jack for Mr. Chrysler":* Letter from Margaret Bourke-White to Parker Lloyd-Smith, December 6, 1929, Margaret Bourke-White Papers at Department of Special Collections, Syracuse University Library (Syracuse, New York).

233 *"Industry is huge and vital":* Typescript Notes in Margaret Bourke-White Papers at Department of Special Collections, Syracuse University Library (Syracuse, New York).

233 *"In this battle of the skyscrapers":* Bourke-White, *A Portrait of Myself,* pp. 76–77.

233 *Ivy Lee had cut his teeth:* Gene Fowler, *Skyline: A Reporter's Reminiscence of the 1920s* (Viking Press, 1961), p. 194.

234 *"special staff of brokers, canvassers":* Press Releases, December 15, 1929, and March 13, 1930, in Ivy L. Lee Papers, Seeley G. Mudd Manuscript Library, Princeton University Library (Princeton, New Jersey).

234 *"With three men holding the tripod":* Vicki Goldberg, *Margaret Bourke-White: A Biography* (Harper & Row, 1986), p. 114.

235 *"was worried that Walter Chrysler":* Glenn Fowler, "Tall Lady Is Gainly and Gainful at 40," *New York Times* (May 9, 1971).

235 *"You see, this spike":* A. S. Foster, "Here and There and This and That," *Pencil Points* (1930).

235 *"What this building needs is a hat":* Theodore James, Jr., *The Empire State Building* (Harper & Row, 1975).

236 *If there was one thing that challenged:* Ann Douglas, *Terrible Honesty: Mongrel Manhattan in the 1920s* (Farrar, Straus, and Giroux, 1995), pp. 434–84; Joseph J. Corn, *The Winged Gospel: America's Romance with Aviation, 1900–1950* (Oxford University Press, 1983).

236 *In Akron, Ohio, the Goodyear Zeppelin Company:* "Smith Plans Zeppelin Mast Atop 1,100 Foot New Building," *New York Herald Tribune* (December 12, 1929).

236 *As a way to win the skyscraper race:* John Tauranac, *The Empire State Building: The Making of a Landmark* (Scribner's, 1995), p. 187.

237 *"the Little Nemo school of architecture":* Theodore James, Jr., *The Empire State Building.*

237 *"Hear No Dirigible—See No Dirigible":* R. H. Shreve, *Travel Log* (1931–32).

237 *"The directors of Empire State":* "Smith Plans Zeppelin Mast Atop 1,100 Foot New Building," *New York Herald Tribune* (December 12, 1929).

238 *"I am interested in constructing buildings":* "Smith in Capital; Explains Air Mast," *New York Evening Post* (December 13, 1929).

238 *"if it was bein' put up":* Empire State Building Scrapbooks, Empire State

Building Archive, Avery Drawings and Archives, Avery Architectural and Fine Arts Library, Columbia University (New York, NY), no source on newspaper article.

238 *"definitely as the tallest"*: Press Release, December 16, 1929, in Ivy L. Lee Papers, Seeley G. Mudd Manuscript Library, Princeton University Library (Princeton, New Jersey).

239 *"she's the most beautiful"*: Faith Hackl Ward, telephone interview.

239 *"the battle for the possession"*: Andrew Eken, "The Ultimate in Skyscrapers," *Scientific American* (May 1931).

239 *In secret they continued*: "Bank of Manhattan Tower Not Being Lifted," *New York Herald Tribune* (March 14, 1930).

239 *"Chrysler's only sixty-eight stories"*: Chester Morrison, "Bold Post Climber Explores Bank of Manhattan Peak," *New York Evening Post* (December 26, 1929).

240 *"This skyscraper was built"*: David Bareuther, "Japanese Designs Great Towers," *New York Sun* (January 11, 1930).

240 *"the great pyramid of Cheops"*: O. F. Semsch, ed., *A History of the Singer Building Construction: Its Progress from Foundation to Flag Pole* (Shumway & Beattie, 1908), p. 9.

240 *After that, the Singer Building*: Anthony Robins, "The Continuing Saga of the Tallest Building in the World," *Architectural Record* (January 1987).

CHAPTER 17

241 *"I feel like my own boss"*: Vicki Goldberg, *Margaret Bourke-White: A Biography* (Harper & Row, 1986), p. 115.

241 *"I descended fifty steps"*: Margaret Bourke-White, *A Portrait of Myself* (Simon & Schuster, 1963), p. 77.

242 *"Box Scores of the Havoc"*: *Variety* (November 6, 1929).

242 *"Sing it for the corpses"*: William Klingaman, *1929: The Year of the Great Crash* (Harper & Row, 1989), p. 270.

242 *"Everywhere was the atmosphere"*: Arnold Shaw, *The Jazz Age: Popular Music in the 1920s* (Oxford University Press, 1987), pp. 285–86.

242 *Attendance spiked at the long-shunned*: John Brooks, *Once in Golconda: A True Drama of Wall Street 1920–1938* (W. W. Norton & Company, 1969), pp. 116–29.

243 *"the newest New York became"*: Elmer Davis, "Too Stately Mansions," *New Republic* (June 1, 1932).

243 *"we were about five years"*: "Realty Notes," *New York Sun* (July 19, 1930).

243 *Even after several friends sat him*: Benjamin G. Raskob, Patsy R. Bremer, and Mary Louise ("Boo") Duffy, personal interview.

244 *"I don't know whether"*: Bourke-White, *A Portrait of Myself*, p. 77.

244 *Those who spoke of the Empire State:* Empire State, Inc., *Empire State: A History* (Selecting Printing Company, 1931).

244 *Raskob secured the money:* Empire State, Inc., "Resolutions for Board of Directors, March 11, 1930," in John Jakob Raskob Papers at the Hagley Museum and Library (Wilmington, Delaware).

245 *"I was to build the world's tallest"*: Paul Starrett, *Changing the Skyline* (Whittlesey House, 1938), pp. 3–14; John Taurenac, *The Empire State Building: The Making of a Landmark* (Scribner's, 1995), p. 284.

245 *With seventeen oxyacetylene torches and five derricks:* Carol Willis, *Building the Empire State* (W. W. Norton, New York, 1998), Notes from the Construction of the Empire State.

246 *"In this Box Lies Adolph Ochs"*: Thomas Shreve, email interview.

246 *"the powers of Aladdin's genii"*: R. H. Shreve, "The Economic Design of Office Buildings," *Architectural Forum* (1931).

246 *In reality, Shreve worked out:* Thomas Shreve, email interview.

247 *"They knew when we would need"*: R. B. Shreve, "RHS—The Life of Richmond Harold Shreve" (August 1, 1984).

247 *"Stone of this size"*: David Bareuther, "Unique Brilliance for New Tower," *New York Sun* (March 4, 1930).

248 *"produce a blaze of light"*: Ibid.

248 *"so far above the earth"*: *New York Evening Post* (March 1, 1930).

248 *"It is the first time"*: "Lauds Safety Record," *New York Times* (January 19, 1930).

249 *"You men are responsible"*: "Chrysler Gives Credit to Men," *New York Telegram* (January 24, 1930).

249 *In press statements:* Press Releases, January 24, 1930, April 13, 1930, and July 26, 193, in Ivy L. Lee Papers, Seeley G. Mudd Manuscript Library, Princeton University Library (Princeton, New Jersey).

249 *"Generally speaking, one thinks"*: Yasuo Matsui, "Architect Explains Tower Height," *New York Sun* (March 1, 1930).

250 *"No, the rumor is baseless"*: "Manhattan Bank Men Deny Plan to Top Chrysler Peak," *New York Evening Post* (March 12, 1930).

251 *"there wasn't going to be any celebration"*: "New Quarters Opening," *Manhattan Family* (May–June 1930).

252 *Bringing everything together was:* Chrysler Tower Corporation, *The Chrysler Building* (Chrysler Tower Corporation, 1930), p. 15.

252 *Each elevator cab was unique:* Ibid., pp. 10–21.

253 *"The king for a day"*: "Chrysler's Spire Formally Opened," *New York World* (May 27, 1930).

CHAPTER 18

254 *"Never before in the history"*: Paul Starrett, *Changing the Skyline* (Whittlesey House, 1938), pp. 295–96.

255 *On April 29, 1930, they started:* Empire State Building Scrapbooks, Empire State Building Archive, Avery Drawings and Archives, Avery Architectural and Fine Arts Library, Columbia University (New York, NY), no source on newspaper article (April 29–May 5, 1930).

255 *To compete with Margaret Bourke-White:* John Taurenac, *The Empire State Building: The Making of a Landmark* (Scribner's, 1995), pp. 279–95.

255 *Not yet satisfied, the major players:* Empire State Building Scrapbooks (1930–1931).

256 *"The prestige of having the tallest"*: Press Release—July 24, 1930, in Ivy L. Lee Papers, Seeley G. Mudd Manuscript Library, Princeton University Library (Princeton, New Jersey).

256 *"The world's tallest structure"*: Press Release—July 26, 1930, in Ivy L. Lee Papers, Seeley G. Mudd Manuscript Library, Princeton University Library (Princeton, New Jersey).

256 *"During the daytime the sun"*: Press Release—July 31, 1930, in Ivy L. Lee Papers, Seeley G. Mudd Manuscript Library, Princeton University Library (Princeton, New Jersey).

256 *"Temporarily is the tallest"*: Empire State Building Scrapbooks (July 1930).

257 *The Empire State rose four and one-half stories:* Carol Willis, *Building the Empire State* (W. W. Norton, New York, 1998), pp. 11–30.

257 *August 14 marked the busiest:* Carol Willis, *Building the Empire State* (W. W. Norton, New York, 1998), Notes from the Construction of the Empire State.

259 *When Richmond Shreve was not chatting:* Thomas Shreve, email interview.

259 *"Windows, spandrels, steel mullions"*: William Lamb, "The Empire State Building—The General Design," *Architectural Forum* (January 1931).

259 *The pace on the Empire State:* Carol Willis, *Building the Empire State* (W. W. Norton, New York, 1998), p. 28.

260 *"Following one of the trucks"*: C. G. Poore, "Greatest Skyscraper," *New York Times* (July 27, 1930).

260 *"If all the materials"*: Empire State, Inc., *Empire State: A History* (Selecting Printing Company, 1931).

261 *"it will automatically keep glittering"*: "Chrysler Spire Looks on Town," *New York Sun* (August 4, 1930).

261 *He wanted to be paid:* Supreme Court of the State of New York, "William Van Alen versus Cooper Union for the Advancement of Science and Art, Reylex Corporation, W.P. Chrysler Building Corporation and National Surety Company," 1930–31 (New York, NY).

262 *"a lesson to other architects"*: "Chrysler Architect Sues Owner," *The American Architect* (January 1930).

CHAPTER 19

263 *"Mightiest peak of New York's"*: Empire State, Inc., *Empire State: A History* (Selecting Printing Company, 1931).

263 *"Eighty years ago, a very short time"*: Empire State Building Scrapbooks (September 1930), no source.

264 *"the black skeleton of a new mammoth"*: Empire State Building Scrapbooks (August 8, 1930), no source. [Note: Raskob later decided to have his office on the 80th floor.]

264 *"flag of triumph"*: John Taurenac, *The Empire State Building: The Making of a Landmark* (Scribner's, 1995), p. 212.

264 *"You should have heard"*: Ibid., p. 213.

265 *Photographs of the flag raising*: Empire State Building Scrapbooks (September–December 1931).

265 *The six men who died*: Carol Willis, *Building the Empire State* (W. W. Norton, New York, 1998), Notes from the Construction of the Empire State. [Note: Despite the heroic framing of their deaths, the details of the unfortunate events were given less attention. One tumbled down an elevator shaft; one fell from a scaffold; one was hit by a hoist; one stepped into an area where they were blasting; and the sixth's death went unrecorded.]

265 *"A King and a Queen Meet"*: Empire State Building Scrapbooks (October 9, 1930), no source.

265 *On November 18, the last beams*: "Topping Out the Empire State Building," *Engineering News Record* (January 22, 1931).

266 *Al Smith stood next to his two grandchildren*: Taurenac, *The Empire State Building*, pp. 227–57; Theodore James, Jr., *The Empire State Building* (Harper & Row, 1975); Empire State Building Scrapbooks (May–June 1930). [Note: This scene draws upon these two books and scores of newspaper articles in the scrapbooks.]

267 *"It belongs to the kids"*: Walter P. Chrysler in collaboration with Boyden Sparkes, *Life of an American Workman* (Dodd, Mead & Company, 1950), p. 208.

EPILOGUE

273 *"From the ruins, lonely"*: Ric Burns and James Sanders, *New York: An Illustrated History* (Knopf, 1999), p. 386.

274 *It was one of the city's great social events*: "Motif of Fantasie to Predominate

at Beaux-Arts Ball," *New York Herald Tribune* (January 4, 1931); Christopher Gray, "An Architect Called the Ziegfeld of His Profession," *New York Times* (March 22, 1998).

275 *"it is distinctly a stunt design"*: T-Square, "The Skyline," *New Yorker* (July 12, 1930).

275 *The* Architectural Forum *offered*: Eugene Clute, "The Chrysler Building, New York," *The Architectural Forum* (October 1930).

275 *"it embodies no compelling"*: Douglas Haskell, "Architecture—Chrysler's Pretty Bauble," *Nation* (October 22, 1930).

275 *Curiously, it was Severance's suit*: Robert A. M. Stern, Gregory Gilmartin, and John Montague Massengale, *New York 1930: Architecture and Urbanism Between Two World Wars* (Rizzoli, 1987), p. 8.

276 *"provided everything for their customers"*: William E. Leuchtenburg, *The Perils of Prosperity, 1914–32* (University of Chicago Press, 1958), pp. 246–47.

276 *Over a million men in New York*: Paul Johnson, *A History of the American People* (Weidenfeld & Nicolson, 1997), pp. 727–45; William Klingaman, *1929: The Year of the Great Crash* (Harper & Row, 1989), pp. 320–27.

277 *"It is becoming clear"*: Klingaman, *1929*, p. 333.

277 *Not surprisingly, the construction*: John Tauranac, *The Empire State Building: The Making of a Landmark* (Scribner's, 1995), pp. 268–73.

277 *"only for one day"*: Faith Severance Hackl Stewart, personal interview.

277 *"a promise, a hope, a gambler's optimism"*: *New Republic* (July 8, 1931).

277 *"From the stories [I read]"*: R. H. Shreve, *Travel Log* (1931–32).

278 *"So there they stand"*: "Too Stately Mansions," *New Republic* (June 1, 1932).

278 *For publicity purposes, Al Smith*: Tauranac, *The Empire State Building*, pp. 267–311; Matthew Josephson and Hannah Josephson, *Al Smith: Hero of the Cities* (Houghton Mifflin Company, 1969), pp. 445–52.

279 *"a victim of overwork"*: Paul Starrett, *Changing the Skyline* (Whittlesey House, 1938).

280 *"with such clean beauty"*: Tauranac, *The Empire State Building*, p. 17.

280 *"Poets in Steel"*: John Fistere, "Poets in Steel," *Vanity Fair* (December 1931).

280 *"it was the first time"*: R. B. Shreve, "RHS—The Life of Richmond Harold Shreve" (August 1, 1984).

281 *"John [Raskob] should be set up"*: Letter from Pierre S. du Pont to General Hugh Drum, May 21, 1948, Pierre S. du Pont Papers at the Hagley Museum and Library (Wilmington, Delaware).

281 *"Go ahead and do things"*: online article (www.rfca.org).

281 *In the crash, the boy wonder*: Maggie Ohrstrom Bryant, telephone interview; Thomas Sutton, personal interview.

282 *"less than we paid"*: 40 Wall Street, Inc., "Report as of June 30, 1956," JPMorgan Chase Archives (1956).

282 *Chrysler maintained control of his skyscraper:* Chrysler Corporation, *The Story of an American Company* (Chrysler Corporation: Department of Public Relations, 1955), pp. 26–27; Vincent Curcio, *Chrysler: The Life and Times of an Automotive Genius* (Oxford University Press, 2000), pp. 603–65.

283 *Like Shreve Lamb & Harmon, Severance designed:* Faith Severance Hackl Stewart, personal interview.

284 *"Dear Faith":* Letter from Bill Gowen to Faith Griswold Hackl, September 4, 1941, courtesy of George Hackl.

284 *"unloved and unmourned":* Letter from Chesley Bonestell to Bill Estler, no date, courtesy of Ron Miller.

284 *Desperate for someone to accept:* William Edwin Squire Jr., personal interview.

285 *"The ornamental treatment":* Lewis Mumford, "Notes on Modern Architecture," *New Republic* (March 18, 1931).

285 *On May 20, 1946, an army transport:* Jay Shockley, *Manhattan Company Building* (Landmarks Preservation Commission, 1995).

286 *Decades after the raising of the Chrysler:* David Michaelis, "77 Stories—The Secret Life of a Skyscraper," *Manhattan, Inc.* (June 1986)

286 *On Saturday morning, July 28, 1945:* Taurenac, *The Empire State Building*, pp. 317–31.

288 *"Remember that our sons":* Paul Starrett, *Changing the Skyline*, p. 319.

289 *"the spirit of men working":* Walter Chrysler, "Skyscrapers and Pyramids," *American Legion Monthly* (1930).

Bibliography

SELECTED BOOKS

Abramson, Daniel, *Skyscraper Rivals: The AIG Building and the Architecture of Wall Street* (Princeton Architectural Press, 2001)

Adams, James Truslow, *The Epic of America* (Little, Brown, & Company, 1931)

Allen, Frederick Lewis, *Only Yesterday: An Informal History of the Nineteen-Twenties* (Harper & Row, 1931)

Allen, Frederick Lewis, *Since Yesterday: The Nineteen-Thirties in America* (Harper & Brothers Publishers, 1940)

Ambrose, Stephen, *Nothing Like It in the World: The Men Who Built the Transcontinental Railroad, 1863–69* (Simon & Schuster, 2000)

Andersen, Stanley Peter, *American Ikon: Response to the Skyscraper, 1875–1934* (University of Michigan, Ph.D. dissertation, 1960)

Bacon, Mardges, *Ernest Flagg: Beaux-Arts Architect and Urban Reformer* (MIT Press, 1968)

Baker, Paul R., *Richard Morris Hunt* (MIT Press, 1980)

——, *Stanny: The Gilded Life of Stanford White* (Free Press, 1989)

Bank of the Manhattan Company, *Manna-hatin: The Story of New York* (Ira J. Friedman, Inc., 1929)

Beach, W. W., *The Supervision of Construction* (Charles Scribner's Sons, 1937)

Benson, Robert Alan, *Douglas Putnam Haskell (1899–1979): The Early Critical Writings* (University of Michigan, 1987)

Blake, Curtis Channing, *The Architecture of Carrère & Hastings* (Columbia University, Ph.D. dissertation, 1976)

Bletter, Rosemarie Haag, and Cervin Robinson, *Skyscraper Style: Art Deco New York* (Oxford University Press, 1975)

Bourke-White, Margaret, *A Portrait of Myself* (Simon & Schuster, 1963)

Brierly, J. Ernest, *The Streets of Old New York* (Hastings House, 1953)

Brooks, John, *Once in Golconda: A True Drama of Wall Street 1920–1938* (W. W. Norton & Company, 1969)

Brown, Wheelock, Harris, Vought & Company, *Chrysler Building: 42nd Street and Lexington Avenue* (Chrysler Tower Corporation, 1930)

Burchard, John, and Albert Bush-Brown, *The Architecture of America: A Social and Cultural History* (Little, Brown & Company, 1961)

Burns, Ric, and James Sanders, *New York: An Illustrated History* (Knopf, 1999)

Bush-Brown, Harold, *Beaux Arts to Bauhaus and Beyond: An Architect's Perspective* (Whitney Library of Design, 1976)

Chase, W. Parker, *New York, The Wonder City* (Wonder City Publishing Company, 1932)

Chrysler Corporation, *The Story of an American Company* (Chrysler Corporation: Department of Public Relations, 1955)

Chrysler Tower Corporation, *The Chrysler Building* (Chrysler Tower Corporation, 1930)

Chrysler, Walter P. in collaboration with Boyden Sparkes, *Life of an American Workman* (Dodd, Mead & Company, 1950)

Cochran, Edwin, *The Cathedral of Commerce* (Broadway Park Place Company, 1916)

Corn, Joseph J., *The Winged Gospel: America's Romance with Aviation, 1900–1950* (Oxford University Press, 1983)

Cram, Ralph Adams, *My Life in Architecture* (Little, Brown, and Company, 1936)

Curcio, Vincent, *Chrysler: The Life and Times of an Automotive Genius* (Oxford University Press, 2000)

Di Donato, Pietro, *Christ in Concrete* (Signet Classic, 1939)

Douglas, Ann, *Terrible Honesty: Mongrel Manhattan in the 1920s* (Farrar, Straus, and Giroux, 1995)

Douglas, George H., *Skyscrapers: A Social History of the Very Tall Building in America* (McFarland & Company, 1996)

Einbinder, Harvey, *An American Genius: Frank Lloyd Wright* (Philosophical Library, 1986)

Eksteins, Modris, *Rites of Spring: the Great War and the Birth of the Modern Age* (Houghton Mifflin, 1989)

Ellis, Edward Robb, *The Epic of New York City* (Coward-McCann, 1966)

Emery, Edwin, and Henry Ladd Smith, *The Press and America* (Prentice-Hall, 1954)

Empire State, Inc., *Commemorating the Completion of Empire State* (1931)

———, *Empire State: A History* (Selecting Printing Company, 1931)

Federal Writers' Project of the Works Progress Administration in New York City, *The WPA Guide to New York City: A Comprehensive Guide to the Five Boroughs of the Metropolis—Manhattan, Brooklyn, the Bronx, Queens, and Richmond* (The New Press, 1992)

Fenske, Gail G., *The "Skyscraper Problem" and the City Beautiful: The Woolworth Building* (Arizona State University, Ph.D. dissertation, 1988)

Ferriss, Hugh, *The Metropolis of Tomorrow* (I. Washburn, 1929)

Fitzgerald, F. Scott, *The Crack-Up: with Other Uncollected Pieces*, edited by Edmund Wilson (New Directions, 1956)

Fowler, Gene, *Skyline: A Reporter's Reminiscence of the 1920s* (Viking Press, 1961)

Galbraith, John Kenneth, *The Great Crash: 1929* (Houghton Mifflin Company, 1988)

Geisst, Charles R., *Wall Street: A History* (Oxford University Press, 1997)

Gillen, Edmund Vincent, *Beaux-Arts Architecture in New York* (Dover Publications, 1988)

Goldberg, Vicki, *Margaret Bourke-White: A Biography* (Harper & Row, 1986)

Goldberger, Paul, *The Skyscraper* (Knopf, 1981)

Goldman, Jonathan, *The Empire State Building Book* (St. Martin's Press, 1980)

Gordon, J. E., *Structure: Or, Why Things Don't Fall Down* (Plenum Press, 1978)

Gournay, Isabelle Jeanne, *France Discovers America, 1917–1939, French Writings on American Architecture* (Yale University, 1989)

Gray, Susan, ed., *Architects on Architects* (McGraw-Hill, 2001)

Handlin, Oscar, *Al Smith and His America* (Little, Brown and Company, 1958)

Harris, Neil, *Building Lives: Constructing Rites and Passages* (Yale University Press, 1999)

Hine, Thomas, *Burnham of Chicago: Architect and Planner* (Oxford University Press, 1979)

Horowitz, Louis, and Boyden Sparkes, *The Towers of New York: The Memoirs of a Master Builder* (Simon & Schuster, 1937)

Hughes, Robert, *The Shock of the New* (Knopf, 1981)

Huxtable, Ada Louis, *The Tall Building Artistically Reconsidered: The Search for a Skyscraper Style* (Pantheon Books, 1984)

James, Theodore, Jr., *The Empire State Building* (Harper & Row, 1975)

Jencks, Charles, *Skyscrapers—Skyprickers—Skycities* (Rizzoli, 1980)

Johnson, Paul, *A History of the American People* (Weidenfeld & Nicolson, 1997)

Josephson, Matthew and Hannah, *Al Smith: Hero of the Cities* (Houghton Mifflin Company, 1969)

Kahn, Ely Jacques, *A Building Goes Up* (Simon & Schuster, 1969)

King, Ross, *Brunelleschi's Dome: How a Renaissance Genius Reinvented Architecture* (Walker & Company, 2000)

Klingaman, William K., *1929: The Year of the Great Crash* (Harper & Row, 1989)

Koolhaas, Rem, *Delirious New York: A Retroactive Manifesto for Manhattan* (Oxford University Press, 1978)

Landau, Sarah Bradford, *Rise of the New York Skyscraper, 1865–1913* (Yale University Press, 1996)

Landmarks Preservation Commission, *Chrysler Building* (Landmarks Preservation Commission, 1978)

——, *Empire State Building* (Landmarks Preservation Commission, 1981)

Latimer, Margaret, *Two Cities: New York and Brooklyn the Year the Great Bridge Opened* (Brooklyn Educational and Cultural Alliance, 1983)

Lehman, Arnold L., *The New York Skyscraper: A History of Its Development, 1870–1939* (Yale University, Ph.D. dissertation, 1974)

Leighton, Isabel, ed., *The Aspirin Age, 1919–1941* (Simon & Schuster, 1949)

Lescaze, William, *On Being an Architect* (G. P. Putnam's Sons, 1942)

Leuchtenburg, William E., *The Perils of Prosperity, 1914–32* (University of Chicago Press, 1958)

Levinson, Leonard Louis, *Wall Street: A Pictorial History* (Ziff-Davis Publishing Company, 1961)

Matsui, Yasuo, *Skyscraper: Multiple Business Dwellings* (JPMorgan Chase Archives, 1930)

Mehrhoff, Arthur, *The Gateway Arch: Fact and Symbol* (Bowling Green State University Popular Press, 1992)

Messler, Norbert, *The Art Deco Skyscraper in New York* (Peter Lang, 1986)

Miller, Ron, and Frederick C. Durante, *The Art of Chesley Bonestell* (Sterling Publications, 2001)

Mizener, Arthur, *The Far Side of Paradise: A Biography of F. Scott Fitzgerald* (Houghton Mifflin Company, 1951)

Morgan, Marilyn Phelan, *An Icon Within an Icon: The Cloud Club in the Chrysler Building* (Columbia University, M.A. dissertation, 1994)

Morris, Edmund, *The Rise of Theodore Roosevelt* (Modern Library, 2001)

——, *Theodore Rex* (Random House, 2001)

Moses, Robert, *A Tribute to Governor Smith* (Simon & Schuster, 1962)

Mujica, Francisco, *History of the Skyscraper* (Archaeology & Architecture Press, 1930)

Nash, Eric P., *Manhattan Skyscrapers* (Princeton Architectural Press, 1999)

Noffsinger, James Philip, *The Influence of the Ecole des Beaux-Arts on the Architects of the United States* (Catholic University of America Press, Ph.D. dissertation, 1955)

O'Connor, Richard, *The First Hurrah: A Biography of Alfred E. Smith* (G. P. Putnam's Sons, 1970)

Pound, Arthur, *The Golden Earth: The Story of Manhattan's Landed Wealth* (Macmillan Company, 1935)

Reynolds, John B., *The Chrysler Building* (Chrysler Tower Corporation, 1930)

Roosevelt, Theodore, *The Works of Theodore Roosevelt* (Charles Scribner's Sons, 1923–26)

Ruttenbaum, Steven, *Mansions in the Clouds: The Skyscraper Palazzi of Emory Roth* (Balsam Press, 1986)

Saylor, Henry, *The AIA's First Hundred Years* (Octagon, 1957)

——, *The Beaux-Arts Boys on the Boulevard, or The Invasion of Paris in 1931* (New York, 1931)

Scully, Vincent, *American Architecture and Urbanism* (Praeger, 1969)

Secrest, Meryle, *Frank Lloyd Wright* (Knopf, 1992)

Severini, Lois, *The Architecture of Finance: Early Wall Street* (UMI Research Press, 1983)

Shachtman, Tom, *Skyscraper Dreams: The Great Real Estate Dynasties of New York* (Little, Brown & Company, 1991)

Shaw, Arnold, *The Jazz Age: Popular Music in the 1920s* (Oxford University Press, 1987)

Shultz, Earle, and Walter Simmons, *Offices in the Sky* (Bobbs-Merrill Company, 1959)

Silverman, Jonathan, *For the World to See* (Viking Press, 1983)

Slayton, Robert A., *Empire Statesman: The Rise and Redemption of Al Smith* (Free Press, 2001)

Snyder-Grenier, Ellen M., *Brooklyn! An Illustrated History* (Temple University Press, 1996)

Sparling, Earl, *Mystery Men of Wall Street: The Powers Behind the Markets* (Blue Ribbon Books, 1930)

Starrett, Paul, *Changing the Skyline* (Whittlesey House, 1938)

Starrett, Colonel W. A., *Skyscrapers and the Men Who Build Them* (Charles Scribner's Sons, 1928)

Stern, Robert A. M., *Pride of Place: Building the American Dream* (Houghton Mifflin, 1986)

Stern, Robert A. M., *Raymond Hood: Pragmatism and Poetics in the Waning of the Metropolitan Era* (Rizzoli, 1982)

Stern, Robert A. M., Gregory Gilmartin, and John Montague Massengale, *New York 1900: Metropolitan Architecture and Urbanism, 1890–1915* (Rizzoli, 1983)

——, Gregory Gilmartin, and John Montague Massengale, *New York 1930: Architecture and Urbanism Between Two World Wars* (Rizzoli, 1987)

Sullivan, Nell Jane Barnett, and David Kendall Martin, *A History of the Town of Chazy, Clinton County, New York* (Little Press, 1970)

Taurenac, John, *The Empire State Building: The Making of a Landmark* (Scribner's, 1995)

Taylor, William R., *In Pursuit of Gotham: Culture and Commerce in New York* (Oxford University Press, 1992)

Thomas, Dana L., *The Plungers and the Peacocks: An Update of the Classic History of the Stock Market* (William Morrow & Company, 1967)

Thomas, Gordon, and Max Morgan-Witts, *The Day the Bubble Burst: A Social History of the Wall Street Crash of 1929* (Doubleday, 1979)

Tuchman, Barbara, *The Guns of August* (Macmillan, 1962)

Turner, E. S., *The Shocking History of Advertising* (E. P. Dutton & Company, 1953)

Twombly, Robert, *Louis Sullivan: His Life and Work* (Viking, 1986)

Van Alen, Benjamin Taylor, *Genealogical History of the Van Alen Family* (Chicago, 1902)

Van Dyke, John C., *The New New York: A Commentary on the Place and People* (Macmillan, 1909)

Van Leeuwen, Thomas, *The Skyward Trend of Thought: Five Essays on the Metaphysics of the American Skyscraper* (AHA Books, 1986)

Vitruvius, *On Architecture*, edited and translated by Frank Granger (Harvard University Press, 1931)

Vlack, Don, *Art Deco Architecture in New York, 1920–1940* (Harper & Row, 1974)

Ward, James, *Architects in Practice, New York City, 1900–1940* (J&D Associates, 1989)

Warner, Emily Smith, and Hawthorne Daniel, *The Happy Warrior: A Biography of My Father, Alfred E. Smith* (Doubleday & Company, 1956)

Weingarten, Arthur, *The Sky Is Falling* (Grosset & Dunlap, 1977)

Willensky, Elliot, *When Brooklyn Was the World, 1920–1957* (Harmony Books, 1986)

Williamson, Roxanne Kuter, *American Architects and the Mechanics of Fame* (University of Texas Press, 1991)

Willis, Carol, *Form Follows Finance: Skyscrapers and Skylines in New York and Chicago* (Princeton Architectural Press, 1995)

——, ed., *Building the Empire State* (W. W. Norton, New York, 1998)

Wilson, Edmund, *The Shores of Light: A Literary Chronicle of the Twenties and Thirties* (Northeastern University Press, 1985)

Woods, James Playsted, *The Story of Advertising* (Ronald Press Company, 1958)

SELECTED MAGAZINE AND NEWSPAPER ARTICLES

William Van Alen

American Architect, "Chrysler Architect Sues Owner," January 1930.

The Architect, "A Selling Urge," December 1928, pp. 352–53.

Architectural Forum, "Forward House," 1933.

Boyd, John Taylor, "The Newer Fifth Avenue Retail Shop Fronts," *The Architectural Record*, June 1921.

Cret, Paul, "The Ecole des Beaux-Arts and Architectural Education," *American Society of Architectural Historians*, April 1941.

Gray, Christopher, "An Architect Called the 'Ziegfeld of His Profession,' " *New York Times*, March 22, 1998.

——, "Fast Food, Then and Now, On Stylish Fifth Avenue," *New York Times*, November 6, 1988.

New York Herald Tribune, "Beaux-Arts Ball Stages Midnight Pageant Friday," January 12, 1931.

——, "William Van Alen, 71 Dies," May 25, 1954.

New York Sun, "Architect to Build—William Van Alen Assembled Plot on Lexington Avenue," January 14, 1930.

——, "Automobiles in Architecture—Row of Motors Cars Placed in Design of Chrysler Tower," January 1930.

New York Times, "Building Design—Architect Deplores Use of Old Types in Steel Construction," March 22, 1931.

——, "Note Cast from Ship Drifts to Scotland," January 30, 1932.

Society of Beaux-Arts Architects, "Circular of Information Concerning the Paris Prize," 1912.

——, "Final Competition for the Fifth Paris Prize," 1908.

Solon, Leon, "The Passing of the Skyscraper Formula for Design," *The Architectural Record*, 1924, pp. 136–44.

Swales, Francis, "Master Draftsmen, VII, Emmanuel Louis Masqueray," *Pencil Points*, 1917, pp. 59–67.

——, "Master Draftsmen, XVIII, Cass Gilbert," *Pencil Points*, 1926, pp. 583–93.

——, "The Competition Extraordinary," *Pencil Points*, 1928, pp. 39–44.

——, "Draftsmanship and Architecture, V, as exemplified by the work of William Van Alen," *Pencil Points*, August 1929, pp. 515–27.

Van Alen, William, "Architect Finds New Designs in Frame of Steel," *New York Herald Tribune*, September 9, 1930.

Chrysler Building

The Architect, "They Do Say," May 1929, p. 222.

Bareuther, David, "Chrysler Building, Now Tallest in World, Steel Tops Woolworth," *New York Sun*, October 12, 1929.

Buildings and Building Management, "The Tallest Yet," June 16, 1930, pp. 47–53.

Clute, Eugene, "The Chrysler Building, New York," *The Architectural Forum*, October 1930, pp. 403–10.

Comstock, William, "The Chrysler Building," *Architecture and Building*, August 1930, pp. 223–24.

Engineering News Record, "New Alloy Steel to Be Used in Chrysler Building," July 18, 1929, p. 119.

——, "Steel Erection Problems on a 1,000 Foot Building," January 28, 1930.

Goldberger, Paul, "The Chrysler Building Enduring Symbol," *New York Times*, August 18, 1980.

Gray, Christopher, "Chrysler Building's Predecessor," *New York Times*, September 2, 2001.

Haskell, Douglas, "Architecture—Chrysler's Pretty Bauble," *Nation*, October 22, 1930.

Klein, Dan, "The Chrysler Building," *The American Connoisseur*.

Krinsky, Carol Herselle, "The Chrysler Preserved," *Art in America*, July 1979, pp. 80–87.

Lohman, J. P., "Speaking of Real Estate," *New York American*, October 22, 1929.

McHugh, F. D., "Manhattan's Mightiest 'Minaret,' " *Scientific American*, April 1930, pp. 265–68.

Michaelis, David, "77 Stories—The Secret Life of a Skyscraper," *Manhattan, Inc.*, June 1986, pp. 105–31.

Murchison, Kenneth, "The Chrysler Building as I See It," *The American Architect*, September 1930, pp. 24–33, 78.

——, "The Spires of Gotham," *The Architectural Forum*, June 1930.

New York Evening Post, "Architect's 'Race' Jostles the Moon," November 18, 1929.

——, "Chrysler Building to Stand on Height," June 14, 1930.

New York Herald Tribune, "Building Height Crown Now Held by Chrysler—Structure's Frame Was Completed, October 1," October 20, 1929.

——, "Chrysler Building Going Up Four Floors a Week," July 28, 1929.

——, "Chrysler Building Will Be City's Highest Tower," March 8, 1929.

——, "Chrysler Tower Wins Sky Race, Soars 1,030 Ft." November 18, 1929.

——, "Chrysler Will Keep His Tool Chest in Tower," January 19, 1930.

——, "Reynolds's 68 Story Plan Nets $2,500,000 in Sale to Chrysler," October 17, 1928.

New York Sun, "Chrysler Building Workers Honored," September 10, 1929.

——,"Chrysler Plans Are Announced," March 7, 1929.

——,"Forms Chrysler Building Company," October 19, 1928.

New York Telegram, "Chrysler Gives Credit to Men," January 24, 1930.

——, "Chrysler Opens His Skyscraper With Ceremony," May 27, 1930.

New York Times, "Architect Designs Home Using Panels—Man Who Planned the Chrysler Skyscraper Turns Skill to Low-Cost Housing," December 22, 1935.

——, "Chrysler Building City's Highest, Open," May 28, 1930.

——, "Chrysler Building Now Tallest Edifice," October 16, 1929.

——, "Chrysler Tower Suit Off," August 22, 1931.

——, "54 Story Skyscraper, Tallest in Midtown, Planned at Lexington Avenue and 42nd Street," February 2, 1928.

——, "W. H. Reynolds, Builder, Dead at 63," October 14, 1931.

New York World, "Chrysler's Spire Formally Opened," May 27, 1930.

New Yorker, "Up and Up," August 17, 1929, p. 13.

Pierpont, Claudia Roth, "The Silver Spire," *New Yorker*, November 18, 2002, pp. 74–81.

Ralston, Louis, "The Engineer's Problems in Tall Buildings," *The Architectural Forum*, June 1930, pp. 909–20.

Record and Guide, "Plan to Start 67-Story Reynolds Building Soon," August 25, 1928.

Robinson, Cervin, "Chrysler," *Architecture Plus*, 1974.

The World, "World's Highest Building Raises the Stars and Stripes," November 3, 1929, gravure section.

Time, "A Man of the Year—Walter Chrysler," January 7, 1929.

T-Square [George Chappell], "The Skyline," *New Yorker* May 24, 1930.

——, "The Skyline," *New Yorker*, July 12, 1930.

Van Alen, William, "The Structure and Metal Work of the Chrysler Building," *The Architectural Forum*, October 1930, pp. 493–98.

Wheeler, William, "Safeguarding Construction Crews in a Great Skyscraper," *Building and Building Management*, December 2, 1929, pp. 25–29.

Zismer, Gustave, "Chrysler's Loftiest Apartment," April 16, 1930.

Manhattan Company Building

Bankers Magazine, "New Bank of Manhattan Building to Be New York's Tallest," 1929, pp. 897–900.

Bareuther, David, "Japanese Designs Great Towers," *New York Sun*, January 11, 1930.

Boston Herald, "Planning 63-Story Wall Street Building," April 14, 1929.

Bridges, William, "New York's Highest Lookout," *New York Sun*, May 31, 1930.

Comstock, William, "The Manhattan Company Building," *Architecture and Building*, July 1930.

Engineering News Record, "Building a 71-Story Skyscraper in 33 Weeks," May 15, 1930, pp. 800–803.

Evening Post, "Manhattan Bank Men Deny Plan to Top Chrysler Peak," March 12, 1930.

Evening World, "Take 18 Workers Playing Craps in Lofty Structure," December 13, 1929.

——, "Views Camera Caught 925 Feet Above Wall Street," November 18, 1929.

Forbes, B. C., "Romance Behind World's Tallest New Skyscraper," *Boston American*, April 17, 1929.

Fortune, "40 Wall: X-Ray of a Skyscraper," 1937.

40 Wall Street Building, Inc., "Report as of June 30, 1956," JPMorgan Chase Archives, 1956.

40 Wall Street Corporation, "Manhattan Company Building," December 1929.

40 Wall Street Corporation, "The Manhattan Company Building—First Mortgage Fee and Leasehold," November 1, 1958.

Grid, "The Rise, Fall, and Rise of 40 Wall Street," spring 1999, pp. 117–18.

Holson, James, "New Skyscraper Race Is Won by Bank of Manhattan," *New York Telegram*, October 18, 1929, p. 20.

Matsui, Yasuo, "Architect Explains Tower Height," *New York Sun*, March 1, 1930.

McIntosh, W. T., "Unusual Foundation Procedure for 71-Story Building," *Engineering News Record*, April 24, 1930, pp. 691–95.

Michigan State Journal, "War Time Aviator to Erect Big Bank," May 1, 1929.

Morrison, Chester, "Bold Post Climber Explores Bank of Manhattan Peak," *New York Evening Post*, December 26, 1929.

New York Evening Post, "Manhattan Tower Opened to Public," May 26, 1930.

New York Herald Tribune, "Bank of Manhattan Tower Not Being Lifted," March 14, 1930.

——, "Half-ton Block Crashes from 70-Story Bank," November 13, 1929.

——, "64-Story Bank Building to Rise in Wall Street," April 7, 1929.

——, "World's Highest Office Building Being Rushed Up in Record Time," September 15, 1929.

New York Sun, "Wall Street Tower to Rise 850 feet," April 13, 1929.

New York Times, "Andrew Eken, Builder, 83, Dies," June 12, 1965.

——, "Denies Altering Plans for Tallest Building," October 20, 1929.

——, "47-Story Building to Rise in Wall Street," March 2, 1929.

——, "G. L. Ohrstrom, 61, Financier, Dead," November 11, 1955.

——, "Holding Company to Unite Utilities," April 24, 1929.

——, "Paul Starrett, Builder, 90, Dies," July 6, 1957

——, "Plane Hits Wall Street Tower," May 21, 1946.

——, "Wall Street Site Leased by Iselins," September 5, 1928.

New York World, "Only a Few Slightly Hurt as Derrick Cable on Bank of Manhattan Company Building Snaps," November 13, 1929.

Sieder, O. F., "Steel Design and Erection on a 900-Foot Tower Building," *Engineering News Record*," May 8, 1930, pp. 756–61.

The Manhattan Family, Series of Articles Related to the Bank of the Manhattan Company Building, JP Morgan Chase Archives, November 1928–June 1930.

Unknown, "A formation of three Salmsons," *Electronic: members.livingalbum. net/robert110/pages/pageeight.html*

Empire State Building

The Architect, "Mr. Murchison of New York Says——," January 1929.

——, "Mr. Murchison of New York Says——," February 1929, p. 589.

Bareuther, David, "Unique Brilliance for New Tower," *New York Sun*, March 4, 1930.

Bridges, William, "Looking Down from 1,050 Feet," *New York Sun*, January 10, 1931.

Building and Building Management, "A Promising Contestant for the Office Building Height-and-Size Record," May 19, 1930, p. 36.

Carmody, John, "The Empire State Building—Field Organization and Methods," *Architectural Forum*, April 1931.

Eken, Andrew, "The Ultimate in Skyscrapers," *Scientific American*, May 1931, pp. 318–20.

Engineering News Record, "Planning and Control Permit Erection of 85 Stories of Steel in Six Months," August 21, 1930, pp. 280–84.

———, "Topping Out the Empire State Building," January 22, 1931, p. 153.

Evening Post, "Ex-Governor Smith to Talk on Realty," November 9, 1929.

———, "Waldorf Razing Started by Smith," October 1, 1929.

Evening Telegram, "Empire Building to Be 1,248 Feet," July 21, 1930.

Fortune, "Governor Smith of the Empire State," September 1930.

———, "Skyscrapers: The Paper Spires," September 1930, pp. 54–59, 119–26.

Fowler, Glenn, "Tall Lady Is Gainly and Gainful at 40," *New York Times*, May 9, 1971.

Glassman, Don, "City's Zeppelin Port Nears Completion," *The World*, November 23, 1930.

Gray, Christopher, "A Red Reprise for a '31 Design," *New York Times*, June 14, 1992.

Harmon, Arthur Loomis, "The Design of Office Buildings," *Architectural Forum*, June 1930, pp. 819–20.

Hill, Edwin, "Al Smith, Realtor," *New York Sun*, January 11, 1930.

———, "It's a Tremendous Event," *New York Sun*, May 1, 1931.

Huxtable, Ada Louise, "Tinsel in the Sky," *New York Times*, June 4, 1992.

Johnston, Alva, "Waldorf Passes as Auctioneers Chant Dirge and Guests Feast," *New York Herald Tribune*, May 2, 1929.

Lamb, William, "The Empire State Building—The General Design," *Architectural Forum*, January 1931, pp. 2–7.

Literary Digest, "Personal Glimpses: Sky Boys Who 'Rode the Ball' on Empire State," May 23, 1931

McManus, Robert Cruise, "Raskob," *North American Review*, 1931, pp. 10–13.

New York Evening Post, "Smith in Capital, Explains Air Mast," December 13, 1929.

———, "Smith Skyscraper to Rise 102 Stories," July 21, 1930.

New York Evening Telegram, "J. J. Riordan Ends His Life," November 9, 1929.

New York Herald Tribune, "Empire State Gets More Financing," April 23, 1930.

———, "Raskob Plans to Aid Workers by Investments," May 7, 1929

———, "Riordan Friends Call Resources of Bank Ample," November 10, 1929.

———, "Smith Extends Site for World's Highest Tower," November 19, 1929.

———, "Smith Plans Zeppelin Mast Atop 1,100 Foot New Building," December 12, 1929.

——, "Smith Plays Hurdy-Gurdy in His Hotel Apartment," March 13, 1929.

——, "Smith to Head Firm Erecting 80-Story Tower," August 30, 1929.

——, "Syndicate Gets Waldorf Site," June 4, 1929.

——, "$25,000,000 Giant Proposed for Waldorf," December 23, 1928.

——, "Will Design Big Building for Al Smith," September 11, 1929.

New York Sun, "80-Story Tower Will Rise Soon," August 30, 1929.

——, "John Raskob of General Motors Made 80 Millionaires in 4 Years," March 12, 1928.

——, "New Plans for Tallest Skyscraper," November 18, 1929.

——, "Wreckers Busy on Old Waldorf," September 27, 1929.

New York Times Magazine, "The Candidates as They Really Are," October 14, 1928.

New York Times, "Notable at Ceremony Opening the Empire State Building," May 2, 1931.

——, "Observation Roof 1,050 Feet in Air," January 12, 1930.

——, "Raskob Is New Type in the Political Field," July 15, 1928.

——, "Sightseers Gallery 1,222 Feet Above 5th Avenue," July 21, 1930.

——, "Smith at Funeral of Young Raskob," July 8, 1928.

——, "Smith Lays Stone for Tallest Tower," September 10, 1930.

Poore, C. G., "Empire State Building Defeats Time," *New York Times*, July 27, 1930.

——, "Greatest Skyscraper Rises on a Clockwork Schedule," *New York Times*, July 27, 1930.

Record and Guide, "Shreve Outlines Economics of Office Building," November 23, 1929.

Shreve, R. H., "The Economic Design of Office Buildings," *Architectural Forum*, 1931, pp. 340–59.

——, "The Empire State Building Organization," *The Architectural Forum*, June 1930.

Starrett, William A., "Making Buildings from Blueprints," *Engineering News Record*, February 19, 1931.

Time, "Raskobism," November 18, 1929, p. 16.

Walsh, James, "John J. Raskob," *Irish Studies Quarterly*, September 1928.

Weber, Hamilton, "Empire State Figures Quoted," *New York Telegram*, July 1, 1930.

Zismer, Gustave, "Architect Reveals Cost Problems," *New York Sun*, November 23, 1929.

——, "Greater City in Skyscrapers," *New York Sun*, January 1930.

Craig Severance

The Architect, "A Practical Point," November 1929.

——, "Modern Architecture," May 1930.

The Architectural Record, "The Work of Messrs. Carrère & Hastings," January 1910.

Gray, Christopher, "Restoring the City's Oldest High-Rise Artists' Studios," *New York Times*, October 6, 1991.

New York Times, "Faith Severance Weds G. F. Hackl Jr.," January 10, 1929

——, "H. C. Severance, 62, Architect, Is Dead," September 2, 1941.

Price, Matlack, "A Renaissance in Commercial Architecture," *Architectural Record*, May 1912.

Sullivan, Bell B., "Severance," *J. C. Hubbell Papers*, County History, Clinton and Franklin County.

T-Square [George Chappell], "The Skyline—Cheap Architecture," *New Yorker*, October 16, 1926.

——, "The Skyline," *New Yorker*, November 27, 1926.

Zismer, Gustave, "45 Stories for 7th Avenue and 34th Street," *New York Sun*, October 18, 1929.

Height Contest

The Architect, "Mr. Murchison of New York Says," April 1928.

——, "Mr. Murchison of New York Says," November 1929.

——, "Mr. Murchison of New York Says," December 1929.

Bareuther, David, "Reaching for the Sky," *The Nation*, November 20, 1929.

Beals, Allen, "Daily Building Reports," *Architects' Weekly Building Material Price Supplement*, November 16, 1929.

Brock, H. I., "New York Completes Highest Office Buildings in All the World," *New York Times*, February 9, 1930.

Engineering News Record, "The Contest Skyward," September 5, 1929.

Evening Post, "Figures Belittle Skyscrapers Here," July 26, 1930.

Evening Telegram, "Los Angeles to Have Airport," November 16, 1929.

Gray, Christopher, "A Race for the Skies, Lost by a Spire," *New York Times*, November 15, 1992.

New York Evening Post, "Bank Skyscraper to Rise 925 Feet," October 2, 1929.

New York Herald Tribune, "150-Story Super-Skyscraper Being Considered for Two Broadway Blocks," October 6, 1929.

——, "The Race Upward," November 23, 1929.

New York Sun, "Skyscraper Now a National Institution with Cities in Race," January 1, 1929.

New York Telegram, "83-Story Tower to Rise on Site of Hippodrome," December 16, 1929

New York Times, "Building in Chicago to Be World's Tallest," May 5, 1929.

———, "Mussolini to Build Highest Skyscraper," September 30, 1924.

———, "110-Story Building, Highest in World," December 1926.

———, "Sees 200-Story Buildings," October 24, 1929.

———, "Tallest Building to Rise in Times Square Area; Lefcourt Will Erect 1,050 Foot Skyscraper," October 4, 1929.

Potter, Robert, "Every Day Sees a New Mark," *New York Evening Post*, December 21, 1929.

Record and Guide, "Thirteen of the World's Fifteen Tallest Buildings in New York," May 24, 1930.

Review of Reviews, "A Race into the Sky," February 1930.

Robins, Anthony, "The Continuing Saga of the Tallest Building in the World," *Architectural Record*, January 1987.

The World, "Continued Stories," November 19, 1929

Zismer, Gustave, "100-Story Building Looms," *New York Sun*, October 4, 1929.

New York in the Roaring Twenties

Brock, H. I. "Again Manhattan Shifts Its Backdrop," *New York Times Magazine*, March 29, 1931.

———, "The City That the Air Traveler Sees," *New York Times Magazine*, March 11, 1928.

———, "From Flat Roofs to High Towers," *New York Times Magazine*," April 19, 1931.

Business Week, "Put Skyscrapers on Ticker Tape," December 14, 1929.

———, "What the Wall Street Crash Means," November 2, 1929.

Corbett, Harvey Wiley, "A Vision of Midtown," *New York Times Magazine*, October 6, 1929.

Evening Post, "Autos Jam Roads Until After Dawn," September 3, 1929.

Evening World, "Wall Street in All-Night Rush," October 25, 1929.

Gould, Bruce, "Night Shows the Airman Manhattan's Beauty," *Evening Post*, February 8, 1930.

Morrison, Chester, "Clanking Ash Cans," *Evening Post*, January 2, 1930.

———, "Post Owl Writers Nocturne to Gotham's Lobster Shift," *Evening Post*, December 30, 1929.

New York Herald Tribune, "New York, a City That Never Will Be Finished," October 28, 1928.

———, "Operators and Brokers Confident," January 26, 1930.

New York Times, "Building Scenes Along 42nd Street," January 6, 1929.

———, "Stocks Collapse," October 30, 1929.

———, "Topics in Wall Street," March 15, 1929

Record and Guide, "Manhattan's Growth Reviewed by Joseph Day," June 8, 1929.

Simpich, Frederick, "This Giant That Is New York," *National Geographic Magazine*, 1930.

Skyscrapers

Arnaud, Leopold, "The Tall Building in New York in the Twentieth Century," *Journal of the Society of Architectural Historians*, XI, 2.

Bareuther, David, "Structure on End," *New York Sun*, January 12, 1929.

Bragdon, Claude, "The Frozen Fountain," *Pencil Points*, October 1931.

Brock, H. I., "Architecture Styled International," *New York Times Magazine*, February 7, 1932.

———, "Our Towers Take on Decoration," *New York Times Magazine*, January 16, 1927.

Corbett, Harvey Wiley, "The Limits of Our Skyscraping," *New York Times Magazine*, November 17, 1929.

Davis, Elmer, "Too Stately Mansions," *New Republic*, June 1, 1932.

Engineering News Record, "Life of Modern Building Set at 30 Years," June 20, 1929.

Gray, George, "The Future of the Skyscraper," *New York Times Magazine*, September 13, 1931.

Harbeson, John, "Design in Modern Architecture," *Pencil Points*, January 1930.

Jacobs, Harry Allan, "New Architecture Based on Utility," *New York Times*, November 30, 1930.

Jones, Chester Henry, "Architecture Astray," *Atlantic*, January 1931.

Mumford, Lewis, "Notes on Modern Architecture," *New Republic*, March 18, 1931.

New York Times, "Building in the Spirit of the Age," October 14, 1928.

———, "75-Story Skyscrapers Found Economical," September 22, 1929.

Pole, Grace, "Sire of the Skyscraper," *New York Times Magazine*, November 21, 1926.

Pope, Virginia, "Architecture of America Molds Beauty Anew," *New York Times Magazine*, December 19, 1926.

Record and Guide, "Dr. Wynne Discusses Housing and Skyscrapers," November 24, 1928.

Rybczynski, Witold, "The Future Up," *New York Times*, December 9, 2001.

The World, "Mayans Reared First Skyscraper," October 27, 1929.

Webster, J. Carson, "The Skyscraper: Logical and Historical Considerations," *Journal of the Society of Architectural Historians*, XV, 3.

Weisman, Winston, "New York and the Problem of the First Skyscraper," *Journal of the Society of Architectural Historians*, XII, 1.

Woolf, S. J., "An Architect Hails the Rule of Reason," *New York Times Magazine*, November 1, 1931.

Building and Skyscraper Construction

Bridges, William, "In the Eyes of a Steel Worker," *New York Sun*, January 29, 1930.

Collins, William, "Our Queerest Building Custom," *Pencil Points*, March 1931.

Coyle, David, "Skyscrapers Vibrate Like the Tuning Fork," *New York Times*, March 31, 1929.

Fortune, "Skyscrapers," 1930.

——, "Skyscrapers: Builders and Their Tools," 1930.

——, "Skyscrapers: Life on the Vertical," 1930.

——, "Skyscrapers: Pyramid in Steel and Stock," 1930.

——, "Skyscrapers: The Paper Spires," 1930.

Jones, Bassett, "The Modern Building Is a Machine," *The American Architect*, January 30, 1924.

McClain, Harold, "The Recollections of a Construction Worker," *Empire State Building Commemorative Issue*, April 30, 1981.

New Republic, "The Steel Mills Today," February 19, 1930.

New York Times, "Novel Methods Are Tried," June 30, 1929.

——, " 3½ Tons of Girders Plunge 22 Stories," *New York Times*, April 21, 1929.

New York Times Magazine, "Watching a Skyscraper Grow Out of a Hole," February 17, 1929.

Norris, Margaret, and Brenda Ueland, "Riding the Girders," *Saturday Evening Post*, April 11, 1931.

Poore, C. G., "The Riveter's Lofty Panorama," *New York Times Magazine*, January 5, 1930.

Pope, Virginia, "The Miracle of Mounting Skyscrapers," *New York Times Magazine*, March 2, 1930.

Rasenberger, Jim, "When They Were Young and the Towers Were New," *New York Times*, September 23, 2001.

Scientific American, "The Story of Steel," January–September 1924.

On Being an Architect

Anonymous, "The Story of an Architect," *Century Magazine*, 1917.

Architecture, "The Editor's Diary," 1928–31.

Fistere, John, "Poets in Steel," *Vanity Fair*, December 1931.

Fouilhoux, J. Andre, "Drawings, Specifications and Inspection," *New York Engineering News Record*, February 19, 1931.

Hood, Raymond, "Behind the Scenes in Building Planning," *Engineering News Record*, February 19, 1931.

Hood, Raymond, "Choosing the Right Career for Success," *New York Evening World*, May 13, 1930.

Illinois Society of Architects, "Just What Does an Architect Do for His Client," *Pencil Points*, December 1929, pp. 866–67.

Keller, Allan, "For Rockefeller Center Or a Small Home. It's Harrison and Fouilhoux," *New York World-Telegram*, February 16, 1938.

Ludlow, William, "The Owner and The Architect," *Pencil Points*, 1928, pp. 47–49.

Magonigle, H. Van Buren, "Office Principles, Policies and Practice," *Pencil Points*, 1925, pp. 43–46.

Pencil Points, "How an Architectural Project Is Carried on," July 1931.

———, "What Is an Architect?" July 1930.

Sturges, R. Clipston, "The Relationship Between the Architect and the Draftsman," *Pencil Points*, August 1926, pp. 457–58.

Talmey, Allene, "Raymond Hood—Man Against Sky," *New Yorker*, April 11, 1931.

Wills, Royal Barry, "The Pursuit of the Elusive Client," *Pencil Points*, June 1931.

ARCHIVES AND SPECIAL COLLECTIONS

Clarence S. Stein Papers at Division of Rare and Manuscript Collections, Cornell University Library (Ithaca, New York)

Cooper Union, "Minutes of Trustees Meetings," Cooper Union Library (New York, New York)

Empire State Building Archive, Avery Drawings and Archives, Avery Architectural and Fine Arts Library, Columbia University (New York, New York)

Ely Jacques Kahn Papers, Avery Drawings and Archives, Avery Architectural and Fine Arts Library, Columbia University (New York, New York)

Harold Van Buren Magonigle Papers, Manuscripts and Archives Division, The New York Public Library, Astor, Lenox and Tilden Foundations (New York, New York)

Ivy L. Lee Papers, Seeley G. Mudd Manuscript Library, Princeton University Library (Princeton, New Jersey)

John Jakob Raskob Papers, Hagley Museum and Library (Wilmington, Delaware)

JP Morgan Chase Archives (New York, New York)

Margaret Bourke-White Papers, Department of Special Collections, Syracuse University Library (Syracuse, New York)

Nicholas Kelley Papers, Manuscripts and Archives Division, The New York Public Library, Astor, Lenox and Tilden Foundations (New York, New York)

Pierre S. du Pont Papers, Hagley Museum and Library (Wilmington, Delaware)

Ralph Walker Papers, Department of Special Collections, Syracuse University Library (Syracuse, New York)

"Reminiscences of Nicholas Kelley," Columbia University Oral History Research Office Collection, Columbia University (New York, New York)

"Reminiscences of Eddie Dowling," Columbia University Oral History Research Office Collection, Columbia University (New York, New York)

Supreme Court of the State of New York, "William Van Alen versus Cooper Union for the Advancement of Science and Art, Reylex Corporation, W.P. Chrysler Building Corporation and National Surety Company," 1930–31 (New York, New York)

Supreme Court of the State of New York, "William Van Alen versus H. Craig Severance," 1924–26 (New York, New York)

Yasuo Matsui Papers, Avery Drawings and Archives, Avery Architectural and Fine Arts Library, Columbia University (New York, New York)

CARMEL CLAY PUBLIC LIBRARY

690 01008 0787

WITHDRAWN FROM
CARMEL CLAY
PUBLIC LIBRARY

CARMEL CLAY PUBLIC LIBRARY
55 4th Avenue SE
Carmel, IN 46032
(317) 844-3361
Renewal Line: (317) 814-3936
www.carmel.lib.in.us

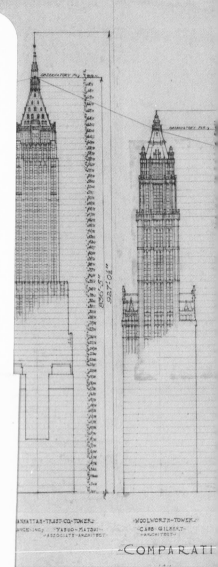